Exhibitions, Trade Fairs and Industrial Events

T0384168

This book is the first to take an in-depth examination of the breadth and scope of exhibitions, trade fairs and other industrial events as a marketing tool or channel. Industrial Events are planned events that are staged with the primary aim of marketing businesses, industries and products. This may lead to direct sales through these events, as well as the development of brand image or building brand awareness; penetration of new markets; trials of new products and knowledge diffusion. These business goals might be future-focused, with meetings of strategic players from across an industry or sector contributing to the shaping of future innovations and development. Industrial events act as a marketplace, but rather than seeing them as temporary or isolated activities, they can be understood as cyclical clusters.

This is a multidisciplinary book written by an international group of leading academics, offering a wide range of case studies that feature countries such as the United Kingdom, United States of America (USA), Japan, South Korea, Saudi Arabia, Australia and New Zealand. It will appeal to students and researchers in the fields of cultural studies, history, tourism, sociology, economics and management.

Warwick Frost is an Associate Professor in the Department of Management, Sport and Tourism at La Trobe University, Melbourne, Australia. His research interests include heritage, events, nature-based attractions and the interaction between media, popular culture and tourism. Warwick is a co-editor of the Routledge *Advances in Events Research* series and has co-edited five books and co-authored five research books.

Jennifer Laing is an Associate Professor in the Department of Management, Sport and Tourism at La Trobe University, Melbourne, Australia. Her research interests include travel narratives; the role of events in society; rural and regional regeneration through tourism and events; and health and wellness tourism. Jennifer is a co-editor of the Routledge *Advances in Events Research* series and was recognised in 2017 as an Emerging Scholar of Distinction by the International Academy for the Study of Tourism.

Routledge Advances in Event Research Series

Edited by Warwick Frost and Jennifer Laing
Department of Management, Sport and Tourism,
La Trobe University, Australia

For a full list of titles in this series, please visit www.routledge.com/tourism/series/
RAERS

Exhibitions, Trade Fairs and Industrial Events

Edited by Warwick Frost and Jennifer Laing

Routledge
Taylor & Francis Group

LONDON AND NEW YORK

First published 2018
by Routledge
2 Park Square, Milton Park, Abingdon, Oxon OX14 4RN

and by Routledge
605 Third Avenue, New York, NY 10017

First issued in paperback 2021

Routledge is an imprint of the Taylor & Francis Group, an informa business

British Library Cataloguing-in-Publication Data
A catalogue record for this book is available from the British Library

Library of Congress Cataloging-in-Publication Data
A catalog record for this book has been requested

ISBN 13: 978-1-03-224209-5 (pbk)
ISBN 13: 978-1-138-21935-9 (hbk)

DOI: 10.4324/9781315415291

Typeset in Times New Roman
by Apex CoVantage, LLC

Contents

Figures

Tables

Contributors

Gary Best is an Honorary Associate of La Trobe Business School, La Trobe University, Australia. He is an independent consultant and author whose research and writing focuses on cultural tourism, gastronomy, festival and event management, and automobility. His most recent publication was: Best, G. (2017) 'Media Memories on the Move: Exploring an Autoethnographic Heritage of Automobility and Travel', *Journal of Heritage Tourism*. 12 (1).

Dr Vern Biaett is an Assistant Professor of Event Management in the Nido R. Qubein School of Communication's Event and Sport Management Department at High Point University, North Carolina, US. His research interests include the behaviour of attendees during festivity with implications for peak liminality, increased social capital and community development; socially constructed grounded theory research method; the estimation of attendance at large events. Vern worked in leisure services for 30 years, the last 20 as event manager for the cities of Phoenix and Glendale, Arizona, prior to entering the world of academia in 2006.

Dr Hilary du Cros is a Senior Research Assistant in the Dean's Unit at the University of Technology, Sydney. Her research interests include cultural heritage management and tourism, specifically as it relates to Asia. She is currently an expert member of the ICOMOS International Scientific Cultural Tourism Committee (ISCTC) (1999 – present), a HKIEd representative to the UNESCO and ICCROM-sponsored Asian Academy Heritage Management Network (2005 – present).

Dr Alison Dunn lectures in Tourism Management and is the Bachelor of Business Honours Coordinator in the Tasmanian School of Business at the University of Tasmania. Her main research interests are in niche, premium products as tourist attractions including craft beverages, tourism education and tourism in protected areas.

Dr Alain Fayolle is a Professor of Entrepreneurship and the founder and director of the entrepreneurship research centre at EM Lyon Business School, France. His current research works are focusing on the dynamics of entrepreneurial processes, the influences of cultural factors on organisations' entrepreneurial orientation and the evaluation of entrepreneurship education. His last published research has appeared in *Academy of Management Learning & Education, Entrepreneurship and Regional Development, International Journal of Entrepreneurship and Innovation,* and *Frontiers of Entrepreneurship Research.* He is Academy of Management ENT Division Chair.

Dr Warwick Frost is an Associate Professor in the Department of Management, Sport and Tourism at La Trobe University, Melbourne, Australia. His research interests include heritage, events, nature-based attractions and the interaction between media, popular culture and tourism. Warwick is a co-editor of the Routledge *Advances in Events Research* series and has co-edited five books and co-authored five research books.

Bokyung Kang is a PhD candidate at Rikkyo University in Japan. Ms Kang's research interests include urban tourism and events, ethnic tourism, and tourist area cycle of evolution.

Melissa Kennedy is a doctoral researcher in the Community Planning and Development Programme at La Trobe University. Her research interests focus on rural cultural and creative economies. She is particularly interested in the relationship between community economic transformation and practices of communing

Dr Sangkyun (Sean) Kim is Associate Professor of Tourism at Edith Cowan University in Australia. His research interests include tourism and creative industries, film tourism, community engagement and empowerment, cultural heritage (e.g. food as intangible heritage) and identity, tourist behaviour and events and festivals in Asia. Associate Professor Kim is a co-editor of the Springer *Film Tourism in Asia: Evolution, Transformation and Trajectory* (2017).

Gerry Kregor is Senior Educational Developer in the Tasmanian Institute for Learning and Teaching at the University of Tasmania. His research interests include: how craft beverage makers use tourism as part of their business strategy; higher education pedagogies and learning designs: and learning technologies. Personal interests include travel, craft brewing and cider making.

Dr Jennifer Laing is an Associate Professor in the Department of Management, Sport and Tourism at La Trobe University, Melbourne, Australia. Her research interests include travel narratives; the role of events in society; rural and regional regeneration through tourism and events; and health and wellness tourism. Jennifer is a co-editor of the Routledge *Advances in Events Research* series and was recognised in 2017 as an Emerging Scholar of Distinction by the International Academy for the Study of Tourism.

Dr Jennifer Lukow is Chair of the Event and Sport Management Department and an Associate Professor of Sport Management at High Point University in High Point, North Carolina. Her research interests include gender equity in collegiate athletics and the media representation of female athletes. Jennifer is a member of the North American Society for Sport Management and the North American Society for the Sociology of Sport.

Dr Judith Mair is a Senior Lecturer in Events in the School of Business, University of Queensland, Australia. Her research interests include the impacts of events on community and society; consumer behaviour in events and tourism; the relationship between events and climate change; and business and major events. She is the author of '*Conferences and Conventions: A Research Perspective*' and '*Events and Sustainability*', both published by Routledge in 2015.

Emad Monshi is an Event and Tourism Management Lecturer in the Tourism and Hospitality Management Department at King Saud University, Saudi Arabia. His research interests include developing best practices in event design, event management and event evaluation; and developing Saudi tourism. Emad is a leading academic practitioner in event management in Saudi Arabia and was awarded in 2015 the Excellence Award for his research by the Saudi Arabian Cultural Mission in Australia.

Dr Eerang Park is Lecturer in Tourism Management at Victoria University of Wellington in New Zealand. Her research interests include community development and tourism, community empowerment, event tourism, the tourist experience and tourism in Asia. Her recent research project focuses on benefits and challenges of sustainable tourism development in the context of Cittaslow, especially in relation to community empowerment and quality of life for various stakeholders.

Dr Veland Ramadani is an Associate Professor at South-East European University, Republic of Macedonia where he teaches both undergraduate and postgraduate courses in entrepreneurship and small business management. His research interests include entrepreneurship, small business management, family businesses and venture capital investments. He has authored or co-authored around 80 research articles and 15 books. Dr Ramadani received the Award for Excellence 2016 – Outstanding Paper by Emerald Group Publishing (*Journal of Enterprising Communities: People and Places in the Global Economy*).

Dr Vanessa Ratten is an Associate Professor (Entrepreneurship and Innovation) at La Trobe Business School, La Trobe University. She is the Discipline Coordinator of Entrepreneurship and Innovation at La Trobe Business School. Her main research areas include entrepreneurship (especially sport entrepreneurship, developing country entrepreneurship and international entrepreneurship) and innovation (focusing on technological innovation, cloud computing, and mobile commerce). She has published on a wide range of subjects including European entrepreneurship, Asian entrepreneurship and tourism marketing.

Dr Claudia Sima is a Lecturer in Tourism in Lincoln International Business School at University of Lincoln, Lincoln, United Kingdom. Her research interests include tourism development and marketing in Central and Eastern

European countries; communist heritage tourism; tourism and mental health; unusual and fringe events; and street food and street art. Claudia has worked as a marketing officer for a London-based DMO, Tour East London, and on exhibition stands for ACE – The Association of Conferences and Events in the UK.

Franziska Vogt is currently teaching on a range of tourism and events-related modules at the University of Sunderland in London, UK. Her research interests include urban tourism with a focus on visitors' experiences in off the beaten track areas, urban regeneration and gentrification, culture and heritage tourism, and events and unusual venues. She holds an MSc in Cultural Tourism Development and a BSc in Tourism Management (University of Sunderland, UK).

Dr Trudie Walters wrote this chapter while working at the University of the Sunshine Coast in Australia, and she is now a Lecturer at the University of Otago in Dunedin, New Zealand. Her research interests include second homes (with a particular focus on the New Zealand context) and events (centring on how events are utilised, perceived and valued). Trudie is Associate Editor and Reviews Editor for *Annals of Leisure Research.*

1 Understanding international exhibitions, trade fairs and industrial events

Concepts, trends and issues

Warwick Frost and Jennifer Laing

Prologue: Steve Jobs and Alexander Graham Bell

The launch of the NeXT computer was a meticulously planned event. At Apple, Steve Jobs was seen as a genius in combining marketing and technical innovation. However, in 1986 he had lost control of the company he had founded and had departed to set up his new enterprise. Two years later he was ready to launch. Renowned for his flair with the 1984 launch of the Macintosh computer, Jobs wanted to go much further with a product launch that would gain international media publicity, generate sales and justify his strategy.

The venue was the Louise M. Davies Symphony Hall, the home of the San Francisco Symphony Orchestra. Over 3000 invited industry and media guests were present. Jobs took centre stage and proceeded to deliver a two and a half hour long speech on his new computer. Running through its features, he constructed an argument that with this computer, he had been able to do what he couldn't at Apple. Coming towards the end of his pitch, with audience fatigue a factor, he unveiled his finale. The computer contained a music synthesizer software application and it now played Gamelan music from Indonesia. Next, Jobs welcomed San Francisco Symphony Orchestra Concertmaster Dan Kobialka on to the stage. What followed was a five-minute violin duet performed by Kobialka and the NeXT computer. The finale garnered a standing ovation and effusive reviews. The NeXT computer was launched to the world (Schlender and Tetzeli 2015).

A century earlier, another giant of telecommunications innovation used an event to launch his new technology. In 1876, Alexander Graham Bell exhibited his telephone at the Centennial International Exposition in Philadelphia. At 29 years old, he was slightly younger than Jobs, who was 31 years old when he launched the NeXT computer. As a static exhibit, his equipment gained little attention during the normal course of the exposition. The key part of the event was the awarding of the prizes in the category of 'electrical apparatus', for this was the opportunity to provide a practical demonstration. The judging was held in the area of the Western Union Telegraph Exhibit, with the head judge being Sir William Thomson, famed for overseeing the trans-Atlantic undersea telegraph cable. Taking place on a Sunday when the exposition was closed to the public, there was a small crowd of distinguished guests and Bell's rivals (Grosvenor and Wesson 1997).

Chief amongst the VIPs in attendance was the Emperor Dom Pedro II of Brazil (the last emperor of Brazil, who reigned from 1831 to 1889). Just as Bell was about to begin his demonstration, the Emperor rose and walked over to him, greeting him warmly. They had met previously through the Boston School for the Deaf and shared an interest in helping deaf people. To the bewilderment of many of those present, the Emperor accompanied Bell and Sir William Thomson up a flight of stairs to where the apparatus was. None of this was planned, but clearly no official was willing to tell the Emperor to sit down. Fascinated by new technology, the Emperor enthusiastically proceeded to take part in the presentation. With Bell speaking into the telephone in another room, both Sir William Thomson and Emperor Dom Pedro exclaim that they can hear Bell's voice electrically projected down the line. Bell's triumph was complete as he was awarded a prize which would help him to further develop and market his invention (Grosvenor and Wesson 1997).

In these two instances, there was a long chain of product development, as these entrepreneurs journeyed from concept and prototype to release on the mass market. Critical to this development pathway was an event – a product launch and an international exhibition respectively – in which the new technology was demonstrated and gained media attention. These events were staged with the objective of highlighting innovation and generating sales and extending market penetration. Such a commercial imperative is an entirely different way of understanding events and their roles in society.

Introduction

Typically, research in Events Studies is divided into two broad fields. The first considers the role of events in promoting tourism. The second focuses on social impacts, conceptualising events as vehicles for disseminating persuasive social messages. In this book, our aim is to introduce a third core area for understanding events and their impacts. This is what we term *industrial events* – which are staged with the primary objective of selling goods and services.

The concept of industrial events is extended from that of *industrial tourism*. As defined by Otgaar, industrial tourism involves visits by tourists, residents and day trippers and not only comprises 'company visit/ tours, but also visits to company museums and brand parks such as the World of Coca Cola and Autostadt [Volkswagen]' (2012: 87). His two examples may also be termed *brand museums*, where visitors to a purpose-built centre are immersed in the culture and heritage of global brands (Hollenbeck, Peters and Zinkhan 2008). Another example of this, visited by us as fieldwork for this book, is La Cité du Vin, in Bordeaux, France. Opened in 2016, at a cost of 81 million Euros, this promotes the brand of Bordeaux wines. Given its cost, it is a good illustration of how critical industrial tourism can be for a region. However, while such centres are important, a focus on industrial tourism misses the substantial devotion of resources by businesses to marketing through events.

Common examples of industrial events include world's fairs, trade shows, industry exhibitions, food and wine festivals and product launches. While these make up a major part of the events industry, their scope and meanings as a category of events have tended to get lost. Yes, they might attract tourists and engender social changes, but for their organisers and other stakeholders, their main role is to *sell*. These are commercial events, operating within a business paradigm, in which success is measured by the increased sales generated through participation in the event. Similarly, for those who attend, the main attraction is to try and buy.

In this introductory chapter, our aim is to sketch out some basic concepts, issues and examples. We start with considering stakeholders and their motivations for being involved in industrial events. In the second and largest section, we provide some examples of the main types of industrial events, identifying key features and the relevant prior literature. In the third section, we qualify the commercial paradigm associated with these events, explaining that they may also have social and tourism aspects as well. In the final section, we detail the scope and structure of this book.

Stakeholders

Industrial events function as a marketplace, with the key stakeholders including sellers, buyers and organisers.

Sellers

Sellers, exhibitors, traders, stallholders or merchants – these are all common terms for those businesses that participate at industrial events. Most of these events feature large numbers of sellers who congregate in the temporary marketplace to exhibit, market and sell their goods and services. Generally a common theme or industry connection binds them together. For example, a hospitality industry trade show includes food and beverage wholesalers, manufacturers and sellers of glasses, crockery, cutlery and furniture and staff training colleges. Intermingled with these industry specific operators are providers of more generic products that could be of interest to a wide range of industries. These include suppliers of cash registers, business services and interior design.

Sales revenue from industry events is generated in the short and long term. The former includes what is sold during the period of the event, the latter occurs afterwards, but is due to interactions with the customers that took place at the time. Another divide is between the markets targeted. Some sellers may be seeking customers from among industry operators; such sales are characterised as wholesale or business-to-business (B2B). Other sellers may be more focused on consumers and their involvement at industrial events is aimed at reducing their reliance on wholesalers and retail businesses.

Sellers may utilise industrial events as just one part of a broader marketing portfolio, complementing existing shops, showrooms and online sales systems. An alternative business model adopted by some – generally smaller operators – is to use these events as the sole or major sales outlet. For example, a manufacturer of premium cheeses told us how they initially opened a shop on their farm. In choosing this option they were encouraged by their regional tourism organisation, keen on promoting agri-tourism. However, these farmers found this model frustrating and ineffective, for low sales were matched by the inefficiency of having to leave farm tasks to attend to visitors at irregular and unpredictable times during the day. On the advice of a friend, they participated in a farmers' market and found that they sold their entire stock in a couple of hours. As a result, they closed their farm shop and focused on farmers' markets, partitioning production and sales into separate parts of the week and their lives.

Selling at industrial events provides businesses with the following advantages:

1   They are able to directly interact with potential consumers, providing samples and advice. Industrial events provide an important opportunity to reach new customers.
2   Building brand knowledge and loyalty. The personal interaction provides the opportunity to effectively tell brand stories or impart persuasive messages.
3   Cheaper sales costs, paying for a temporary outlet with high customer flows.
4   Controlling their own sales outlet. In contrast, conventional retail channels such as supermarkets or department stores are outside the control of suppliers and while they act as 'agents' during customer interaction, they have their own objectives which may conflict with those of suppliers.
5   They complement the trend towards online shopping and promotion via social media. Businesses can use customer interaction at these events to market their websites and sign attendees up to their various social media platforms.
6   Valuable marketing intelligence, both through direct feedback from customers and through observation of the trends amongst competitors.
7   The opportunity to promote new or little-known products, which might be overlooked by customers in conventional outlets.
8   Educating customers on the features of their products, such as the health benefits of certain foods or the energy efficiency of electrical goods.
9   There may be public relations opportunities. For example aerospace companies exhibiting at airshows will interact with the general public, even though their customers are major businesses. Exhibiting to the public might not generate any sales, but it promotes technical, environmental and safety advances in the aerospace industry.
10 At some industrial events there are prizes for the best exhibitors, often spread across a range of categories. This recognition is then used for brand differentiation in future marketing and may be reinforced by media coverage. Examples of intense competition for prizes include garden shows (such as the Chelsea Flower Show in London), beer shows and wine festivals.

Buyers

Buyers at industrial events may be businesses or consumers. Businesses – commonly referred to as *trade* – use these events to view, try and discuss new products and trends. As these events are tightly focused on a particular industry and occur within a concentrated space and time, they allow business operators to efficiently explore new commercial possibilities.

Consumers are primarily motivated by the opportunities to shop. As with businesses, they value that the event is focused in theme, space and time and they are strongly interested in new developments and technical innovations. Cheaper prices may be a motivation, as many industrial events offer discounts and specials for attendees. Apart from making purchases, there is a strong leisure component to these events, with attendees seeing them as an entertaining and relaxing day out. Much of the research on consumers at industrial events concerns their motivations, an issue of high practical value for organisers and business participants (see for example Dodd, Yuan, Adams and Kolyesnikova 2006; Hall 2013; Lee, Kang and Lee, 2013; Yuan, Cai, Morrison and Linton 2005).

Organisers and venues

The highly commercial nature of industrial events leads to professional specialisation in organisers and venues, particularly in regards to the larger scale events. As distinct from most festivals, which are usually organised by community and not-for-profit groups, many industrial events are staged by events management companies that own the event. Undertaking these events as an entrepreneurial activity, these companies rent venues, recruit exhibitors and engage in its marketing. Their revenue comes from a combination of entry fees, stall rentals and sponsorship. A purely business undertaking, these companies take the full financial risk for any profit or loss. Intriguingly, there has been very little research into this little-known niche sector of the events industry.

A wide range of venues are used for industrial events. Most prominent are purpose-built exhibition centres. Particularly in recent years, these have been viewed as major drivers of economic growth and diversification for cities. A common model has been the funding and building of exhibition centres by municipal, regional or national governments as *anchors* for tourism/entertainment/events precincts (Figure 1.1). These are often situated on the fringes of central business districts, in areas of economic decline and de-industrialisation, such as former ports or docklands. The building of an exhibition centre is thus an initiative to generate *service economy* business and jobs, whilst providing a major economic heart for a precinct development.

Venues may also be temporary adaptations of existing structures. For example, in conducting fieldwork for this study, we visited two events – the Melbourne Leisure Fest and the Lost Trades Fair – that were held at racecourses

Figure 1.1 A purpose-built exhibition centre, Motorclassica 2016 at the Royal Melbourne
Exhibition Building

Source: Photo courtesy of Gary Best

(Figures 1.2 and 1.3). In both cases the racecourses provided large areas for displays, car parking, catering, toilet facilities and office space. The racing clubs gained rentals for weekends when they were not conducting race meetings and the organisers gained a prominent established venue. Another intriguing example was that the launch of the NeXT computer was held at a purpose-built symphony orchestra concert hall. Holding it in such a prestigious high-quality

Figure 1.2 Demonstration of constructing a dry-stone wall at the Lost Trades Show 2016, held at Kyneton Racecourse, Australia

Source: Photo courtesy of Warwick Frost

Figure 1.3 Exhibits at the Melbourne Leisure Fest 2016, held at Sandown Racecourse, Melbourne

Source: Photo courtesy of Warwick Frost

event venue was deliberately planned to emphasise sophistication, a quality that the manufacturers wanted to be associated with their new product.

Major types

World's Fairs and international exhibitions

Held every few years at different cities around the globes, these are *mega-events*, due to their attendance numbers in the millions, international media coverage, large scale of facilities construction and need for government endorsement and funding (Frost and Laing 2011). As with other mega-events like the Olympics, cities make competitive bids to win the right to host World's Fairs. These bids are evaluated by the Bureau International des Expositions, established in 1928, based in Paris and with 169 country members (Frost and Laing 2011; International Bureau des Expositions 2016).

The concepts of mega-events and hallmark events are closely associated with the tourism impacts of events and are worth considering here to better understand the role and importance of World's Fairs. While mega-events are attractive to policy-makers due to their promise of high numbers of tourists – thereby justifying the high levels of public investment in facilities – they come with three limitations. The first is that it is the brand of the mega-event that is internationally recognisable and reinforced by the repetition of the event and this might outshine the tourist brand of the one-off host destination (Richards and Palmer 2010). Second, despite the promises of organisers to governments, it is often the case that most attendees are locals rather than international tourists (Craik 1992). Third, rapid changes in fashion and taste have led to some World's Fairs being failures, most strikingly in the USA late in the 20th century. Planned World's Fairs at Philadelphia (1976) and Chicago (1992) were cancelled due to financial difficulties and New Orleans (1984) – the last World Fair staged in the USA – went bankrupt (Frost and Laing 2013; Gold and Gold 2005). Such concerns with the high-risk nature of mega-events lead many places to focus on hallmark events instead. These are events that are staged regularly in one place and consequently the brand is more closely associated with that place (Frost and Laing 2011; Richards and Palmer 2010). As we explore later in this section, with the exception of World's Fairs, industrial events tend to follow the hallmark events model.

The history of World's Fairs dates back to the 19th century, a period of rapid technological and social change in the Western world. A rapidly expanding middle class was drawn to World's Fairs that showcased the latest innovations and developments in trade. The 1851 Great Exhibition in London provided a template for future events, particularly in the audacity of its modernist glass and steel venue in the Crystal Palace (Auerbach 1999; Roche 2000). The French were enthusiastic adopters of the concept, with their 1889 Exposition Universelle attracting 32 million attendees – roughly the then population of France – and leaving a significant legacy in the Eiffel Tower. The USA staged a World's Fair at Philadelphia in 1876 to commemorate the centenary of the Declaration of Independence. Rather than a single stupendous building, they opted for what would become the common model of a range of themed pavilions. This was followed by a successful World's Fair in 1893 in Chicago, staged to commemorate the 400th Anniversary of Columbus. In Australia, Melbourne and Sydney followed suit, with Melbourne's 1880 Royal Exhibition Building gaining UNESCO World Heritage status in 2004 (Frost and Laing 2013; Greenhalgh 1988; Hoffenberg 2001; Roche 2000; Rydell 1984).

In the first two thirds of the 20th century, the USA became most closely associated with the World's Fairs and there was a gradual shift from 19th century imperialism towards consumer culture (Becker and Stein 2011; Rydell 1993; Rydell and Kroes 2005). This Americanisation of the concept is best exemplified in the successful Elvis Presley film *It Happened at the World's Fair* (1963). However, the Americans did not have a monopoly and European countries remained enthusiastic stagers of these events, resulting in the 1928 creation of the Bureau International des Expositions to manage the bidding of potential host cities.

Late in the 20th century, enthusiasm for World's Fairs in the USA rapidly declined, with the focus shifting more to Europe and Asia, where Osaka hosted the first Asian World's Fair in 1970 (Gold and Gold 2005). In the 21st century, World's Fairs have been staged at Hanover (Germany), Aichi (Japan), Zaragoza (Spain), Shanghai (China), Yeosu (South Korea) and Milan (Italy). A new chapter is now being written in their history with the 2017 World's Fair being staged in Astana (Kazakhstan) and the 2020 one in Dubai (UAE).

With this new wave of World's Fairs, there has been a range of research studies focusing on them as mega-events. Examples of these include:

* Economic Impact, Yeosu 2012

  (Lee, Mjelde and Kwon, 2017)

* Reinforcing and refashioning destination image, Milan 2015

  (Ferrari and Guala 2017)

* Environmental certification, Milan 2015

  (Guizzardi, Mariani and Prayag 2017)

* Visitor motivation and segmentation, Shanghai 2010

  (Lee et al., 2013)

* Community participation, Shanghai 2010

  (Lamberti, Noci, Guo and Zhu 2011)

Trade shows

Trade shows are primarily directed at businesses within a particular industry. In simple terms, they are opportunities for retailers to view and sample the offerings of wholesalers, manufacturers and ancillary service providers. Examples include Lineapelle Milano and Swiss Pel (leather goods), the Automotive Interiors Expo and the Automotive Testing Expo (both in Stuttgart, Germany), the World Travel Market (London), the Mobile World Congress Barcelona (mobile phones and technology), the Frankfurt Book Fair, the East China Fair (textiles and homewares, in Shanghai) and Foodex Japan (food and beverages).

Originally, trade shows developed as specialised fairs where buyers could examine samples and place sales orders for delivery at a later date. Generally, they were held regularly – often once a year – thereby becoming fixed in the business calendar and were held either at central trading cities or in regions which specialised in manufacturing certain products. In the 20th century, they developed further foci in being places where the latest trends were on show and where industry participants could come together to network and develop business-to-business relationships (Bathelt, Golfetto and Rinallo 2014; Lampel and Meyer 2008). Generally, trade shows have a low profile in the media and public perception, an exception is high-end fashion shows. However, the majority tend to be more prosaic, concentrating on volume and mass markets and pitched at small to medium enterprises (Skov 2006).

The research into trade shows is mostly concerned with what businesses attending are seeking. This includes:

*   How businesses evaluate the value they gain from attending
                (Alberca-Oliver, Rodriguez-Oromendia and
            Parte-Esteban 2015; Berné and Garcia-Uceda 2008)

*   How attendees behave and what attracts them to individual stalls, particularly in comparison to retail shoppers
                (Gopalakrishna, Roster and Sridhar 2010)

*   The opportunities for building networks to better understand technical developments and access new markets
                (Evers and Knight 2008; Lampel and Meyer 2008)

*   Sociological research into the roles played by buyers and sellers and the power relationships and symbolic status of participants
                (Entwistle and Rocamora 2006)

*   How trade shows are integrated into the regular cycle of business, requiring ongoing and overlapping planning for multiple trade shows
                (Power and Jansson 2008)

*   The place of trade shows in the production and marketing value chain
                (Skov 2006)

*   The role of prizes and awards in disseminating innovations
                (Aldebert, Dang and Longhi 2011)

In addition, there is research into how such trade shows are organised, including:

- *Concertation*, whereby the trends and latest styles to be highlighted are developed in the lead-up period by the organisers working with exhibitors and industry leaders. Such a process happens in the background, presenting the impression to the public that such developments in fashions were organic.
  (Bathelt et al. 2014)

- The building of a distinctive and attractive brand for the event as part of a strategy to ensure its sustainability
  (Jin and Weber 2013)

- Factors considered in choosing a host city, including synergies between its industry and the event
  (Jin, Weber and Bauer 2012)

Consumer-orientated industry shows

In contrast to trade shows, these events are focused on marketing and sales to consumers rather than other businesses. That said, there are overlaps, with some trade shows having special days reserved for the public and some consumer events reserving set periods for the trade only. Examples of this hybridity include the Melbourne Fashion Festival (Weller 2013) and the Australian International Airshow.

Examples of such consumer-orientated shows include those themed on weddings, automobiles and recreational vehicles, leisure, gardening, travel, cosmetics and beauty products, popular culture and food and beverages. Research on these types of events is surprisingly limited, perhaps because there is an assumption that they simply follow the same patterns as trade shows. Two exceptions are festivals themed on food and wine and those relating to popular culture (which are considered separately below) and the recent study by Song, Bae and Lee (2017) of Cosmetics and Beauty Expos in South Korea.

Food and wine festivals

Amongst the most popular and well-known of industrial events are food and wine festivals. These fall into two main categories (Frost et al. 2016):

1 General food and wine festivals, usually developed by cities as hallmark events. An example is the Melbourne Food and Wine Festival. Such events are developed to attract a mass market, utilising the widespread consumer appeal of food and wine and their increased prominence in the modern media. In some cases, organisers are seeking to develop or reinforce a destination image that highlights a strong gastronomic culture and agricultural hinterland. The Melbourne Food and Wine Festival provides an interesting

example of how and why such general festivals are created. In 1990, Melbourne had lost out to Atlanta in bidding for the 1996 Olympics. Peter Clemenger was an advertising executive involved in the failed bid. Dejected, he went on holidays to Thailand, but kept mulling over alternative events that could promote Melbourne. He came up with three possibilities where Melbourne excelled: fashion, gardens and food and wine. Evaluating the three, he concluded, 'you build on your strengths, but fashion was going to be too expensive and I didn't know much about gardens. So I chose food and wine because it is part of Victoria's way of life. It is very important to us.'(quoted in Money 2012)

2   Specifically themed food and wine events. Examples include the Galway International Oyster and Seafood Festival (Ireland), the Melbourne Salami Festival (Australia), the Mundaring Truffle Festival and Truffle Kerfuffle, Manjimup (Western Australia) and the Stockton Asparagus Festival (California). In most cases, these are created by specialist producers. For example, the initiative for the Galway International Oyster and Seafood Festival came from the company Kelly Oysters (Frost et al. 2016). In others there is greater complexity. The Bluff Oyster Festival in New Zealand was organised by a regional government promotion agency. When they tried to move it to a larger city, the townspeople of The Bluff reclaimed their festival and re-orientated it from a corporate to a community festival (Frost et al. 2016). In Stockton, California, the local tourism organisation and agricultural businesses wanted to develop a festival themed around one of the wide range of crops the region produced. They strategically chose asparagus because they viewed it as a distinctive and high-status gourmet food. (Lewis 1997)

Farmers' Markets may be regarded as a subset of food festivals, though they tend to be held regularly – weekly or monthly – throughout the year. These are becoming increasingly popular as consumers search for high quality organic food and value the alternative to conventional supermarket distribution chains. The common model is to only allow stallholders who actually grow their produce in the local region. For these producers, farmers' markets are a means of directly interacting with and selling to their customers, whilst avoiding wholesaler and supermarket margins (Frost et al. 2016; Hall 2013; Hede and Stokes 2009; Kirwan 2005).

Research into these food and wine events has considered:

• strategic planning, including linkages to tourism and regional development
(Beverland, Hoffman and Rasmussen 2001; Cavicchi and Santini 2014; Higham and Ritchie 2001; Jolliffe, Bui, and Nguyen 2008; Laing and Frost 2013; Lee and Arcodia 2011; Lewis 1997);

• critical success factors
(Taylor and Shanka 2002);

- consumer characteristics and motivations
                    (Dodd et al. 2006; Hall 2013; Yuan et al. 2005);

- the link between *festivalscape* (the physical environment and atmosphere) and satisfaction
                    (Mason and Paggiaro 2012);

- heritage
                    (Laing and Frost 2013; Timothy and Pena 2016);

- the increased use of websites and social media
                    (Frost and Laing 2015; Strickland, Williams, Laing and Frost 2016).

Popular culture themed festivals

These industrial events take as their theme elements of popular culture, such as music, cinema, science fiction or fantasy. Examples include:

- Comic-Con (Jenkins 2012)
- South by South West
- Film festivals (De Valck 2007; Frost 2009; Grunwell, Inhyuck and Martin 2008; Stevens 2016)
- The Doctor Who Festival
- Star Trek Conventions (Kozinets 2001)

The major popular culture events are commercial enterprises attracting large numbers of fans, as in the example of Comic-Con, held annually in San Diego. Established in 1970, it initially focused on fans of comic books. In order to attract more attendees, the organisers recruited groups with other youth popular culture interests. By 1980, attendance reached 5,000 people; in 2000 it was 48,000. At the 2011 Comic-Con, held over five days at the San Diego Convention Center, attendance was over 140,000 (Jenkins 2012).

Comic-Con allows creative industries such as television, film and games to gauge potential audience reactions to their new productions. In essence, they are able to launch prototypes and test them on the market. South by South West in Austin, Texas functions in a similar way for the music industry. As Jenkins observes, Comic-Con is 'the meeting place between a transmedia commercial culture and a grassroots participatory culture, the place where an uncertain Hollywood goes when it wants to better understand its always unstable relations with its audience' (2012: 23).

Social media has given the attendees a role as *influencers* or *trend-leaders*, 'intermediaries [who] help to inform and shape the ticket-buying habits of more casual audience members' (Jenkins 2012: 26). Whilst this role has always been there, societal changes have increased the importance of such fan events:

> Comic-Con is a microcosm of the dramatic changes transforming the US entertainment industry. As media options proliferate, attention is fragmenting and audience loyalty is declining. The entertainment industry depends on its fans like never before. As social media allows fans to connect with each other and actively spread the word about their favourites, fans are exerting an unprecedented impact on decisions regarding which films to finance and which [tv] series to put on the air.
>
> (Jenkins 2012: 36)

In this highly competitive temporary marketplace, 'Hollywood studios and television networks have to pull out all stops if they want to play, from clips of previously unreleased footage or surprise appearances by crowd-pleasing celebrities to costumes, props and sets on the floor of the Exhibit Hall' (Jenkins 2012: 26). Though there had been some talk that the major studios were less interested in what happened at Comic-Con, the 2010 event saw Marvel Studios introduce the entire cast of the upcoming *Avengers* film. In 2011, the main attraction turned out to be the television series *Game of Thrones*, with 7,000 fans turned away from a panel discussion of the show. In contrast, some shows garnered negative reactions, with attendees being very open about voicing their displeasure in preview screenings (Jenkins 2012).

At the other end of the scale, there are smaller events, some of which are staged by fans independently of the producers of the popular culture. The Gilmore Girls Fan Fest, which began in 2016, is an example of this. *Gilmore Girls* (2000–07) was a Warner Brothers' television series about a single mother and her teenage daughter who move to a small New England town. For that fictional setting, the series was shot in the town of Washington in Connecticut. The festival was created by Jennie Whitaker, who was inspired after she passed through the town on a trip. As she explained, 'I'm an avid, rabid fan and so when we drove through I thought, how come no one has done anything before? We should do something' (quoted in Zeitchik 2016). Fired with enthusiasm, she issued a press release and began selling tickets. Within a few hours, she had sold over a thousand tickets and then realised she had to organise the event. Whilst she could not get the main stars, she did recruit over a dozen supporting actors and production staff who made presentations about various aspects of the show. In all, 1,200 people attended the weekend event in the small town of 3,600 inhabitants (Zeitchik 2016).

The Gilmore Girls Fans Festival highlights the paradoxical nature of popular culture themed events initiated by fans. For participants, the event offers the opportunity for communitas with like-minded members of a fan subculture, forging a social world based on immersion in a fictional universe, through a process of co-creation with the original cultural production and their imagination (Frost and Laing 2014; Jenkins 2012). In this case, the television series producers in Warner Brothers had no involvement, though they also had no opposition. Such non-participation, however, does not mean that they have no commercial involvement. Fan subculture, including events, may influence future directions for popular culture brands. As with *Star Trek* and *Doctor Who*, the ongoing existence of a strong and committed fan base has led to the revival of the *Gilmore Girls*.

Product launches

These are one-off events designed to focus attention on a new product entering the marketplace. That new product might be a tangible item (for example, the launches of iPod, iPhone and iPad, which are available on Youtube and which we show to our students), or an event or service (for example in 2016 we attended the launch of the Cricket World Cup). While the focus may be on attracting the attention of other businesses (including retailers and wholesalers) or consumers, the key target of many product launches will be the media. Organisers are hoping to maximise that media coverage, turning the hype into ongoing trends, interest and sales. Accordingly, the design of these events is critically important, with the application of flair and spectacle in order to attract media outlets. Until recently the focus was primarily on the mainstream media, such as print and television, whereas now there is increasing emphasis on specialised bloggers and social media. Of all the types of industrial events examined in this chapter, product launches are by far the most under-researched. This may be partly due to their ephemeral nature and it may be because their importance in business and marketing strategies is under-recognised.

A qualification – just business?

As we have argued, industrial events are defined by their commercial focus. Their intention is to make money through the sales of goods and services. However, it is important to understand that some industrial events may also have secondary objectives – matching those we conventionally associate with events – of encouraging tourism and effecting social change.

Research into industrial events and tourism has generally fallen into two categories. The first is World's Fairs as mega-events and recognises that in order to gain government approval and funding, there is a need to attract tourists. It is the expenditure of these tourists flowing into the economy that justifies this public expenditure. Whilst in the past, this tourism impact was assumed rather than evaluated (Craik 1992), in recent years there has been increased research into the reinforcing and refashioning of the host city's destination image (Ferrari and Guala 2017), visitor motivation and segmentation (Lee et al. 2013) and the calculation of economic impact (Lee et al. 2017).

The second area of tourism research relates to regional and rural festivals, particularly wine and food. A number of studies have considered how such events have been developed with a strong purpose of encouraging tourism. In these cases, the rationale has been to utilise the key attributes of such rural destinations, namely their links with the land, farming and various agricultural products (Beverland et al. 2001; Cavicchi and Santini 2014; Hede and Stokes 2009; Higham and Ritchie

2001; Jolliffe et al. 2008; Laing and Frost 2013; Lee and Arcodia 2011; Lewis 1997). In taking such an approach, organisers are both distinguishing the characteristics of the country from the city and aiming to draw in urban tourists keen to experience those differences.

The social impacts and legacy of industrial events are also important. One of the chief social roles that industrial events may have is of revitalising cities. This is particularly clear with the construction of exhibition centres, often as an anchor for major redevelopments of run-down industrial and docklands precincts and for World's Fairs (Gold and Gold 2005; Richards and Palmer 2010). Such major undertakings usually require strong government support for planning permissions and funding and their justification is couched in terms of economic benefit and urban improvement. The impetus for the 1962 Seattle's World Fair, for example, was that civic leaders saw it as an opportunity to build a concert hall and city auditorium that would continue to be used after the event (Becker and Stein 2011).

Organisers and stakeholders of industrial events may have the objective of utilising the event as a medium for disseminating social messages and encouraging changes in society. The degree to which this occurs varies. It may be that the event is primarily about change, as in the case, for example, of an event promoting renewable energy. Alternatively, it may be that the event is more general, but the sponsors are promoting a social message. The Winery Walkabout, a wine festival staged annually since 1974 in Rutherglen, Australia, is sponsored by the government Transport Accident Commission. That agency uses the event to get across messages about not drinking and driving and the need to have a designated driver.

Food and wine festivals often feature social marketing. A few studies are worth noting. At farmers' markets and rural food festivals, the messages tend towards organic methods of production, the value of small producers, healthy eating and the need for urban dwellers to reconnect with food producers (Frost et al. 2016). Slow Food festivals concentrate on educating the public and have taken to social media to promote the concept of Slow Food to potential attendees (Frost and Laing 2015). The Nottingham Food and Drink Festival in the UK was partly developed to combat an image of central Nottingham as having a heavy-drinking culture and being dangerous and unattractive at night. Through this festival, a strategy was promoted of encouraging families to visit the city centre at night and that food and drink should be enjoyed together (Hollows, Jones, Taylor and Dowthwaite 2014). Many food and wine festivals have ethnic themes and aim to promote a sense of heritage and identity amongst the community (Laing and Frost 2013; Timothy and Pena 2016).

All of the above may be seen as desirable social messages. However, it must also be acknowledged that there are some industrial events that provoke controversy and dissonance, as they promote products, (and associated attitudes and behaviours) that some sections of society would like to see restricted or even banned. In the USA, for example, there is the Shooting, Hunting and Outdoor Trade (SHOT) Show. Held annually in Las Vegas, the 2016 show comprised 1,600 booths, 64,000 attendees and a presentation by then presidential candidate Donald Trump (Rowley 2016). In contrast, in South Korea, the Busan City Council tried to shut down the Busan Film Festival as they felt that it had become politically too left wing in screening a documentary that criticised the government (Brasor 2016). Such examples demonstrate that while industrial events are about sales, like many events they reflect issues within societies. Given that there is a 'heritage of events as places of ferment and political dialogue' (Laing and Frost 2010: 265), the highly commercial nature of industrial events may from time to time stimulate such socio-political controversies.

Scope and structure of this book

Our aim in this book is to tell the story of industrial events and encourage readers – whether they are academics, students or industry practitioners – to take a different view of events. As the field of events studies grows and matures, it is time that we looked more deeply at those events that are designed to sell goods and services. Whilst there is now widespread understanding of the tourism and social impacts of events, we also need to consider that a significant component of the events industry is very commercially focused and that events are an effective marketing medium used widely across many industries.

This book is divided into three parts. The first examines international exhibitions, industry and trade shows and comprises Chapters 2 to 6. The second focuses on food and beverage festivals and also consists of five chapters (Chapters 7 to 11). The third analyses the trend towards using industrial events to promote social messages regarding sustainability, comprising Chapters 12 to 15.

References

Alberca-Oliver, P., Rodriguez-Oromendia, A. and Parte-Esteban, L. (2015) 'Measuring the efficiency of trade shows: A Spanish case study', *Tourism Management*, 47, 127–137.

Aldebert, B., Dang, R. and Longhi, C. (2011) 'Innovation in the tourism industry: The case of Tourism@', *Tourism Management*, 32, 1204–1213.

Auerbach, J. (1999) *The Great Exhibition of 1851: A Nation on Display*, New Haven, CT: Yale University Press.

Bathelt, H., Golfetto, F. and Rinallo, D. (2014) *Trade Shows in the Globalizing Knowledge Economy*, Oxford: Oxford University Press.

Becker, P. and Stein, A. (2011) *The Future Remembered: The 1962 Seattle World's Fair and Its Legacy*, Seattle: Seattle Center Foundation.

Berné, C. and Garcia-Uceda, M. (2008) 'Criteria involved in evaluation of trade shows to visit', *Industrial Marketing Management*, 37(5), 565–579.

Beverland, M., Hoffman, D. and Rasmussen, M. (2001) 'The evolution of events in the Australasian wine sector', *Tourism Recreation Research*, 26(2), 35–44.

Brasor, P. (2016) 'Despite controversy, the Busan International Film Festival is as strong as ever', *Japan Times*, 13 October, www.japantimes.co.jp/culture/2016/10/13/films/despite-controversy-busan-international-film-festival-strong-ever/#.WB-nsCQrbVc (accessed 31 October 2016).

Cavicchi, A. and Santini, C. (Eds.). (2014) *Food and Wine Events in Europe*, London and New York: Routledge.

Craik, J. (1992) 'Expo 88: Fashions of sight and politics of site', in T. Bennett, P. Buckridge, D. Carter and C. Mercer (eds.), *Celebrating the Nation: A Critical Study of Australia's Bicentenary* (pp. 142–159), Sydney: Allen & Unwin.

De Valck, M. (2007) *Film Festivals: From European Geopolitics to Global Cinephilia*, Amsterdam: Amsterdam University Press.

Dodd, T., Yuan, J., Adams, C. and Kolyesnikova, N. (2006) 'Motivations of young people for visiting wine festivals', *Event Management*, 10(1), 23–33.

Entwistle, J. and Rocamora, A. (2006) 'The field of fashion materialized: A study of London fashion week', *Sociology*, 40(4), 735–751.

Evers, N. and Knight, J. (2008) 'Role of international trade shows in small firm internationalization: A network perspective', *International Marketing Review*, 25(5), 544–562.

Ferrari, S. and Guala, C. (2017) 'Mega-events and their legacy: Image and tourism in Genoa, Turin and Milan', *Leisure Studies*, 36(1), 119–137.

Frost, W. (2009) 'Projecting an image: Film-induced festivals in the American West', *Event Management*, 12(2), 95–103.

Frost, W. and Laing, J. (2011) *Strategic Management of Festivals and Events*, Melbourne: Cengage.

Frost, W. and Laing, J. (2013) *Commemorative Events: Memory, Identities, Conflicts*, London and New York: Routledge.

Frost, W. and Laing, J. (2014) 'The role of fashion in subculture events: Exploring steampunk events', in K. Williams, J. Laing and W. Frost (eds.), *Fashion, Design and Events* (pp. 177–190), London and New York: Routledge.

Frost, W. and Laing, J. (2015) 'Communicating persuasive messages through slow food festivals', *Journal of Vacation Marketing*, 19(1), 67–74.

Frost, W., Laing, J., Best, G., Williams, K., Strickland, P. and Lade, C. (2016) *Gastronomy, Tourism and the Media*, Bristol: Channel View.

Gold, J.R. and Gold, M.M. (2005) *Cities of Culture: Staging International Festivals and the Urban Agenda, 1851–2000*, Aldershot, UK: Ashgate.

Gopalakrishna, S., Roster, C. and Sridhar, S. (2010) 'An exploratory study of attendee activities at a business trade show', *Journal of Business & Industrial Marketing*, 25(4), 241–248.

Greenhalgh, P. (1988) *Ephemeral Vistas: The Expositions Universelles, Great Exhibitions and World Fairs, 1851–1939*, Manchester: Manchester University Press.

Grosvenor, E.S. and Wesson, M. (1997) *Alexander Graham Bell: The Life and Times of the Man Who Invented the Telephone*, New York: Abrams.

Grunwell, S., Inhyuck, H. and Martin, B. (2008) 'A comparative analysis of attendee profiles at two urban festivals', *Journal of Convention & Event Tourism*, 9(1), 1–14.

Guizzardi, A., Mariani, M. and Prayag, G. (2017) 'Environmental impacts and certification: Evidence from the Milan World Expo 2015', *International Journal of Contemporary Hospitality Management*, 29(3), 1052–1071.

Hall, C.M. (2013) 'The local in farmers' markets in New Zealand', in C.M. Hall and S. Gössling (eds.), *Sustainable Culinary Systems: Local Foods, Innovation, Tourism and Hospitality* (pp. 99–121), London and New York: Routledge.

Hede, A.-M. and Stokes, R. (2009) 'Network analysis of tourism events: An approach to improve marketing practices for sustainable tourism', *Journal of Travel & Tourism Marketing*, 26(7), 656–669.

Higham, J. and Ritchie, B. (2001) 'The evolution of festivals and other events in rural southern New Zealand', *Event Management*, 7(1), 39–49.

Hoffenberg, P. (2001) *An Empire on Display: English, Indian and Australian Exhibitions from the Crystal Palace to the Great War*, Berkeley, CA: University of California Press.

Hollenbeck, G., Peters, C. and Zinkhan, G. (2008) 'Retail spectacles and brand meaning: Insights from a brand museum case study', *Journal of Retailing*, 84(3), 334–353.

Hollows, J., Jones, S., Taylor, B. and Dowthwaite, K. (2014) 'Making sense of urban food festivals: Cultural regeneration, disorder and hospitable cities', *Journal of Policy Research in Tourism, Leisure & Events*, 6(1), 1–14.

International Bureau des Expositions (2016) *International Bureau des Expositions*, www.bie-paris.org/site/en/ (accessed 23 September 2016).

Jenkins, H. (2012) 'Superpowered fans: The many worlds of San Diego's Comic-Con', *Boom: A Journal of California*, 2(2), 22–36.

Jin, X. and Weber, K. (2013) 'Developing and testing a model of exhibition brand preference: The exhibitors' preference', *Tourism Management*, 38(5), 94–104.

Jin, X., Weber, K. and Bauer, T. (2012) 'Impacts of clusters on exhibition destination attractiveness: Evidence from mainland China', *Tourism Management*, 33(6), 1429–1439.

Jolliffe, L., Bui, H. and Nguyen, H. (2008) 'The Buon Ma Thuot Coffee Festival, Vietnam: Opportunity for tourism?', in J. Ali-Knight, M. Robertson, A. Fyall and A. Ladkin (eds.), *International Perspectives of Festivals and Events: Paradigms of Analysis* (pp. 125–137), Oxford: Elsevier.

Kirwan, J. (2005) 'The interpersonal world of direct marketing: Examining the conventions of quality at UK farmers' markets', *Journal of Rural Studies*, 22(3), 301–312.

Kozinets, R. (2001) 'Utopian enterprise: Articulating the meaning of Star Trek's culture of consumption', *The Journal of Consumer Research*, 28(1), 67–88.

Laing, J. and Frost, W. (2010) '"How green was my festival": Exploring challenges and opportunities associated with staging green events', *International Journal of Hospitality Management*, 29(2), 261–267.

Laing, J. and Frost, W. (2013) 'Food, wine . . . heritage, identity? Two case studies of Italian diaspora festivals in regional Victoria', *Tourism Analysis*, 18(3), 323–334.

Lamberti, L., Noci, G., Guo, J. and Zhu, S. (2011) 'Mega-events as drivers of community participation in developing countries: The case of Shanghai World Expo', *Tourism Management*, 32, 1474–1483.

Lampel, J. and Meyer, A.D. (2008) 'Field-configuring events as structuring mechanisms: How conferences, ceremonies, and trade shows constitute new technologies, industries, and markets', *Journal of Management Studies*, 45(6), 1025–1035.

Lee, C.-K., Kang, S. and Lee, Y. (2013) 'Segmentation of mega-event motivation: The case of Expo 2010 Shanghai China', *Asia Pacific Journal of Tourism Research*, 18, 637–660.

Lee, C.-K., Mjelde, J. and Kwon, Y. (2017) 'Estimating the economic impact of a mega-event on host and neighbouring regions', *Leisure Studies*, 36(1), 138–152.

Lee, I. and Arcodia, C. (2011) 'The role of regional food festivals in destination branding', *International Journal of Tourism Research*, 13(4), 355–367.

Lewis, G. (1997) 'Celebrating asparagus: Community and the rationally constructed food festival', *Journal of American Culture*, 20(4), 73–78.

Mason, M. and Paggiaro, A. (2012) 'Investigating the role of festivalscape in culinary tourism: The case of food and wine events', *Tourism Management*, 33, 1329–1336.

Money, L. (2012) 'Food for thought brings festival to life', *The Age*, 1 March, 24.

Otgaar, A. (2012) 'Towards a common agenda for the development of industrial tourism', *Tourism Management Perspectives*, 4, 86–91.

Power, D. and Jansson, J. (2008) 'Cyclical clusters in global circuits: Overlapping spaces in furniture trade fairs', *Economic Geography*, 84(4), 423–448.

Richards, G. and Palmer, R. (2010) *Eventful Cities: Cultural Management and Urban Revitalisation*, Oxford and Burlington, VT: Butterworth-Heinemann.

Roche, M. (2000) *Mega-Events & Modernity: Olympics and Expos in the Growth of Global Culture*, London and New York: Routledge.

Rowley, T. (2016) 'Under the gun', *The Age*, Good Weekend section, 12 March, 14–17.

Rydell, R. (1984) *All the World's a Fair: Visions of Empire of American International Expositions, 1876–1916*, Chicago and London: University of Chicago Press.

Rydell, R. (1993) *World of Fairs: The Century of Progress Expositions*, Chicago and London: University of Chicago Press.

Rydell, R. and Kroes, R. (2005) *Buffalo Bill in Bologna: The Americanization of the World, 1869–1922*, Chicago and London: University of Chicago Press.

Schlender, B. and Tetzeli, R. (2015) *Becoming Steve Jobs: The Evolution of a Reckless Upstart into a Visionary Leader*, New York: Crown Business.

Skov, L. (2006) 'The role of trade fairs in the global fashion business', *Current Sociology*, 54(5), 764–783.

Song, H.J., Bae, S.Y. and Lee, C.-K. (2017) 'Identifying antecedents and outcomes of festival satisfaction: The case of a cosmetics and beauty expo', *International Journal of Contemporary Hospitality Management*, 29(3), 947–965.

Stevens, K. (2016) 'From film weeks to festivals: Australia's film festival boom in the 1980s', *Studies in Australasian Cinema*, 10(2), 250–263.

Strickland, P., Williams, K., Laing, J. and Frost, W. (2016) 'The use of social media in the wine event industry: A case study of the High Country Harvest Festival in Australia', in G. Szolnoki, L. Thach and D. Kolb (eds.), *Successful Social Media & Ecommerce Strategies in the Wine Industry* (pp. 74–92), New York: Palgrave Macmillan.

Taylor, R. and Shanka, T. (2002) 'Attributes for staging successful wine festivals', *Event Management*, 7(3), 165–175.

Timothy, D. and Pena, M. (2016) 'Food festivals and heritage awareness', in D. Timothy (ed.), *Heritage Cuisines: Traditions, Identities and Tourism* (pp. 148–165), London and New York: Routledge.

Weller, S. (2013) 'Consuming the city: Public fashion festivals and the participatory economies of urban spaces in Melbourne, Australia', *Urban Studies*, 50(14), 2853–2868.

Yuan, J., Cai, L., Morrison, A. and Linton, S. (2005) 'An analysis of wine festival attendees' motivations: A synergy of wine, travel and special events?', *Journal of Vacation Marketing*, 11(1), 41–58.

Zeitchik, S. (2016) 'Gilmore Girls fans bring zeal – and a dash of Comic-Con – to the real Stars Hollow', *Los Angeles Times*, 17 October, www.latimes.com/entertainment/tv/la-et-st-stars-hollow-returns-20161022-snap-story.html (accessed 29 October 2016).

2   Modernity on show

World's Fairs, international exhibitions
and expos, 1851–2020

Warwick Frost, Gary Best and Jennifer Laing

It Happened at the World's Fair (1963)

Most of the musical-romance films of Elvis Presley followed a standard formula. He was a young ex-serviceman trying to achieve success, usually through expertise with exciting modern technology, such as helicopters, racing cars, scuba gear or motorbikes. In many cases, the backdrop was a trendy leisure destination. Examples of these included Hawaii, Las Vegas and Fort Lauderdale. These elements come together in *It Happened at the World's Fair*, where pilot Elvis finds his life transformed through adventures at the 1962 Seattle World's Fair.

Mike (Presley) and Danny (Gary Lockwood) are crop-dusting pilots down on their luck. In essence, they and their rickety biplane are emblematic of the old economy. When Elvis reluctantly agrees to escort a young girl Sue-Lin (Vicky Tiu) to the World's Fair, he is gradually exposed to modernity and new opportunities. When Sue-Lin gets sick from over-eating junk food, Elvis meets and falls for nurse Dianne (Joan O'Brien). To meet her again, he engineers an injured shin through paying a young Kurt Russell to kick him. Worried that he might sue them, the Fair's management insist that Joan help him home via a restaurant meal atop the Space Needle.

The film is just a light-weight confection, but it does make some interesting points about the roles and features of international exhibitions. With an official title of the Century 21 Exposition, the Seattle World's Fair was conceived as showcasing future technology, particularly highlighting Seattle as a hub for the aerospace industry. Initially, the fair had been conceived as a modest 50th anniversary for Seattle's 1909 Alaska-Yukon-Pacific Exposition. Plans changed, however, with the launch of the Soviet satellite *Sputnik* in 1957. In the USA, this news was greeted with dismay. The USSR had shot to the lead in the 'Space Race', whilst America had not even planned to compete. Under immense public and media pressure, America began to invest large amounts in science and engineering with the view of restoring national pride. For the organisers of Seattle's World's Fair, here was an opportunity and they shifted their focus towards science and space (Becker and Stein 2011; Findlay 1992).

However, very little of this comes through in the film, with the Fair being represented as not much more than a normal state fair. For Sue-Lin, her day out is all about eating as much junk food as she can. At no stage is either she or Elvis viewing the exhibits with any interest. Some do appear – such as the monorail, Space Needle and the futuristic General Motors Firebird III – but their screen time is fairly limited. Indeed, it is curious that as a pilot, Elvis shows little interest in the jet-like Firebird, one of a series of prototypes that General Motors developed specifically for displays at World's Fairs and Motorama auto shows. Ford's counterpart – the Seattle-ite XXI, with six wheels and pre-internet computerised navigation – does not even appear, nor does the Science Pavilion, the centrepiece of the Fair. In the musical finale of the film, Elvis joins a cheesy marching band as it performs – a concluding vignette that looks backwards to small-town Americana, rather than towards the future.

Nonetheless, the film does present some sort of futuristic vision. When they first meet, Joan tells Mike that she has applied for the Space Medical Corps. Grabbing his arm with enthusiasm, she says that the future is in outer space and they need pilots. Mike starts to think about this. Conveniently, he and Danny are able to sign up at the National Aeronautics and Space Administration (NASA) stand at the World's Fair. Rather than just being crop-dusters, they now see they will have the right stuff to help the USA win the space race.

NASA had been created in 1958 and with President John Kennedy's 1961 pronouncement that the USA was going to the Moon, its programme and budget was rapidly expanding. The Seattle World's Fair provided an excellent public relations opportunity. General Motors had their rocket-like concept car (which they had no intention of putting into production). In contrast, the NASA exhibit had an authentic Mercury space capsule on display and brought in a real astronaut in John Glenn – as the first American to orbit the Earth, he was arguably as big a celebrity as Elvis (Becker and Stein 2011).

NASA's strategy at Seattle was not to sign up adult pilots and nurses, but to win over the support of the general public, particularly children. One such child was Bonnie Dunbar, a 13-year-old local girl. As she recalled her visit to the NASA exhibit:

> I was excited to go because I was told there would be space, I'd get to see the future. That was the most exciting part for me . . . I wanted to fly in space and I knew NASA was someplace I wanted to work. This was about going into the future . . . It was educating and inspiring and I was part of that audience. If that was what they intended to do, it worked on me.
>
> (quoted in Baskas 2012)

Though at the time astronauts were all male, Dunbar pursued the idea implanted by the World's Fair. In 1981, she was admitted to NASA's space programme and successfully completed five missions into space (Baskas 2012).

Understanding World's Fairs

World's Fairs are the grand examples of industrial events. In the typology used for events, they are *Mega-Events*, drawing participants and media attention from around the world and attracting millions of attendees. Like the Olympics, they are gained through an international bidding process and shift from city to city (Frost and Laing

2011). Seattle, for example, has hosted just the two World's Fairs of 1909 and 1962. These events also stand out in having a long history, becoming popular in the 19th century. In this chapter our aim is to better understand these industrial events by examining their history and how they have changed over time. Initially starting as exhibitions promoting imperialism and national achievements, they have changed to placing a greater emphasis on a vision of the future for industry and society.

Displaying trade, industry and empire

The 1851 Great Exhibition in London has come to be regarded as the template for all future World's Fairs. Even though the Great Exhibition itself was inspired by a series of earlier French Industrial Expositions, its scale and impact greatly out-stripped its forebears. It was simply 'Great' and all others that followed aspired to being comparable. Through its steel and glass exhibition hall that became known as the Crystal Palace, it gained immense media coverage and attracted six million visitors during the five and a half months that it was open (Auerbach 1999). Prince Albert was the chairman of the organising committee and saw the Exhibition 'as a forum where the nations would come together in both celebration and competition, where swords would be beaten into steam engines, barometers and piano rolls' (Gill 2010: 245). His wife, Queen Victoria, was equally enthusiastic and was a regular attendee, allowing the Koh-i-Noor diamond to be put on display as one of the British exhibits (Gill 2010).

With such an audacious design using new building materials, the Great Exhibition and Crystal Palace became enduring symbols of modernism and the peak of the British Empire (Buzard, Childers and Gillooly 2007). With its ordered group-ings of manufactured items, available under one roof to see, experience and perhaps buy, it suggested later developments in department stores and was the harbinger of modern consumer society (Gurney 2007). Whilst organisers wanted to downplay national divisions, they were ultimately unsuccessful, with the layout emphasising national achievements. Like the modern Olympics, the media quickly became obsessed with the counting of the medals awarded to the competing countries (Buzard 2007). Its success as an event revolutionised tourism. To attract people from outside of London, especially skilled mechanics and their families, innovative thinking was required. Thomas Cook was contracted to organise tours, complete with rail-tickets, accommodation and admission (Auerbach 1999; Roche 2000). Entry prices differed depending on the day, and it was occasionally free, which made it accessible to a broad, yet remarkably well-behaved audience (Gill 2010).

With the success of the Crystal Palace, the concept was quickly picked up by two other super-powers. The USA staged a World's Fair at New York in 1853 and then one to commemorate the Centenary of the Declaration of Independence at Philadelphia in 1876. The turn of the century saw a flurry of American World's Fairs, including New Orleans (1884), Chicago (1893), Omaha (1898), Buffalo (1901), St Louis (1904), Portland (1905), Norfolk (1907), Seattle (1909), San Francisco (1915) and San Diego (1915). These established the USA as the centre of this concept. As Gold and Gold comment, 'it is difficult nowadays to realise how much significance expositions once had in the USA' (2005: 83).

France also quickly imitated its rival. World's Fairs were held at Paris in 1855, 1867, 1878, 1889 and 1900. Of these, the 1889 one was the most prominent, commemorating the centenary of the French Revolution and leaving a legacy in the Eiffel Tower. Other European countries to stage World's Fairs in the 19th century were Italy, Spain, Portugal, Austria and Belgium. The success of an international event, rotating through major cities and bringing together a range of nations in one place provoked other ideas of internationalism. When the 1889 Paris Exposition included an athletics games, it provided Pierre de Coubertin with inspiration to revive the Olympic Games (Roche 2000). Indeed, the Olympics would be staged parallel to World's Fairs at Paris (1900) and St Louis (1904). The latter was originally awarded to Chicago, but was strategically moved so that St Louis would host both events.

As with the Crystal Palace, the chief objectives of these exhibitions were to promote manufacturing and trade. Staging a World's Fair allowed the promotion of the regional economy and the opportunity to develop trading networks and new markets. Just getting organised to exhibit could be a stimulus for innovation. For the 1855 Paris International Exhibition, the Emperor Louis Napoleon requested the wine merchants of Bordeaux to develop some sort of classification to allow visitors to make sense of the extensive wine displays. The result was the Bordeaux Wine Official Classification, dividing vineyards into five *crus* (or growths) on the basis of reputation and price at the time. Still in use today, it provides a classification of terroir and continues to be criticised for its rigidity (Simpson 2011).

These 19th century World's Fairs were self-consciously aimed at the rapidly-growing urban middle classes. In this and their focus on major cities, they set patterns that still exist today (Roche 2000). These were events that were strategically positioned to win the support of the new elites and bind them to a strong vision of the future. As Ley and Olds remarked, these events combined culture and consumerism and education and entertainment, in reimagining modernity:

> Part of the fantasy of the expositions was their optimistic portrayal of a middle-class present and future, aesthetic, hygienic, pleasurable, self-improving, and consensual, where conflict and scarcity were no more evident than in any other middle-class setting.
>
> (1988: 200)

Imperial conquests on show

As well as promoting manufacturing, the World's Fairs before World War One were focused on imperialism and colonies. This approach had a twofold purpose: reinforcing home support for such expansionist policies and demonstrating one's expansionist achievements to external audiences. Such promotion, however, entailed some risks. For example, British authorities were concerned at German enthusiasm for the 1880 World's Fair in Melbourne, where the German Emperor funded a prize for the best colonial manufactured item (which was won by wine-maker Hubert de Castella). The worry was that the Germans were using the event to further their trade interests at the expense of the British (Hoffenberg 2001).

Within the British Empire, exhibitions at home, Australia and India 'were part of the self-conscious reworking of fluid national and imperial identities' (Hoffenberg 2001: xiv). The Australian colonists were enthusiastic imitators, organising their own exhibitions and building a magnificent Italianate domed building for their 1880 World's Fair (Dunstan 1996; Young 2008). At the time of federation in 1901, it was the largest building by far in Australia and accordingly was chosen as the venue for the first parliament. Restored as part of the Centenary of Federation, in 2004 this Royal Exhibition Building was added to the UNESCO World Heritage List as one of the last remaining intact structures from the great exhibitions of the 19th century (Frost 2012). In contrast, Indian exhibitions were planned by colonial officials and omitted references to the possibilities of independence (Hoffenberg 2001).

Whilst often characterised as mainly primary producers, the self-governing Australian colonies were interested in diversifying their production base. World's Fairs were a conduit for their economic independence. Heavily invested in the Victorian values of progress and modernity, their World's Fairs were a showcase for the latest technology. Intriguingly, they juxtaposed British industrial power against colonial import-replacement innovations (Figures 2.1 and 2.2). Though mainly focused on maintaining their links with Britain (Young 2008), they also featured exhibits that indicated pride in their distinctive natural environment (Figure 2.3) and included exhibits from their neighbours in Asia and the Pacific (Figure 2.4).

Figure 2.1 Made in Melbourne, colonial manufactured locomotives, Melbourne International Exhibition 1880

Source: Photo courtesy of State Library of Victoria

Figure 2.2 Melbourne as an imperial market, British machinery on display, Melbourne
International Exhibition 1880

Source: Photo courtesy of State Library of Victoria

Figure 2.3 Landscape nationalism, an Australian scenic diorama, Melbourne International
Exhibition 1880

Source: Photo courtesy of State Library of Victoria

Figure 2.4 Trade with Asia, the Japanese booth promotes raw silk, tea and rice, Melbourne
    International Exhibition 1880

Source: Photo courtesy of State Library of Victoria

A trio of American World's Fairs – Chicago (1893), St Louis (1904) and Portland (1905) – promoted the concept of Manifest Destiny. All three were commemorative events: Chicago being the 400th Anniversary of Columbus, St Louis
the Centenary of the Louisiana Purchase (through which the USA had gained
territories west of the Mississippi) and Portland the Centenary of the Lewis and
Clark Expedition which explored these new territories. These historical commemorations were all linked to the idea of Manifest Destiny, a popular view that it was
clearly America's destiny to keep expanding westwards, even ultimately further
into the Pacific Ocean and South America. The turn of the century saw this concept
at its height and it played out in the 1898 acquisitions of Hawaii, the Philippines
and Puerto Rico (Frost and Laing 2013).

Following on from the recent takeover of the Philippines, the St Louis Fair
featured a 'Philippine Reservation', with 1,200 Filipinos. About half of these were
presented as living in a supposedly traditional tribal manner, whereas the other half
were auxiliary veterans from the recent war with Spain. The juxtaposition of the
two groups was intended to represent progress (Frost and Laing 2013; Rydell
1984). The official guide for the World's Fair made the link between historical and
contemporary progress very clear, stating 'the time is coming when the purchase

and retention of the Philippine Islands will seem as wise to our descendants as does the Louisiana Purchase seem to us who live today' (quoted in Rydell 1984: 167).

The use of the term 'Reservation' was deliberately suggestive of American policies towards Native Americans. Reinforcing this view of racial and imperial superiority, St Louis contained displays of Native Americans to complement that of the Filipinos. Earlier World's Fairs had also exhibited Native Americans, though in the case of Philadelphia in 1876 this was tempered by the national shock arising from the defeat of George Custer at the Battle of Little Bighorn in that centennial year. By the turn of the century, hostilities were almost at an end and an elegiac view of Native American culture as fast disappearing was more in evidence. At Chicago in 1893, Buffalo Bill's Wild West Show was extremely popular, though it was not part of the official exhibition, Buffalo Bill simply renting an adjoining field. Approximately 170 Native Americans from the Great Plains were employed in Buffalo Bill's Show at Chicago, both performing daily and providing a supposedly traditional camp that visitors could wander through (Rydell and Kroes 2005). The Chicago World's Fair was also the venue for historian Frederick Jackson Turner to present his influential thesis that the now closed frontier had made the USA exceptional. St Louis in 1904 featured the Apache warrior Geronimo in its display and he was so popular that President Theodore Roosevelt included him in his inauguration parade (Frost and Laing 2013).

Selling culture: art nouveau and haute couture

The 1900 Exposition Universelle in Paris attracted an estimated 50 million people, which was 'more than the French population at the time' (Greenhalgh 2011: 28), although projected attendance had been 60 million (Mandell 1967). The Paris Olympic Games were held concurrently with the Exposition, as was to happen in St Louis in 1904, adding to the city's vibrancy. It was the last hurrah for the great 19th century French exhibitions (Wilson 1991), with many concessionaires losing money and discounted tickets towards the end. There was also perhaps less desire for demonstrations of 'cultural imperialism' (Mandell 1967: 110). Yet there was evidence that the Exposition had had positive economic benefits for the city, and brought Paris alive. The liberal use of electricity and a sustained period of good weather saw crowds amass to enjoy a night's entertainment, although Mandell (1967: 84) notes that 'despite the electric lighting, the grounds [of the Exposition] were disappointingly empty in the evening'.

Architectural legacies from the 1900 Exposition continue to form part of the backdrop of Paris for modern visitors, namely the Grand and Petit Palais and the Pont Alexandre, which were built in monumental, yet a 'somewhat restrained' style, given they were designed to be permanent (Mandell 1967: 72). They can be contrasted with the temporary buildings which were often overblown, with every surface covered and decorated with allegorical sculptures, statues and friezes (Mandell 1967), and the giant Ferris Wheel, which was a standard attraction at World's Fairs by then and later demolished in 1920. One of the great acts of historical vandalism was thwarted when plans to dismantle the Eiffel Tower down to the first stage and build a Museum of Mankind on top were scrapped due to the prohibitive costs (Arwas 2002).

Perhaps the greatest legacy of the Exposition is its presentation of two forms of artistic expression – French high fashion or *haute couture* and the new art movement known as *art nouveau*. This reflected the desire of Napoleon III in his decree of 1853 to put the fine arts centre-stage at expositions: 'May it be particularly the role of France, whose industry owes so much to the fine arts, to grant them the place they deserve at the forthcoming universal exhibition' (quoted in Green 2013: 5).

The links between Paris and its fashion industry were made clear as soon as the visitor entered the exhibition through the Monumental Gateway or Porte de la Concorde. Created by René Binet, the Orientalist fantasy structure was topped by a gargantuan 15-foot statue of a woman, *La Parisienne*, wearing a gown by couturière Jeanne Paquin, rather than the classical garments worn by traditional allegorical symbols of France such as Liberty (Dymond 2011; Tolini Finamore 2003). The statue was meant to be the symbol of modernity – 'bespeaking a world of luxury, elegance, and ease, a world accessible through commodities' (Wilson 1991: 148) – and illustrating France's position as a leader in luxury goods, notably fashion (Tolini Finamore 2003), but this new powerful symbol of women polarised some people and was criticised as 'the triumph of prostitution' (Julian 1974: 38).

All French World's Fairs had included a pavilion or display centred on fashion (Tolini Finamore 2003). In 1900, the focus was on the Palais du Costume, which showcased a historical display, and the Palais des Fils, Tissus et Vêtements, highlighting current clothing and fabric (Dymond 2011). Traditional provincial attire, which was presented as unchanging, was juxtaposed with the latest urban styles aimed at the chic and wealthy (Dymond 2011). The garb was arranged on wax mannequins and tableaus were created, everything from 'Departure for the Opéra' to 'Fitting the Wedding Gown' (Steele 1988). It was clearly an aspirational experience for many of the visitors, who were mostly 'the lower bourgeoisie' (Julian 1974: 199) and it was no coincidence that the organisational team included the director of the Magasins du Bon Marché department store, given the close relationship between the great 19th-century exhibitions and department store displays of the period and the shared objective to awaken consumer demand (Greenhalgh 2011; Steele 1988). Wilson (1991: 149) labels the Exposition 'an occasion for instruction in progressive, patriotic consumption', which was particularly aimed at women.

Examples of art nouveau could be seen at various exhibitions at the turn of the 20th century, but its apotheosis is acknowledged as the 1900 Paris Exposition (Olsen Theiding 2006), with the greatest number of exponents of this movement yet assembled (Greenhalgh 2011: 215). Sadly, it was also the herald of its decline, with the movement not lasting 'long beyond the [twentieth] century's first decade' (Olsen Theiding 2006: 227). Its legacy in modern Paris can still be seen in some of the Métro railway entrances designed by Guimard (Greenhalgh 2011) and the décor of Maxim's restaurant. The first leg of the underground opened during the Exposition (Arwas 2002) in order to assist with the movement of people.

Art nouveau is characterised by motifs that were held to be timeless by being drawn from nature, such as swans, seaweed, lily-pads and peacocks (Mandell 1967: 75). Its 'ephemeral vogue' (Julian 1974: 208) is therefore ironic, and can be attributed to two factors. First, the commodification of the art movement in the form of everyday household items 'vulgarised' it, as did the 'facile imita-tions' of artistic works such as Lalique glass or furniture by Majorelle (Julian 1974: 211). The craftsmanship and much of its delicate nuances were lost when industrial production took over. Second, much of what was seen at the Exposi-tion was not the full glory of art nouveau, but simply 'the elaborate concoctions of the architects of the Beaux-Arts who were anxious to appear modern' (Julian 1974: 208). Conservative control over the art that was presented was manifest (Mandell 1967). Instead, the contribution to art made by the Exposition was chiefly in the display of work from places such as Asia, Africa and South America, leading to the 'birth of a new aesthetic system' (Julian 1974: 208). Other exceptions included the German, Austrian and Hungarian displays of art nouveau (*Jugendstil* in Germany), the American exhibits of Tiffany glass, Rodin's sculptures and the privately curated Bing Pavilion, named for S. Bing, the dealer and patron of art nouveau (Mandell 1967), which housed 'the most elegant and *avant-garde* specimens of Art Nouveau furniture and hangings' (Julian 1974: 115) by artists such as de Feure and Grasset. De Feure was responsible for the frescoes of 'peacock-women' who adorned the façade of the pavilion.

The presentation of art nouveau at the 1900 Exposition was the subject of much debate in Great Britain, with the movement described as corrupt and degenerate (Olsen Theiding 2006). Conversely, it was also criticised as an imitation of earlier British work by the likes of William Morris and his Arts and Crafts movement. One of the jurors in 1900, George Donaldson, gave some samples of furniture, pottery and glassware that were exhibited in Paris to the Victoria and Albert Museum, but there were protests from various artists of the time, printed in *The Times* in 1901, and the exhibits, after touring the regions, were kept in storage in an annex until 1985 (Olsen Theiding 2006).

A New Deal

Following the Great Depression, 100 million Americans attended six successful World's Fairs between 1933 and 1939 (Rydell 1993). At first glance, this seems extraordinary, especially as poor attendances at the 1926 Philadelphia World's Fair had been thought to indicate that the public was tiring of the concept. At a time of maximum economic, social and political uncertainty, surely people would be con-servative in their leisure expenditures. Two forces seemed to be at play. The first was that – as with the success of Hollywood cinema at this time – the public was seeking escapism. The second was that organisers and governments followed a conscious strategy of reinforcing stability and brighter prospects through these exhibitions. World's Fairs were seized upon as part of the marketing of President Franklin Roosevelt's New Deal.

Roosevelt was familiar with the power of World's Fairs through being involved with the organisation of the 1915 San Diego Exhibition. He was aware that expenditure on such a project could help stimulate the economy. The 1933 Chicago World's Fair, for example, employed 22,000 workers for its construction (Gold and Gold 2005). Even more importantly, his administration saw the symbolism of what these World's Fairs offered to the American people. Accordingly, themes of a better future based on scientific and economic progress were emphasised. These World's Fairs became a *medium* for disseminating messages that supported the government's reform programme and 'were designed to restore popular faith in the vitality of the nation's economic and political system and, more specifically, in the ability of government, business, scientific and intellectual leaders to lead the country out of the depression' (Rydell 1993: 9).

The organisers of these 1930s World's Fairs were very aware of the brief they had been given and the need for subtlety in promoting these persuasive messages. As Frank Sewett, President of the Scientific Advisory Committee for Chicago reported, the exhibits needed to provide:

> a quite unconscious schooling to the thoughtful people [who will] . . . pass through the fair and go out of it, largely without any consciousness of having being educated [but they] . . . go educated to the idea that science is the root of most of the material things, and many of the social things, which make up modern life.
>
> (quoted in Rydell 1993: 96)

By the time of the 1939 New York World's Fair, confidence in the power of these exhibitions led to the abandonment of the need for subliminal messaging. New York – staged to commemorate the 150th anniversary of the inauguration of George Washington as President – boldly promoted a message of the desirability of democracy. Britain, which had tended to focus on colonial achievements, happily changed its emphasis to fit in with the USA, and its exhibiting of the Magna Carta was one of the most popular displays. In contrast, Nazi Germany felt snubbed by promotion of democracy as the ideal political system and chose not to exhibit (Greenhalgh 1988).

The automobile takes over

World War Two brought a temporary hiatus, with there being a gap until World's Fairs were staged at Brussels, Belgium in 1958 and Seattle in 1962. However, prior to British Prime Minister Chamberlain's declaration of war against Germany on September 3, 1939, four months earlier, on April 30, the 1939 New York World's Fair, billed as 'The World of Tomorrow', opened spectacularly on the site of a former garbage dump and, amongst other displays, 'laid out a glorious vision of the automobile: General Motors' Futurama designed by Norman Bel Geddes, depicted the multilane highways of the future' (Patton 2014). Despite Futurama's crowd-pleasing fabulous futurism, Fotsch drew attention to the fair's fundamental dichotomy operationalized through a blending of information and promotion, and counterpointed by an uncritical celebration of technology by, and for, corporate interests (2001: 68). Those corporate interests were the three major US automotive manufacturers – General Motors, Ford and Chrysler – each of which had a distinctive corporate pavilion that, not surprisingly, made no mention of the 1937/38 recession that resulted in a fall in Michigan's manufacturing employment as well as a decline in automobile production and sales of more than 40%, yet saw at the same time a rise in automobile prices (see Raff, 1991 and Hausman 2016: 442–445). Whilst Geddes controlled the GM design vision, Ford's guru was Walter Dorwin Teague and Chrysler's creative vision was generated by Raymond Loewy. According to Brandon: 'These freelance industrial designers were an altogether new species: between them, they would influence the look of a generation' (2002: 253).

Economic challenges to the industry notwithstanding, the future as presented to Futurama visitors provided some reassuringly familiar forms but frequently on a monumental scale, with one model having a very strong resemblance to Los Angeles's current interstates 405/10 interchange (Meikle 1979: 203). The seductive, 'streamlined' curvature of the model's freeway ramps were largely free of model vehicles which, had the 'intersection' been built in 1939, would probably have been the case, but Bel Geddes's vision of 1960 didn't appear to have considered either inevitable increases in population growth nor the associated increased demands for, as well as dependence upon, automobility. Bel Geddes's '1960' was, however, alluringly Utopian but also flawed in its continuing dependency on roads where:

> the automobile would solve virtually every urban problem . . . It was an undeniably attractive, if hopelessly idealistic, portrayal. But to a consumer society emerging from the throes of the most prolonged period of economic hardship in the country's history, it was a vision worth embracing.
>
> (Coffey and Layden 1998: 121–122)

An integral element of Futurama's automotive vision was a range of initiatives including seven-lane highways with varying lane speeds and traffic control towers, curved lanes similar to luge tracks, and radio controls to monitor safe distances between cars as they travelled at speeds approaching 100 miles an hour (Curts 2015: 734). Whilst an excited public's superficial reading of Futurama's functionalism may have concluded that the automotive future would be a much safer experience, the embedded mechanisms of social control in the guise of such safety anticipated those of Orwell's *1984* (1949) by a decade. Visitors who undertook the Futurama experience were 'afforded a new experience . . . of mobile freedom . . . in 'carry-go-rounds' [read: chairs] simulating an airplane ride over a diorama . . . [of] 50,000 scale-model automobiles with 10,000 in motion' (Curts 2015: 734). Futurama, it seems, offered one prescient future vision: a freeway with only one in five cars moving.

Full-size 1939 GM models from Cadillac, Buick, Oldsmobile, Pontiac and Chevrolet were displayed to consolidate corporate consumerism in the minds of visitors and to counterpoint the tiny diorama models. Whilst most were regular production models, one notable exception was a transparent 'ghost' 1939 Pontiac Deluxe Six made of Plexiglass with a chrome-plated dashboard and white rubber tyres (www.autoblog.com/2011/08/01/). The 'ghost' Pontiac wasn't exactly futuristic, but it no doubt stimulated diverse discussions about driving and dating. Thomas (1999: 12–15) writes of a second 'X-ray' 1940 Pontiac, but no evidence of its survival exists.

The second major automotive manufacturer at the Fair was the Ford Motor Company which, in 1937 was first in US automotive production, then second in 1938 and 1939 (Hausman 2016: 442–445). Walter Dorwin Teague had designed 'smash hit' corporate exhibits for Ford at both the 1933–34 and 1936 expositions in Chicago and Dallas respectively, but the undisputed 'smash hit' of the 1939–40 fair was not Teague's 'gear-shaped Ford building with a spiralling outdoor test ramp' (Meikle 1979: 195) but Bel Geddes's Futurama (Marchand 1992: 23). Teague's Ford pavilion, however, offered visitors: 'a collection of exhibits, demonstrations and performances that together proclaimed a dynamic future achieved through a vertically integrated, materially converted, efficiently assembled Ford machine' (Curts 2015: 737). The pavilion entrance displayed a statue of the Roman god Mercury evoking not only 'fleet, effortless travel' but also serving to remind visitors of Ford's latest addition to the company's automotive range, the Mercury (Gunnell 1994:13). Given Henry and Edsel Ford's insistence on the necessity of educational content, Teague developed a huge animated cyclorama depicting the manufacturing process as well as a technicolor movie ('Melody in F') in which Disneyesque animated cartoon figures came to life and shared the Ford production story (Marchand 1991: 15). Despite being able to ride in the latest Ford cars through part of its exhibit and watch racing car drivers on the aforementioned endless figure 8 roof-top track, Teague and Ford had to concede to running a distant second in popularity to Bel Geddes's Futurama to the extent that 1000 departing fairgoers awarded 39.4% to the GM exhibit but only 8.5% to second place Ford, with 47.5% of those respondents keen to re-visit GM but only 3.8% prepared to re-visit Ford (Marchand 1991: 24).

Teague had observed that: 'the danger of being fantastic in a Wellsian sense, and of being too definitely prophetic, must be avoided' (Meikle 1979: 189), but Bel Geddes had done just that, and to huge acclaim, leaving only Raymond Loewy to rely on already familiar and somewhat conventional forms in his Chrysler Building at the Fair with: 'its ovoid center section flanked by slender pylons with streamlined chevrons' (Meikle 1979: 196). Burkhart and Hunt observed that Loewy was: 'offering a smooth, frictionless, machine-age future to cure a post-Depression hangover' (2000: 52).

Upon entering the Great Hall of the Chrysler Motors' building by James Gamble Rodgers, the visitor could choose between exhibits. One was a display by Raymond Loewy depicting transport through the ages beginning with the trudge of bare feet and concluding with a rocket flight taking passengers to London. Another featured a talking Plymouth sedan being assembled, and a third Chrysler's Air-Temp air conditioning that took the form of a glittering frozen forest which displayed Plymouth, Dodge, De Soto and Chrysler vehicles (Wood 2004:55). Tré-tiack observed that 'Raymond Loewy was the embodiment of the twentieth century; it is understandable that he would sometimes consider himself a star' (1999:13).

The automotive experience at the 1939 New York World's Fair was a celebration of mobility, design, industry and consumerism. All, however, would be profoundly compromised by the events of later that year but the societal dependency upon, as well as the necessity of, the automobile would ensure its continued, if reduced, production into the years of war to follow.

New trends and names: World's Fairs become Expos

The late 20th century saw a massive swing in the geography of World's Fairs. America's love affair with the concept abruptly came to a halt. While Seattle and New York in the early 1960s were successful, rapid social changes led to diminished interest. World's Fairs suddenly seemed old-fashioned and unsophisticated to the Woodstock Generation. Montreal in 1967 took the bold step of discarding the title of World's Fair and rebranding itself with the more modern nomenclature of an Expo. Planned World's Fairs at Philadelphia (1976) and Chicago (1992) were cancelled due to financial concerns and New Orleans (1984) – the last World's Fair staged in the USA – went bankrupt (Dimanche 1996; Frost and Laing 2013; Gold and Gold 2005). In Australia, the Brisbane Expo in 1988 provided mixed results (Craik 1992) and no World's Fair has been staged in that country since, nor has France staged a World's Fair since before World War Two.

Montreal not only reflected a new world in its name change, but also in how it portrayed shifts in the global economy. The Australian exhibit illustrated how some countries were no longer satisfied with their international economic image as simple primary producers. Australia had not exhibited since New York in 1939 and for such an event staged by its colonial cousin, it was prepared to spend big to present a new vision of its post-war economy. Coming at a time when Britain's entry into the Economic Union and the rise of the East Asian economies were reshaping trading relationships, a statement was made:

> Australia now emphasised its scientific and technical proficiency with large scale models of the Snowy Mountains Hydroelectric Scheme and the Parkes radio telescope, as well as evidence of manufacturing capacity through examples of modernist furniture and product design . . . exhibits included displays of world-class Australian research in medicine and agricultural science . . . [and] a replica of Canberra as a modern city.
> (Barnes and Jackson 2008: 20.6 and 20.12)

Osaka in 1970 was testament to Japan's reconstruction and rehabilitation after World War Two. Like South Korea, Japan was strategically important to Western foreign policy regarding the communist powers. Awarding it a World's Fair, recognised both its place in international politics and the success of the 1964

Olympics in Tokyo. Most importantly, Osaka demonstrated the economic rise of East Asia and what would become known as the Asian Century. Japan was increasingly becoming a major trading partner and countries like Australia used the opportunity to emphasise both economic links and the general need to keep building friendship and co-operation (Barnes and Jackson 2008).

In the USA, World's Fairs got smaller, before disappearing. Whereas 50 million attendees were recorded for New York on 1964–65 and Montreal in 1967, Knoxville in 1982 received 11 million visitors and New Orleans just seven million. New Orleans only aimed for 11 million – based on Knoxville – but its failure to meet that modest target resulted in a $US75million loss. This poor performance was partly due to changing tastes, competition from the Los Angeles Olympics and the rise of Reaganomics, which drastically reduced federal government investment in the event. Whilst a financial failure, this World's Fair did leave a positive legacy, particularly in the development of an attractive tourism precinct along the Mississippi River (Dimanche 1996).

At Vancouver in 1986, a key point of conflict arose in the aftermath of the failure of New Orleans. Vancouver was originally planned as Transpo '86, a commemoration of the centennial of the railway reaching the West coast and spanning the continent. Accordingly, the main themes were to be transportation and communication. However, as planning proceeded the emphasis shifted from technology to entertainment. Despite criticisms of Disneyfication, the organisers became primarily concerned that there was enough fun and spectacle to attract sufficient visitors to show a profit (Ley and Olds 1988).

Future of the World's Fair concept

With the decline of interest in traditional host countries like the USA, the focus shifted towards other European countries and Asia. Osaka hosted the first Asian World's Fair in 1970, testament to the industrial development after World War Two (Gold and Gold 2005). In the 21st century, World's Fairs have been staged at Hanover (Germany), Aichi (Japan), Zaragoza (Spain), Shanghai (China), Yeosu (South Korea) and Milan (Italy). This new generation of World's Fairs has tended to focus on the latest technology, particularly new media. In addition there has been a focus on the service economy, including the distinctive offerings of exhibiting countries in tourism and gastronomy. As with most recent mega-events, researchers have focused on measuring their economic impacts, market segmentation and community interactions (Lamberti, Noci, Guo and Zhu 2011; Lee, Kang, and Lee 2013; Lee, Mjelde and Kwon 2017).

A further new direction is the extension of the concept to the Middle East with the 2017 World's Fair being staged in Astana (Kazakhstan) and Dubai (UAE) hosting the next one in 2020. Both of these instances are part of a broad strategy of these countries to utilise events to promote tourism development and a modern, developed identity. The success of these recent World's Fairs – the attendance for Shanghai was 73 million and for Aichi and Milan it was over 20 million – suggest that this mega-event is still very much alive.

References

Arwas, V. (2002) *Art Nouveau: The French Aesthetic*, London: Papadakis.

Auerbach, J. (1999) *The Great Exhibition of 1851: A Nation on Display*, New Haven, CT: Yale University Press.

Barnes, C. and Jackson, S. (2008) 'A significant mirror of progress: Modernist design and Australian participation at Expo '67 and Expo '70', in K. Darian-Smith, R. Gillespie, C. Jordan and E. Willis (eds.), *Seize the Day: Exhibitions, Australia and the World* (pp. 20.1–20.19), Melbourne: Monash University ePress.

Baskas, H. (2012) 'Back to the Future: Seattle's 1962 World Fair', *OPB FM*, radio broadcast, 30 July 2012, transcript, www.opb.org/news/article/back-to-the-future-seattles-1962-worlds-fair/ (accessed 29 July 2016).

Becker, P. and Stein, A. (2011) *The Future Remembered: The 1962 Seattle World's Fair and Its Legacy*, Seattle: Seattle Center Foundation.

Brandon, R. (2002) *Auto Mobile: How the Car Changed Life*, London: Macmillan.

Burkhart, B. and Hunt, D. (2000) *Airstream: The History of the Land Yacht*, San Francisco: Chronicle.

Buzard, J. (2007) 'Conflicting cartographies: Globalism, nationalism and the Crystal Palace floor plan', in J. Buzard, J. Childers and E. Gillooly (eds.), *Victorian Prism: Refractions of the Crystal Palace* (pp. 40–52), Charlottesville, VA and London: University of Virginia Press.

Buzard, J., Childers, J. and Gillooly, E. (2007) 'Introduction', in J. Buzard, J. Childers and E. Gillooly (eds.), *Victorian Prism: Refractions of the Crystal Palace* (pp. 1–19), Charlottesville, VA and London: University of Virginia Press.

Coffey, F. and Layden, J. (1998) *America on Wheels: The First 100 Years: 1896–1996*, Los Angeles: General Publishing Company.

Craik, J. (1992) 'Expo 88: Fashions of sight and politics of site', in T. Bennett, P. Buckridge, D. Carter and C. Mercer (eds.), *Celebrating the Nation: A Critical Study of Australia's Bicentenary* (pp. 142–159), Sydney: Allen & Unwin.

Curts, K. (2015) 'Temples and turnpikes in "The World of Tomorrow": Religious assemblage and automobility at the 1939 New York World's Fair', *Journal of American Academy of Religion*, 83(3), 722–749.

Dimanche, F. (1996) 'Special events legacy: The 1984 Louisiana World Fair in New Orleans', *Festival Management & Events Tourism*, 4(1), 49–54.

Dunstan, D. (Ed.). (1996) *Victorian Icon: The Royal Exhibition Building, Melbourne*, Melbourne: Australian Scholarly Publishing.

Dymond, A. (2011) 'Embodying the nation: Art, fashion and allegorical women at the 1900 Exposition Universelle', *RACAR: revue d'art canadienne/Canadian Art Review*, 36(2), 1–14.

Findlay, J. (1992) *Magic Lands: Western Cityscapes and American Culture after 1940*, Berkeley: University of California Press.

Fotsch, P. (2001) 'The building of a superhighway future at the New York World's Fair', *Cultural Critique*, 48, 65–97.

Frost, W. (2012) 'Commemorative events and heritage in former capitals: A case study of Melbourne', *Current Issues in Tourism*, 15(1/2), 51–60.

Frost, W. and Laing, J. (2011) *Strategic Management of Festivals and Events*, Melbourne: Cengage.

Frost, W. and Laing, J. (2013) *Commemorative Events: Memory, Identities, Conflicts*, London and New York: Routledge.

Gill, G. (2010) *We Two: Victoria and Albert: Rulers, Partners, Rivals*, New York: Ballantine.

Gold, J.R. and Gold, M.M. (2005) *Cities of Culture: Staging International Festivals and the Urban Agenda, 1851–2000*, Aldershot, UK: Ashgate.

Green, A. (2013) *Changing France: Literature and Material Culture in the Second Empire*, London and New York: Anthem.

Greenhalgh, P. (1988) *Ephemeral Vistas: The Expositions Universelles, Great Exhibitions and World Fairs, 1851–1939*, Manchester: Manchester University Press.

Greenhalgh, P. (2011) *Fair World: A History of World's Fairs and Expositions from London to Shanghai 1851–2010*, Winterbourne, UK: Papadakis.

Gunnell, J. (1994) *55 years of Mercury: The Complete History of the Big 'M'*, Iola, WI: Krause

Gurney, P. (2007) 'A palace for the people? The Crystal Palace and consumer culture in Victorian England', in J. Buzard, J. Childers and E. Gillooly (eds.), *Victorian Prism: Refractions of the Crystal Palace* (pp. 138–150), Charlottesville, VA and London: University of Virginia Press.

Hausman, J. (2016) 'What was bad for General Motors was bad for America: The automobile industry and the 1937/38 recession', *The Journal of Economic History*, 76(2), 427–477.

Hoffenberg, P. (2001) *An Empire on Display: English, Indian and Australian Exhibitions from the Crystal Palace to the Great War*, Berkeley, CA: University of California Press.

Julian, P. (1974) *The Triumph of Art Nouveau: Paris Exhibition 1900*, London: Phaidon.

Lamberti, L., Noci, G., Guo, J. and Zhu, S. (2011) 'Mega-events as drivers of community participation in developing countries: The case of Shanghai World Expo', *Tourism Management*, 32, 1474–1483.

Lee, C.-K., Kang, S. and Lee, Y. (2013) 'Segmentation of mega-event motivation: The case of Expo 2010 Shanghai China', *Asia Pacific Journal of Tourism Research*, 18, 637–660.

Lee, C.-K., Mjelde, J. and Kwon, Y. (2017) 'Estimating the economic impact of a mega-event on host and neighbouring regions', *Leisure Studies*, 36(1), 138–152.

Ley, D. and Olds, K. (1988) 'Landscape as spectacle: World's fairs and the culture of heroic consumption', *Environment and Planning D: Society and Space*, 6(2), 191–212.

Mandell, R.D. (1967) *Paris 1900: The Great World's Fair*, Toronto: University of Toronto Press.

Marchand, R. (1991) 'The designers go to the fair: Walter Dorwin Teague and the professionalization of corporate industrial exhibits, 1933–1940', *Design Issues*, 8(1), 4–17.

Marchand, R. (1992) 'The designers go to the fair II: Norman Bel Geddes, the General Motors "Futurama" and the visit to the factory transformed', *Design Issues*, 8(2), 22–40.

Meikle, J. (1979) *Twentieth Century Limited: Industrial Design in America, 1925–1939*, Philadelphia: Temple University Press.

Olsen Theiding, K. (2006) 'Anxieties of influence: British responses to art nouveau, 1900–04', *Journal of Design History*, 19(3), 215–231.

Patton, P. (2014) 'When cars ruled the world's fair', *The New York Times*, 11 April, AU 1.

Raff, D. (1991) 'Making cars and making money in the interwar automobile industry: Economies of scale and scope and the manufacturing behind the marketing', *Business History Review*, 65(4), 721–753.

Ramsey, J. (2011) '1939 Pontiac ghost car commands $308,000 at auction', *Autoblog*, 1 August, www.autoblog.com/2011/08/01/1939-pontiac-ghost-car-commands-308-000-at-auction (accessed 27 March 2017).

Roche, M. (2000) *Mega-Events & Modernity: Olympics and Expos in the Growth of Global Culture*, London and New York: Routledge.

Rydell, R. (1984) *All the World's a Fair: Visions of Empire of American International Expositions, 1876–1916*, Chicago and London: University of Chicago Press.

Rydell, R. (1993) *World of Fairs: The Century of Progress Expositions*, Chicago and London: University of Chicago Press.

Rydell, R. and Kroes, R. (2005) *Buffalo Bill in Bologna: The Americanization of the World, 1869–1922*, Chicago and London: University of Chicago Press.

Simpson, J. (2011) *Creating Wine: The Emergence of a World Industry, 1840–1914*, Princeton and Oxford: Princeton University Press.

Steele, V. (1988) *Paris Fashion: A Cultural History*, Oxford and New York: Berg.

Thomas, J. (1999) *Pontiac Dream Cars, Show Cars and Prototypes 1928–1998 Photo Album*, Hudson, Wisconsin: Iconografix.

Tolini Finamore, M. (2003) 'Fashioning the colonial at the Paris expositions, 1925 and 1931', *Fashion Theory*, 7(3/4), 345–360.

Trétiack, P. (1999) *Raymond Loewy and Streamlined Design*, New York: Universe.

Wilson, M. (1991) 'Consuming history: The nation, the past and the commodity at L'Exposition Universelle de 1900', *American Journal of Semiotics*, 8(4), 131–153.

Wood, A. (2004) *New York's 1939–1940 World's Fair: Postcard History Series*, Chicago: Arcadia.

Young, L. (2008) 'How like England we can be: The Australian international exhibitions in the nineteenth century', in K. Darian-Smith, R. Gillespie, C. Jordan and E. Willis (eds.), *Seize the Day: Exhibitions, Australia and the World* (pp. 12.1–12.19), Melbourne: Monash University ePress.

3 The High Point Furniture Market

A dilemma of eventful place making

Vern Biaett and Jenny Lukow

Introduction

High Point is a city of 110,000 residents nestled between its more well-known neighbours of Greensboro and Winston-Salem in North Carolina, USA. If you are not a resident of the Piedmont Triad region of North Carolina or not associated with the furniture industry, you may have never heard of the 107-year-old High Point Furniture Market (hereafter referred to as the Market). Worldwide, people who work in the home furniture industry, whether they have travelled to North Carolina or not, are very well aware of the Market. Growing from its roots as an established regional trade show, the Market, over the past 40 years, has outpaced other national furniture markets in Chicago, Atlanta, Las Vegas, and Dallas, as well as international competitors in Cologne, Tokyo, Guadalajara, Milan, and San Paulo, to become the largest residential furnishing trade show in the world. Those other cities all offer better entertainment, lodging and attractions and are easier for buyers to walk and work, yet the Market is where they come to stock their stores and meet the needs of their global customers. The event provides a critical source of local jobs and tax revenues and has been referenced as a significant component of the region's creative economic furniture cluster (Florida 2008; Porter 1998). The city of High Point has been described as a 'Niche City' which utilised the Market to fashion for itself a 'global centrality by creating an economic specialization in a specific segment of the global service economy' (Schlichtman 2009: 106). This business-to-business (B2B) hallmark event transmits place-making impacts upon its host city and is recognised as a special place by the furniture industry, specifically because the majority of its annual sales transactions are initiated and negotiated in the Market's showrooms. The unique alliances that engulf the Market truly emphasise that 'place-making is an inherently networked process, constituted by the socio-spatial relationships that link individuals together through a common place-frame' (Pierce, Martin and Murphy 2011: 1).

The Market's roots date to 1901 when a group of 35 manufacturers joined High Point's mayor to discuss a possible furniture exposition. Within a year, 10 of them had pledged a $1,000 each towards a trade show. In 1905, the High Point Furniture Exposition with a 2,000 square foot showroom was created by furniture salesman D. Ralph Parker, followed a year later by the Furniture Manufactures' Exposition with 10,000 square feet of space. By 1909, the rival companies had merged under the banner of the Southern Furniture Market and began hosting an annual event for buyers from North Carolina as well as neighbouring states. In 1913, with 1,000 buyers walking the showroom floors of 100 manufacturers, it became the region's largest display of Southern-made furnishings. In the tradition of other furniture markets, it became a semi-annual event held in January and July each year.

Following World War One, provincial manufacturers raised $35,000 to purchase land for a sizeable showroom in downtown High Point and within two years the 250,000 square foot Southern Furniture Exposition Building was constructed at a cost of $1,000,000. The emerging trade show attracted buyers from over 100 cities across America in 1921and continued to grow in size and stature throughout the 1920s. It was also during this time that it was first informally referred to as the High Point Market. The furniture industry was severely distressed in the early years of the Great Depression with nearly a third of manufacturers going out of business, but recovered quickly and by 1936, the exposition was back on track, reaching attendance levels that approached 2,500 buyers. During World War Two, the trade show was cancelled and the showrooms were occupied by the US Army, but when it reopened in 1947, with pent-up demand for home furnishings, more than 5,000 buyers worked the showrooms.

In 1951, smaller in-between events began to be held during April and October, which by 1960 surpassed the size of the original January and July expositions, and within another 20 years, completely eliminated and replaced the traditional winter-summer dates. Correspondingly, by the early 1960s, the trade show had increased in physical size to approximately 2 million square feet of showroom space. During the 1980s, independent manufacturers began to offer showrooms specialising in accessory items including rugs and lamps which had previously been add-ons in the furniture showrooms. By 1989, the trade show had grown to over 7 million square feet of showroom space and was renamed and rebranded as the International Home Furnishings Market to better represent its emerging global presence.

As the Market's growth cycle continued into the 21st century, the exposition was once again renamed in 2006, this time simply to what people had casually been calling the event for several years . . . The High Point Market. At the same time, the event's organisational body, the High Point Market Authority (HPMA), cautiously opened its International Buyers Center to extend the Market's brand appeal to foreign visitors. The Market is today a semi-annual event of 7-day sessions in both April and October with each period attracting between 75,000 and 80,000 visitors for a total of nearly 160,000 per year, with 10% travelling from abroad representing over 100 countries. Change seems perpetual however, and since 2014, a few exhibitors have begun to experiment with special two day Pre-Market events to entertain, network with and sell to selected invited buyers. The type of manufacturers participating in the Market has also increased from the traditional furniture and accessory manufacturers, retail store buyers and interior and furniture designers, to include many non-traditional sellers of such items as driftwood sculptures, patio furniture and dog beds.

Corporate event impacts and place making

Events can positively heighten a community's identity as a special place (De Bres and Davis 2001; Derrett 2003), not automatically, but with carefully devised and implemented internal and external strategies (Sharpley and Stone 2012). While internally the concentration of event policy is socio-cultural with an emphasis on enhancing identity for the local citizenry and community, externally the purpose is to build and have a financial impact on the economy. The latter has been the almost single-minded focus of the Market until just recently.

A recent study by the Duke University Center on Globalization, Governance, and Competitiveness (Brun and Lester 2013) found the Market generates an economic impact of $5.39 billion as well as annual tax revenues of $539 million, making it both High Point's and North Carolina's largest-single economic event. To arrive at the economic impact figure the Duke researchers employed IMPLAN 3.0 (IMpact Analysis for PLANners) software and focused on specific types of activity including spending by visitors and organisers, spending by vendors to rent space for, construct and operate displays, and furniture sales generated by local manufacturers. Furniture sales generated for manufacturers outside the study area were purposefully excluded as the researchers wanted to 'focus *only* on the activities which are explicitly associated with the Market so that we can feel confident that they would not have occurred *but-for* the Market itself' (Brun and Lester 2013: 6). Further, the researchers stated there were additional 'limitations of the study which result in our figures being on the conservative side' (Brun and Lester 2013: 24) that included the exclusion of data from the Raleigh-Durham and Charlotte Douglas International Airports as they were located outside the study area.

This prominence garnered government support in 2016 with appropriations of $2.9 million from the state legislature with $1.7 million slated for marketing and $1.2 million for transportation. Additional funding support included $2.6 million provided by the city of High Point, $405,000 supplied by Guilford County, $150,000 from the High Point Convention and Visitors Bureau, and $130,000 of resources derived from other sponsors (Kimbrough 2016d). The city's historic downtown, dominated by furniture showrooms, is the highest valued property in the city of High Point. There are roughly 69,000 people regularly employed throughout the Piedmont Triad in the furniture industry with several thousand of those jobs associated directly with the Market.

When event participants arrive, they occupy hotels and motels extending into the nearby cities of Greensboro, Winston-Salem and other smaller communities within a 25-mile radius that encompasses Guilford, Forsythe and Davidson counties. Thousands also rent rooms or entire homes from local residents, or have purchased properties they use only during the Market. The rental car business booms, cabs temporarily relocate from across the state, hundreds of buses are chartered and non-profit organisations generate revenue parking guests in their facility's lots. Florists prepare hundreds of arrangements to decorate showrooms, musicians are booked and college students skip classes to work well-paying part-time jobs. Caterers generate a substantial portion of their annual income, local restaurants and eateries overflow and churches use their kitchen facilities and fellowship halls to prepare and serve meals. *In terms of economic impact to the city of High Point, the Piedmont Triad and the State of North Carolina, the Market is truly an eventful place.*

This industry gathering of manufacturers, designers and buyers encompasses every aspect of the corporate event umbrella categorised as MINCE (Bladen, Kennell, Abson and Wilde 2012) including meetings and conferences, incentives, networking opportunities, corporate hospitality, and exhibitions and trade shows. The Market now physically dominates the central downtown core of the city of High Point with over 11.5 million square feet of showroom space located in 180 buildings that saturate the bulk of a 14-block deep by 9-block wide footprint. Sixteen additional showrooms are located immediately outside of the downtown core. International Market Centers (IMF) has consolidated and owns 14 of these properties comprising 6.7 million square feet and serves as the rental agent for 60% of the total Market showroom space. IMF made a $30 million investment to property improvements in 2011 and in 2016 announced construction of a supplemental showroom while declaring an expression of confidence in Market viability for the next 100 years. Others are adding showroom space or have recently revealed plans for continued Market expansion. In 2016, Fine Furniture Design enlarged its showroom as well as relocated its corporate headquarters to its new space. New York's Art Addiction, after previously renting space, announced the company's intentions to build two new properties. HTL International, a manufacturer of leather sofas with a presence in 52 countries, recently purchased and remodelled a former printing facility, the Enterprise Building with its Art Deco façade and listing on the National Register of Historic Places, for a permanent market district showroom. Likewise, Lacquer Craft USA remodelled a 90-year-old flour mill, with its silos still in place and faded paint advertising 5 cent Coca-Cola for sale still visible on its brick walls, to create a unique showroom. These recent moves were heralded by the city's mayor as proof that the Market continues to increase year-round employment in High Point's downtown core.

There are now typically in excess of 300 manufacturers with over 2,600 different exhibits filling the various showroom spaces, creating a trade show of such proportions that it requires a continual loop of bus and van shuttles throughout the market district for efficient attendee flow. The HPMA hosts two major outdoor evening concerts during each Market for attendees and has engaged in preliminary discussions with both IMF and the city of High Point to develop a permanent stage and a park in the heart of the showroom district. Corporate hospitality and incentives also extend into the showrooms and exhibition areas where hundreds of smaller, intimate receptions and parties replace meeting and conference room spaces during afterhours to provide invaluable networking opportunities. In 2016, two of the popular entertainers found mingling with guests at private parties included Donny Osmond and Kathy Ireland. *Contemplating the words of an eminent human geographer that 'there are as many intimate places as there are occasions when human beings truly connect' (Tuan 1977: 141) in terms of MINCE, and the Market, the largest and most significant gathering of the corporate furniture world, is truly a B2B eventful place.*

Customer service and innovation are embraced by the Market as it progresses into a new century of rapidly changing technology. Originally, registration was a near year-round effort of assembling badges and credentials with a small staff assisted by local women's clubs and the Junior League during event days. In 1992, the HPMA used its first computers and has since continued technologically to keep the Market on the leading edge of customer service. With a grant of $200,000 from the North Carolina General Assembly, a smartphone app was developed and designed to guide trade show attendees as they navigate their way around the multitude of showrooms and exhibits. This MyMarket app features both indoor and outdoor mapping features that allow a user to pick a specific exhibitor and map the most direct route to their showroom building. The app then allows a user once inside a building to be guided step-by-step and floor-by-floor to their selected destination. To further aid interior designers, HPMA publishes a Designer's Guide to the Market, with tips on making a visit as productive as possible, among many other services for its customers. As an imaginative strategic communication twist, HPMA, in partnership with Esteem Media, created a tour for bloggers that brings authoritative furniture design bloggers directly into the Market showrooms. The tour is intended to promote quality online design content and community building as it cooperatively provides exposure for the bloggers as it promotes participating exhibitor products. Also introduced during the April 2016 Market, a virtual reality technology demonstration by Wayfair Design was part of a futuristic design tech summit about mavericks and risk takers driving the reinvention of furniture retail and design. Market-goers donned headsets as they took on a patio design challenge in the virtual setting of a home and surrounding lawn to expose interior designers to an innovation that they could soon use with clients to sell more home furnishings. It is predicted that virtual reality will soon enable shoppers to drag furniture icons from catalogs to see how they would look and fit in their living spaces. *In terms of customer service, forward thinking and innovation, the Market is attempting to truly remain an economically impactful eventful place.*

Security and crisis planning for the Market has also experienced major adjustments in the past two decades. As for all major events, things changed dramatically following the terrorist attacks of September 11, 2001. Prior to 9/11, security was local with the High Point police department focused primarily on pedestrian safety. In the month before the October 2001 Market, local police were joined by state and federal law enforcement, including the FBI and ATF, to quickly create a plan to protect the thousands of people, including international guests, who suddenly became a potential target. Today, parking in the Market district is extremely restricted and all local delivery vehicles must receive prior clearance from authorities and cannot be left unattended. Furniture manufacturers that want to bring in additional merchandise during show hours must make arrangements for vehicles to be inspected off-site. Security practices that formerly embraced casual principles founded on southern hospitality, such as access for guests, caterers, entertainers and dock workers, have also been fundamentally heightened. Everyone, without exception, must be processed through the HPMA's centralised badge registration system before they can enter a showroom.

With thousands of international visitors, there are also potential health issues that must now be addressed. Ebola, Asian bird flu, Zika virus and other infectious diseases are all potential threats to the Market. Guests arriving from foreign countries, such as Nigeria that in 2014 was under a Center for Disease Control and Prevention level 1 travel watch for Ebola, are screened upon arrival and registration. High Point Regional Hospital has trained staff and established emergency procedures in case an infectious disease outbreak arises including front line first responder mobile emergency medical services located within the Market. Details of emergency planning preparedness have also been released to local media to ease public concerns. *In terms of safety and security the Market is ensuring that it remains an economically viable eventful place with aspirations to remain an uneventful place of crisis.*

While the HPMA, IMF and others associated with the Market strive to produce a hospitable, safe and secure sense of place for the furniture industry, the City of High Point local government endeavours to maintain a history of regional furniture manufacturing and identify itself as a distinctive place of substance for those who attend the Market. This heritage can be found in High Point at such places as the Furniture Discovery Center museum, Furniture Walk of Fame, Bernice Beinenstock Furniture Library and the International School of Home Furnishings at High Point University. Probably the most unique building in town is a three-story structure constructed in 1926 that resembles a large-scale chest of drawers, including two massive socks protruding from its second floor drawer. To create a positive visual impression, the market district has been enhanced by the city with numerous historical markers, statuary, international flags, iron benches and modern art.

In the early growth years of the Market, the city found itself embarrassed as visitors poured into a downtown area with limited parking. When yellow school buses were employed to ease congestion, foreign visitors mocked the vehicles as 'cheese buses' (Schlichtman 2009: 114). Transportation services and parking have since been updated and modernised with a state-of-the-art transportation terminal located in the heart of the Market district. City services, including waste management and the recycling of thousands of tons of cardboard and packing material, are purposefully designed and undertaken to craft a favourable impression of High Point. The city council has long been an advocate for the Market and the city may be unique in that its zoning ordinances include specific rules and regulations for exposition buildings and furniture showrooms. *In terms of the city of High Point policy, proactive actions and strong commitment to preserve its furniture heritage, the Market is truly supported by economic development policy to promote it as a modern and efficient eventful place.*

Historical antecedents: an economic impact vs quality of life dilemma

During the early 1970s, as American cities experienced the deindustrialisation of their manufacturing caused by modernisation and globalisation, there emerged a widespread community development strategy to use events for purposes of urban regeneration (Green, Flora, Flora and Schmidt 1990; McGuire, Rubin, Agranoff and Richards 1994; Smith 2012), with a crucial impetus of economic impact. While the preponderance of American cities at this time elected to pursue public festivals, fairs and markets, and many constructed purpose-built public squares and facilities to host these events, the leaders of High Point elected instead to build on their already existing Southern Furniture Market corporate event as a practical approach to maintain their downtown's vitality. These leaders, rather than embrace the newly emerging concept of economic community development (Phillips 2016) relied only on the principles of basic economic development. They single-mindedly focused on economic impact and quantitatively embraced tax dollars, jobs and spending, failing to include the qualitative aspect of social and cultural impacts. Today, while the city of High Point finds itself as the habitat of a global hallmark event with incredible economic impact, it also finds itself with an event that has so overwhelmed its downtown that the quality of life for its citizens in this space has been stripped away. For local residents, their downtown has become placeless and irrelevant (MacLeod 2006) with its focus more closely aligned to the Market and its visitors, than to their city.

A synopsis of business relocation away from High Point's downtown core during a period of urban to suburban flight between 1963 and 2003 (Schlichtman and Patch 2008) underscores the dramatic use of facility changes that occurred. Traditional downtown occupants departed *en masse* from a central city core to new malls, strip centres and office/industrial parks closer to freeways and airports. The number of non-food related retail stores declined from 164 to 17, personal service entities from 177 to 31, third places such as cafes, pool halls and community clubs, from 60 to 11 and offices from 262 to 48. During this period the original Southern Furniture Market, which in the early 1960s was in reality 1 million square feet of showroom space in downtown High Point and 1 million additional square feet spread over other smaller towns connected by 200 miles of rural roads, benefited from this situation by consolidating and expanding into rapidly vacating downtown locations. It was a symbiotic relationship, in that as vacant buildings were converted to furniture market showrooms, more local entities chose to relocate, which further opened spaces for even more showrooms. From the furniture manufacturer point of view, the situation was driven by a competitive advantage that began to develop over participation in other furniture expositions. There was a tremendous cost-effectiveness for manufacturers to maintain single showrooms versus continually designing, transporting, constructing and dismantling travelling trade show exhibits. This permitted transformation over time of otherwise unpretentious spaces into unique, brand-infused, special places that better satisfied both seller and buyer needs. As the square footage of showrooms increased, local residents had fewer reasons to be engaged with the area and their presence in the downtown core, outside of possibly working at the Market, dramatically decreased.

By definition, planned events are both spatial and temporary with an established beginning and end. The Market has delineated opening and closing dates each spring and fall and in that sense it is temporary, but unlike a music festival, carnival, convention or fair, when it is over it does not end. Its 180 buildings and 11.5 million square feet of showrooms are permanent structures and are owned or rented on a permanent year-round basis. Unlike convention centres and fair grounds that may accommodate different events every few weeks, these buildings house only the Market. The temporality of activity in downtown High Point is unlike the distinct pattern of activity in a normal downtown that continually repeats itself, deviated only by holidays or weather. There are no real daily or weekly timepieces in the market district and with the exception of Market dates, it's hard to discern either the day or the week when one is there. Although the area remains marginally active with incessant preparation for the next Market, downtown High Point is not a communal place, not a place that local citizens go to be with each other, a place of shared values or possibilities or a place that fosters a greater sense of humanity. Locals do not gather for pleasure, to sit on a bench to talk, to shop, to eat a meal, to enjoy a night on the town, or except on very limited occasions to view a parade or attend a special event. It is not a public square, not a

> unique venue that includes, welcomes, and bonds every component of the community together under one vision – friends and families, corporate citizens, government agencies, educational institutions, the media, social organizations, the arts, causes . . . cultural backgrounds and political viewpoints.
>
> (Schmader 2016: 10)

High Point's downtown is often referred to by local residents as a ghost town or as a beautiful flower that blooms only twice a year when the market is in session. The Market's re-commodification of a decentralising downtown business district in the second half of the last century was a saving grace and financial windfall for High Point, but it also created a serious dialectical dilemma. Today, residents depend on and embrace the essential and crucial economic impact that the Market dominance of their downtown brings to the region, yet endure the lack of quality of life impacts that coincide with this success, a situation not typical of more progressive community development endeavours.

Diminishing the dialectical dilemma

Throughout the regenerative conversion of High Point's downtown business core into a global Market district, some concerns were expressed that although this provided the community with economic sustainability, it was tearing apart the social and cultural soul of the area. Downtown business proprietors and residents voiced complaints to the city council of excessive Market influences and lack of merchant and citizen input as city leaders revised zoning ordinances, agreed upon purely economic development plans and set policy decisions to favour the Market, often behind closed doors. In the mid-1980s, there was a call for modifications to the still emerging market district to include residential, cultural amenities and retail centres, but these were quickly quashed by influential furniture manufacturers and some property owners hoping to profit from escalating prices.

Non-profit art organisations and city of High Point departments such as parks and recreation have not been able to generate any real significant social and cultural impact for local residents within the market district. The High Point Theater, owned and operated by the city of High Point, was constructed in 1975 as a cooperative venture with the International Home Furnishing Center. The complex includes a 929-seat auditorium and three large exhibition galleries used for meetings, display or receptions. It is rented exclusively for Market programmes when it is in session. Although it does attract people to a schedule of professional and community theatre offerings, concerts and other musical performances, and is used by the Theatre Art Guild to programme multiple exhibitions as well as other educational experiences for the community, attendees have very little else to do before or after their visit. In 2013, the High Point Arts Council acquired Centennial Station, an 80-year-old freight train depot on the edge of the market district, and remodelled it to support and host community-based performing arts. Random community events such as Ignite High Point's Whistle Stop concert series at the High Point train depot, the Carolina Brewfest Craft Beer Festival and HiFest at the Mendenhall Transportation Center, the EbFest Bluegrass Music Festivals at the Market Square Courtyard and holiday parades on Main Street also occur from time to time in the market district attracting small crowds. The organisations that produce these events have been well intentioned, but have lacked the size, and the cohesiveness to create a significant social or cultural synergy without restaurants, retail or other third places.

At the turn of the 21st century, as the Market attained a level of mature sustainability, attitudes of local leaders began to change about the quality of life aspects of downtown. They began to realise that an expanded strategy that included both externally directed economic development and internally directed community development was required for future sustainability. It had become apparent it was time to embrace a concept purported by Teodori and Luloff (1998) that without community involvement in, or attachment to, a space it would never become a quality of life place.

In 2015, the High Point City Council and Chamber of Commerce cooperatively established a public-private redevelopment agency, with a long-range goal of reawakening the social and cultural vibrancy of its historic downtown by making it a more eventful place for local residents. The agency, entitled Forward High Point, was tasked to accomplish this community economic development goal that also included the objectives of adding 500 new private-sector jobs, 15 to 20 new retail and restaurant establishments and 250 new residential units (Kimbrough 2016c). It was understood that this effort would be complimentary to the Market.

The social facets and implications of creating quality of life have been increasingly aligned with local and regional development to enhance social connections and place meanings (Gibson and Connell 2012). To kick start this place-making regeneration effort, the agency has decided to explore a strategy used successfully for downtown redevelopment in other North Carolina cities including Durham and Winston-Salem. It began an investigation into the prospect of a 2,500 to 3,500 seats sport/entertainment venue being constructed within or adjacent to the downtown Market district (Kimbrough 2016a; Kimbrough 2016b). A possible primary tenant of the venue was identified as a local minor league baseball team from nearby Thomasville, roughly 6 miles from downtown High Point. Numerous additional proposed uses for the stadium include foremost hosting events or providing space for the Market and HPMA much in the same way the High Point Theater is being used today. To create a broad communal sense of place, the venue might also be home to High Point University events, touring music concerts, community festivals, fairs, conferences, trade shows and really any activities that would attract visitors to downtown. Not wanting this to be a place for one-and-done visits to only the planned events themselves, it has been imagined the proposed venue would include retail and other commercial space on the first floor. At this point, three potential sites adjacent to the market district have been tentatively identified with careful consideration that they not negatively affect Market activity. The delicately crafted plan for a possible sport/entertainment venue hinges on complementing the economic impact of the Market with a multitude of year-round activities to create the missing quality of life impacts needed to increase the sustainability of High Point's historic downtown core. If this Forward High Point revitalization project can be brought to fruition, or another if it turns out to not be feasible, the city may attract both residents and off-Market tourists to the downtown area throughout the year and diminish the city and region's dialectic dilemma. It is possible that the visibility and centrality a sport/entertainment venue might be predicted to bring to downtown High Point could create a clustering effect among non-profit art organisations, city departments, independent festivals and community events leading to meaningful social and cultural impact. One certainty, however, is that because the Market is High Point's most crucial economic place maker, it will heavily influence and be part of all quality of life place-making strategies.

Conclusion

The High Point Market is a global industrial corporate hallmark event that has both positive and negative impacts on its host city and region. The establishment of a market district in the historic downtown core of High Point proved to be a highly successful financial strategy that produced an exceptionally strong economic impact. At the same time, the establishment of a market district in the historic downtown core of High Point led to the near elimination of any local social and cultural impact in the same space. This 40-year-old dialectical dilemma was the result of a policy decision to utilise only basic economic development concepts to build upon and further develop an existing regional trade show as a strategy to revitalise a decentralising downtown. Today, new policies and strategies that also embrace community development strategies are being employed in hopes of re-energising the local social and cultural soul of the area. City policy, focused on economic development, was at the heart of the dilemma, and now policy focused on quality of life issues will be at the heart of a solution. While economic impact dominated event policy for many years, the leaders of High Point have now come to understand and embrace an idea championed by Foley, McGillvray and McPherson who contend that cities must assign 'greater value to the underlying social and cultural meanings attributable to events' (2012: 177).

References

Bladen, C., Kennell, J., Abson, E. and Wilde, N. (2012) *Events Management: An Introduction*, New York: Routledge.

Brun, L. and Lester, T.W. (2013) *The Economic Impact of the High Point Market*, Durham, NC: Center on Globalization, Governance & Competitiveness, Social Science Research Institute, Duke University.

De Bres, K. and Davis, J. (2001) 'Celebrating group and place identity: A case study of a new regional festival', *Tourism Geographies*, 3(3), 326–337.

Derrett, R. (2003) 'Making sense of how festivals demonstrate a community's sense of place', *Event Management*, 8(1), 49–58.

Florida, R. (2008) *Who's Your City? How the Creative Economy Is Making Where to Live the Most Important Decision of Your Life*, New York: Basic Books.

Foley, M., McGillvray, D. and McPherson, G. (2012) *Event Policy: From Theory to Strategy*, New York: Routledge.

Gibson, C. and Connell, J. (2012) *Music Festivals and Regional Development in Australia*, Farnham, UK: Ashgate.

Green, G.P., Flora, J.L., Flora, E. and Schmidt, F.E. (1990) 'Local self-development strategies: National survey results', *Journal of the Community Development Society*, 21(2), 55–72.

Kimbrough, P. (2016a) 'Ballpark ask could be $10 million', *The High Point Enterprise*, www.hpenews.com/news/ballpark-ask-could-be-million/article_bb5db43e-b00c-11e5-a543-2379b87a3c06.html (accessed 26 May 2016).

Kimbrough, P. (2016b) 'Study supports ballpark idea', *The High Point Enterprise*, www.hpenews.com/news/study-supports-ballpark-idea/article_7d550faa-f4e7-11e5-bad3-97b411a305f6.html (accessed 26 May 2016).

Kimbrough, P. (2016c) 'Council sets plan for millennials', *The High Point Enterprise*, www.hpenews.com/news/council-sets-plan-for-millennials/article_8deb9c9e-ffe6-11e5-9714-e3b25689a405.html (accessed 26 May 2016).

Kimbrough, P. (2016d) 'City to consider market, CVB budgets', *The High Point Enterprise*, www.hpenews.com/news/council-to-consider-market-cvbudgets/article_0cc30a70-22c9-11e6-a45e-27fdd2c50719.html (accessed 26 May 2016).

MacLeod, N. (2006) 'The placeless festival: Identity and place in the post-modern festival', in D. Picard and M. Robinson (eds.), *Festivals, Tourism, and Social Change: Remaking Worlds* (pp. 222–237), Clevedon: Channel View.

McGuire, M., Rubin, B., Agranoff, R. and Richards, C. (1994) 'Building development capacity in nonmetropolitan communities', *Public Administration Review*, 54(5), 426–433.

Pierce, J., Martin, D.G. and Murphy, J.T. (2011) 'Relational place-making: The networked politics of place', *Transactions of the Institute of British Geographers*, 36(1), 54–70.

Phillips, R. (2016) 'Community development and economic development: What is the relationship?', in E. Sharpe, H. Mair and F. Vuen (eds.), *Community Development: Applications for Leisure, Sport, and Tourism* (pp. 183–189), State College, PA: Venture.

Porter, M. (1998) 'Clusters and the new economics of competition', *Harvard Business Review*, November-December, 77–90.

Schlichtman, J.J. (2009) 'The niche city idea: How a declining manufacturing center exploited the opportunities of globalization', *International Journal of Urban and Regional Research*, 33(1), 105–125.

Schlichtman, J.J. and Patch, J. (2008) 'Contextualizing impressions of neighborhood change: Linking business directories to ethnography', *City and Community*, 7(3), 273–293.

Schmader, S.W. (2016) Festivals & events: Playing our roles as the public squares of our community', *The Business of International Events*, Summer, 10.

Sharpley, R. and Stone, P.R. (2012) 'Socio-cultural impacts of events', in S. Page and J. Connell (eds.), *The Routledge Handbook of Events* (pp. 347–361), London: Routledge.

Smith, A. (2012) *Events and Urban Regeneration: The Strategic Use of Events to Revitalize Cities*, New York: Routledge.

Teodori, G. and Luloff, A. (1998) 'Land use and community attachment', *7th International Symposium on Society and Resource Management*, Columbia, MO: University of Missouri.

Tuan, Y. (1977) *Space and Place: The Perspective of Experience*, Minneapolis, MN: University of Minnesota Press.

4 The evolving nature of commercial art fairs

Hilary du Cros

Introduction

International contemporary art fairs (ICAFs) are now fixed dates on the international art calendar and herald the latest trends for the art market. With new art markets opening up in developing countries, pressure on art fairs to offer something different in terms of art experiences is causing the event form to become more inclusive of participants without a deep knowledge of the visual arts.

Quemin (2013) examined the participation of art galleries at ICAFs to evaluate what contribution they could make to theories of cultural globalisation. He was the first to focus on the geographical distribution of major ICAFs worldwide, that is, their concentration in selected geographical locations, such as Europe, as well as the country of origin of the galleries participating in these events. This approach was intended to map out the workings of any territorial forms of dominance affecting the art market, especially if a cluster of one or more ICAFs can occur almost concurrently (in a type of bundling effect) and how art galleries participate in such high-profile events.

This chapter will commence with a brief examination of the nature of ICAFs and their development, and then look at the evolution of Art HK into Art Basel HK. A case study approach is used for the latter where key aspects of the Sustainable Creative Advantage (SCA) assessment tool are then applied to understand more about the events' appeal and ability to sell art.

Venice Biennale: an early example of an evolving and enduring commercial arts event

Since the late 19th century, international visual arts events have attracted commercial interest, tourists and the art world. Biennials are the earliest example of a hallmark international arts event form that is a periodic international art fair or exhibition that only deals with visual arts, as against a major exposition that features multiple sectors. The first of these (and still ongoing) is the Venice Biennale International Art Exhibition first held in 1895. It is the oldest periodic contemporary art exhibition in the world, and one of Italy's most prominent cultural events. It is also one of the first arts events to develop commercial practices still used by many international exhibitions, arts fairs and biennial events today.

The first Biennale ran between April and October 1895, after a series of false starts and abortive efforts. Authorities worked hard to build the demand for a major arts event in the city. West (1995) has concluded that throughout the early history of the event, a tension was clearly evident between national and international ambitions in the organisation and selection ratios of Italian and non-Italian artists and artworks, given that Italy had only recently unified and Venice only became a part of Italy in 1866.

The Biennale nevertheless survived this tension and became an important international event on the arts calendar. The cultural space within the city opened Venice up to a new style of promotion, as its gardens' pleasurable qualities were fully recognised in arts criticism and event marketing for the first time. The event was staged partially in pavilions erected in the Castello Gardens and partially in adjacent civic halls, giving it an indoor/outdoor ambience. The positive image this presented was also supported by arts critics' reviews, whose expenses were financed by the astute Biennale organisers. However, the critic's premium was not the only benefit they received. The first instance of a VIP area at an arts event was intended initially for art critics and journalists in 1903 at the fifth Biennale. It was known as the 'Sala,' very like the French 'Salon' and ancestor of the VIP lounge. It comprised a reception room, a library, a smoking room and a post/telegraph office in line with advances in media and communications technology, in order for critics to publicise the event during its entire run. The Biennale also kept up with the times by instituting electric lighting in 1901 for illuminating artworks in interior spaces. In 1907, a restaurant designed in the 'Byzantine-Venetian Style' was added to the garden area for the use of all fairgoers. The event also had the first instance of an art publication produced especially for the event, where items normally considered 'high art' were depicted alongside advertising of mundane consumer goods and services in a catalogue (West 1995).

Initially, visitor numbers grew from 224,327 in 1895 to 457,960 in 1909. Organisers also noticed similar trends in the artwork sales over this period. There was a major dip as World War One approached. The war caused some interruption, even though Italy did not enter it until after many of its neighbours. In general, the organisers established a model pre-war that worked, attracting a critical mass of artists, artworks, critics, curators and visitors, which made the event viable over the long-term.

Late in the 20th century, the Biennale organisers realised they needed to reinvent their business and marketing practices. Also, a market-positioning problem was identified for the Biennale, as it appeared to be losing its dominance as a taste influencer and market appeal. This was due to a series of changes in its competitive environment both inside and outside of Europe. The internal changes in the art world and the growing complexity of the marketplace in the early 21st century have provided various challenges, which have made the Biennale consider its strategic marketing research as extremely important (Bagdadli and Arrigoni 2005).

Commercial arts events in Asia and Hong Kong

In the early 21st century, the commercial side of visual arts was strengthened in response to the professionalisation of arts events and the growth in popularity of some as sites for commerce. However, for the visual arts, the proliferation of international contemporary art fairs is the clearest evidence of the increasing importance of market influences over that of the wishes of artists and art critics. Originating in the 1960s, ICAFs have become the commercial rivals of the great periodic exhibitions, particularly those such as Art Basel (in Switzerland, Miami and Hong Kong) and the Dubai Art Fair, which are now fixed dates on the international art calendar, and herald the latest trends for the market beyond Europe. In addition to the conventional exposition of art from participating galleries, these fairs are currently offering various ancillary events that are more cultural than commercial in order to build up the loyalty of private collectors and art critics in particular.

Most indicative of change is how the art market and art tourism are driving the creation of new events; for instance, many major hotel chains are now leasing several floors at a time to art fair organisers. Since 2010, each five-star hotel chain represented in Hong Kong has hosted a hotel art fair. For instance, the Conrad Hotel in Admiralty signed up with a local organiser in 2012 to host the Asian Contemporary Art Show (ACAS). From 2013, the event was held twice a year on three of its floors (ACAS 2016). In the same year, five major art fairs (including three hotel art fairs) were held within the same week as Art Basel Hong Kong in May, all offering a high concentration of art on sale and for viewing.

Hong Kong becomes a commercial arts sales hub

That major international arts festivals can be responsible for attracting many international visitors to a location is not in doubt. Boyle, Reaiche, Abdullah and Murad (2016) looked into whether the high-profile major international acts that are selected for a particular festival play an important role in attracting international visitors to the Hong Kong Arts Festival (an annual heavily curated performing arts event). Regional tourists made up the majority of this sample, while many of the acts came from further afield. This study suggested that relevant programming strategies were influential in attracting international visitors and in increasing their interest in arts events of this kind.

Accordingly, art fairs also offer the opportunity to see high quality art from overseas galleries and specially curated exhibitions, in addition to the local private gallery fare. In doing so regularly, they can add to a city's status as an arts hub. However, there is very little academic work directly on the topic of commercial art fairs, as it seems to fall into a gap between *creative cities* and special events management research interests, where it is either too commercial for some researchers to consider studying or too 'artsy' for others. In regard to the latter, there is a massive amount of literature on sports events and their commercial aspects, but not arts events.

For ICAFs, their growing popularity is based on an emerging market of new art collectors who have disposable income for this activity for the first time. In response to this incipient market in Asia, the new mission of art fairs is to provide free education to art tourists from the region, which could be seen as self-serving in that it encourages new collectors who may make current or future purchases at the fair. Accordingly, fun learning experiences are hoped to encourage and educate collectors of the future from amongst the general public, such that these could be considered long-term audience-building exercises (du Cros and Jolliffe 2014).

The example of Hong Kong International Art Fair (ART HK) and its metamorphosis into Art Basel Hong Kong (Art Basel HK) has been tracked from 2008 to 2016, as an example of an ICAF responding to 21st century conditions. It was selected also to demonstrate how co-dependent art fairs in Asia are on each other and on the vagaries of the political and economic conditions. Hong Kong is also one of the few cities in Asia that has excellent conditions for such commercial events, as it hosts seasonal auctions by both Christie's and Sotheby's and has been an Asian arts and antiques sales hub for a number of years (Holloway 2013). Art fairs have begun to move their events away from needing to coincide with art auctions, while Hong Kong's liberal tax and business environment has allowed ICAFs to prosper and independently become a magnet for visual arts investment (Batten 2012). The only sour note occurred in 2015 when Mainland China's anti-corruption campaign was at its height and the country achieved its lowest growth target in the past two decades (7%). The strong US dollar that year also caused the Japanese *yen* and South Korean *won* to depreciate and collectors from these countries also to be less eager (Chow 2015). However, in 2016 it was evident that this trend was over, with fairs experiencing more record sales and art dealers/galleries appeared confident that the increase in sales would continue (Lau 2016).

Art critics and others note that Asia has enormous economic potential, but not a particularly long history of public and private galleries and visiting is not considered an everyday activity for the public (Seno 2013). Increasingly, there has been a steady movement of private galleries to Hong Kong, as a result of the ICAF's success (Lau 2016). Even so, the Hong Kong Tourism Board critiqued Hong Kong as a 'cultural desert' in the late 1990s, which then spurred a massive capital works programme to create new public arts facilities for a cultural district at West Kowloon (du Cros and Leong 2011). While this project has been mired in difficulties and has progressed slowly, Hong Kong has organically developed as a commercial arts sales hub (Wang 2012).

The current situation is clearly evident in Table 4.1, which shows that Hong Kong is becoming a significant player in the international art market. It reflects that in comparison to other countries, it is exporting more than might be expected given its general and arts population. This result also means it is sought after and trusted as a place for making art purchases away from the source by art dealers, collectors and curators.

Table 4.1 Hong Kong and the Asian art world in 2016

Country/City	Hong Kong SAR	Singapore	Republic of South Korea	Japan	People's Republic of China
Population	7,182,724	5,460,302	48,955,203	127,253,075	1,349,585,838
Total Value of Art Exported (US$)	476,031,000	152,535,000	123,301,000	171,331,000	534,302,000
Arts Funding (US$) (all arts)	425,620,224*	184,140,894	Information Not available	1,189,465,874	358,835,494
Student enrolment (visual arts only)	3,400	1,203	15,796	11,683	1,268,368

* Includes only the 2016 cost of funding for construction of the West Kowloon Cultural Hub (based on Art Asia Pacific 2016)

Methodology

The case study is structured using the key elements of the Sustainable Creative Advantage (SCA) approach favoured by du Cros and Jolliffe (2014) for arts events. This is because the influence of the creative process in the design of most arts events makes them a natural part of the 'experience economy', as promoted by Pine and Gilmore (1999), as they showcase the cultural rhythms or creative synergies of a particular place. The definition of such experiential encounters is still being developed in the literature in relation to the creative industries, events and the arts in a tourism context (Kay and Polonsky 2010; Sotiriadis and Gursoy 2016). Quinn (2006) described arts festivals, in particular, as 'socially significant cultural practices,' which deserve consideration beyond their contributions to economic and tourism development or 'as a product to enliven a destination' (Quinn 2006: 301). One danger identified in her study is that running 'a model commercial' event that highlights internationally known artists can mean that regional and local ones could be marginalised and alienated. A balance should be maintained when local, regional and international artists are shown at any ICAF, which seeks to leverage 'place' as part of its marketing and be supported by local/regional arts ecologies (du Cros and Jolliffe 2014).

This chapter will present the ART HK/Art Basel HK transformation as a case study where the SCA assessment approach has been applied. The event has been studied over the last few years using data gathered mainly since 2012 (when it was still the Hong Kong International Art Fair) for an initial SCA analysis supplemented by more recent information and event observation by the author.

Longitudinal event observation is becoming an increasingly important part of evaluation for event organisers, as well as academics (Mackellar 2013).

ART HK fair becomes Art Basel HK

The evolution of Art HK into Art Basel HK will be outlined below using the SCA key aspects of *glocal* support (the global and local support of the art world), brand image, market orientation and position, conceptual uniqueness, event experience and finally, operation and management.

Glocal support

ART HK held its first successful edition in May 2008 at the Hong Kong Exhibition and Convention Centre. Magnus Renfrew, an art promoter with an extensive network in the region, was appointed director. Founders of the event, Tim Etchells, Sandy Angus and Will Ramsay sold a majority stake in it in 2011 to MCH Group, organisers of Art Basel (the original event in Switzerland) and Art Basel Miami (Zaremba 2012). After the 2011 sale of ART HK to Art Basel, the event ran in its existing form for the 2012 edition, then converted to Art Basel HK for the 2013 edition (ART HK 2012).

Art Basel began in the Swiss city of the same name in June 1970 and reached its current event size of 300 galleries in 1975. Miami Beach was added as the US edition after the first successful event in December 2002. Hong Kong was added in response to a 'desire to build a cultural bridge between the long-established Western art world and the vibrant new scenes of the entire (Asian) region' (Art Basel 2016). Next, Art Basel is considering South America for a trial event in Buenos Aires, as part of its new 'Art Basel Cities Initiative' with which it is testing which location might work best for them for a base there. Art Basel still largely controls its name and branding from Switzerland and only takes on partners as sponsors after close vetting (Art Basel 2016).

In Hong Kong since 2013, support has continued from the Hong Kong Gallery Association, critics, auction houses, the media, curators and sponsors (despite the change of name and management). The combination of the Basel brand and the growing reputation of Hong Kong as an art sales hub ensured that the organisers have had the pick of the best international galleries, while collectors, critics and curators have joined the event in increasing numbers. Asia Art Archive (a local arts-focused not-for-profit organisation) continued to support the educational side, whilst working in a more structured programme. Its key sponsor is the Hong Kong government's Home Affairs Bureau.

Considering itself also part of the Hong Kong arts scene, the Art Basel HK (see Figure 4.1) has continued to feature Hong Kong artists prominently, as well as shifting its focus for the 'Encounters' curated exhibition from country to country around Asia and selecting high quality art from galleries based further afield (Batten 2013; Lau 2016). So, it still tries to select artists and galleries from local, regional and further afield. Meanwhile, new arts districts, such as the Married

Figure 4.1 Art Basel in Hong Kong 2017
Source: Photo courtesy of Art Basel

Police Quarters and Art Central, are increasing the number of private art galleries actually based in Hong Kong (Ramsay 2016).

Brand image, market orientation and position

The original event was first held in 2008 with 100 galleries participating and in its last year in 2012 it had 630 applications for the 230 places offered to galleries from 38 countries (Batten 2012). Gallery owners interviewed in 2013 about the new Basel event ventured that it attracted a lot of interest within Hong Kong and outside, which was built on the success of the earlier version. More media interest was generated in connection with the growth of the art market in China – the event is mentioned just as often in the business section of local newspapers, as in the arts and culture section.

The first Hong Kong version of Art Basel in 2013 appeared to be very interested in the views of collectors, critics and journalists and not so much those of the general public. For instance, see an online seven-page questionnaire created by Art Basel that appeared on its website (posted after the first Basel HK in 2013) (see also Table 4.2). Collecting more than basic demographic and psychographic information would assist the organisers in ensuring that the event is establishing its brand, image and position in the eyes of its key market in the Asia-Pacific region, where Basel is a new competitor.

Table 4.2 Online marketing survey topics for the first edition of Basel 2013

Topic area	Typical concerns
Demographic details	Gender, age, place of residence, level of education, nature of profession, income level
Experience of a specific event	Repeat visitor/first to this event/others, time spent, nature of pre-planning, ticket purchased, intentions, expectations, activities undertaken, orientation, nature of social interaction during visit, nature of trends exhibited, galleries representative of art market
Visual arts engagement	Attendance at other art events, private galleries visited, favourite art movements/journals/information sources, purchasing habits, interest in virtual art fairs
Personal arts appreciation and preferences	Other art forms, nature of art appreciation preferred, value of this event's activities in enhancing arts knowledge/appreciation, this event's influence on appreciation/purchase
Art market trends/opinions	Importance/influences on pricing, impact on contemporary arts, opinions on other factors, overall impression of art market and art fairs, capacity of event to provide networking opportunities for professionals

Source: Based on analysis by du Cros and Jolliffe 2014)

Conceptual uniqueness

Currently, there is no other event in Asia with the Basel brand, image and approach to running an ICAF. The edgy ancillary events such as 'Guerilla Talks' and 'Back-room Conversations', were adapted by Art Basel to become 'Salon' and 'Conversations' in line with a more mainstream European format. Some local art critics complained that it had become bland as a result (Batten 2013), whilst others thought it added more sophistication (Tam 2014). Others still welcomed it as another addition to Hong Kong's high society event calendar as celebrities, such as Kate Moss, were invited by Art Basel to add a bit of glamour to the new look fair in 2013 (Chow 2013).

The event experience

Ticketing practices and prices for the public remained largely unchanged over the transformation and later. More VIP tickets and lounges were offered in 2013 sponsored by major European banks (such as UBS and Deutsche Bank). The event typically runs from Thursday night (private viewing for collectors, critics and dealers), through three days of public viewings and talks, until Sunday night (for both ART HK and Art Basel). Art Basel also offered a similar type and number of activities to ART HK with the exception of one headlining talk, co-hosted by Intelligence Squared in 2012 on local cultural politics for ART HK, that was very popular (ART HK 2012). Building on the event-based education activities in 2015, Art

Basel launched the executive-education programme 'Collecting Contemporary Art' through continuing education provider HKU SPACE with content delivered by the Central Saint Martins College of Arts and Design, London (Art Basel 2016).

The experience of participants from each sector (collectors, public, critics and so on) was likely to differ and Art Basel was initially concerned to know more on this topic (see Table 4.2). More tours were available than before and after 2015, specific art tours from outside Hong Kong have been devised to take advantage of all the activities possible during what has become an 'art week' March (see Art Gallery of New South Wales members tour as an example – Ramsay 2016).

Between 2008 and 2012, ART HK grew from attracting 27,000 visitors to 60,000 per edition (ART HK 2012). After the transfer to Art Basel, in excess of 60,000 people in 2013 attended and 10% more in 2014 to 65,000 (Tam 2014). It dropped back to 60,000 in 2015. The 2016 edition attracted the highest number so far of 70,000 with exhibitions from 239 of the world's leading modern and contemporary art galleries promoting more than 1,000 artists (Lam 2016; Art Basel 2016). Reviews were generally favourable; however, no results of the Art Basel online survey are available publicly in order to judge the event in more detail for this analysis. Seno (2013) has observed in relation to the Hong Kong public that 'also providing educational activities and talks to give context to what visitors are seeing' is important given how 'museum-going-for-fun', especially for viewing contemporary art, is a relatively new concept.

Implementation and management

The event had a different layout in 2013 to that of past years, due to the organisers requiring some adherence to the Art Basel brand. It approximately followed the Basel formula of dividing galleries into areas marked out into different colours on the map representing Discoveries, Insights, Encounters and other exhibition areas. The three named areas also included one that was individually curated by Yuko Hasegawa to include large-scale sculptures and installations from around the world (Art Basel 2016).

In regard to content, organisers for both the previous and current event practised a selection process, which has become more particular as time has gone on (Lau 2016). There was less information publicly available about Art Basel's selection process than that for ART HK's, although the selection committee names are publicly available on the Art Basel website (Art Basel 2016). One of the biggest changes concerned its timing. The first few editions took the same time slot of May as before. However, after a 10-month adjustment, it was moved to March in 2015 to fit better within the international art calendar and coincide or overlap with five other art fairs in Hong Kong (Art Basel 2016). Hence, it has become another example of a bundled art experience for tourists (du Cros and Jolliffe 2011).

Connectivity remained quite strong as the event organiser, Magnus Renfrew, stayed with the fair up to 2015, when his protégé, Adeline Ooi, took over the directorship (Chow 2015). New York art dealer, Andrea Rosen, observed 'that's one of the things I like about Hong Kong: You're there evolving new relationships' (quoted in Lau 2016: S1). The Art Basel event design when applied at the Hong Kong Exhibition and Convention Centre allowed for a more coherent allocation of space for this to occur.

Accordingly, in 2013 there was new funding and enthusiasm to build new partnerships, and a lot more media exposure than in previous years in order to herald Art Basel's arrival in Asia to its main orientation, which is the art market, comprising curators (buying for museums and public galleries), dealers and collectors. The event organisers had achieved a level of professionalism in managing resources after six years of holding the event that was passed onto Art Basel, which then added its own stamp on it.

Overall, the event has gone from strength to strength with occasional hiccups, as in 2015, for largely external reasons. In 2016, there was evidence of a bounce back. The event experience of participants from each sector likely differed and requires more research than one page in a seven-page online survey to assess fully. The organisers' continued effort to increase and maintain regional networks in the art world is being supported for this new version of the event to maintain its SCA and position it as a hallmark event in the international arts events calendar.

Discussion

Building glocal support

Knowing more about the nature of the glocal support for an event is important for understanding the enabling conditions for achieving ongoing success in relation to arts events. Such conditions are also important for creating a sustainable advantage that is place-based and makes the most of available creative capital (creativity, creatives, creative processes and global and local cultural/arts ecologies). Not only should the benefits spread outwards to the participants, sponsors and community, if the events are well planned and implemented, but also the connections should ensure that a repeated event is viable for years to come. Support for an event from the local and international (if relevant) arts communities in terms of building on social connections that organisers may already have needs to be carefully scrutinised in any assessment of an event's success. Connectivity is crucial to the public and private goodwill that arts events need to develop and survive (du Cros and Jolliffe 2014).

The Basel group of international art fairs with annual events in Basel (Switzerland), Miami (USA) and Hong Kong Special Administrative Region (SAR), China, use this kind of connectivity to a strong commercial advantage to reinforce its brand image as a market leader internationally. The benefit for Hong Kong is that local artists featured in the event have another avenue for exposure to potential buyers visiting Hong Kong.

Market share

Market share often requires studies of impact and many arts organisations, particularly for the performing arts, conduct these regularly regarding developing audience-building strategies without specific reference to particular events (du Preez and Bailey 2010). The issue then becomes whether market research for arts events should differ greatly from that conducted for other kinds of special events or not. Where the difference might lie is with how to integrate useful information from audience-building/impact studies into the mix. How many extra sources of data beyond those associated with the basic demographic and psychographic questions need to be included in surveys for events depending on their orientation? The interesting example for Art Basel HK in 2013 was an online survey conducted first in German and then translated into English for gathering market research for Art Basel regarding the success of the Art Basel Hong Kong (see Table 4.2).

Another issue is maintaining position in the marketplace. Singapore is likely to start cutting into Hong Kong's art market share, as it now has a refurbished and extended national art gallery, conducts more art fairs (but not Art Basel) and private galleries (local and international). A cluster of international galleries were encouraged to set up at the converted Gillman Barracks in 2012 and are also scattered throughout the city. In addition, the city hosts major art auctions and is exporting more art than it can produce locally (see Table 4.1). From observation, most of this art appears to be sourced from its neighbours in Southeast Asia, whereas Hong Kong sources art more widely.

The event experience

One of the key differences between the earlier ART HK and Art Basel HK, was that the local elements in the activities seemed to have been altered towards a more cosmopolitan and Eurocentric formula aiming to herald a change in direction. The commercial orientation of the event therefore came a little more obviously to the fore as private collectors and dealers were either attracted or 'groomed' to engage more with the art for either status seeking or lifestyle reasons and not cultural politics.

Art Basel HK included private as well as public lectures given by renowned figures in the art world in the programme sessions, 'Conversations' and 'Salon,' in an effort to allow industry networking and cross-cultural discussions in a way that harks back to traditions started by the early biennials. The appearance of extensive review sections in international specialty publications, such as *The Art Newspaper, Flash Art International* (published in New York and Milan, respectively) and *Ocula* e-journal (branches worldwide), testifies to the growing importance of this kind of event for all sectors. This special attention to the media included whole areas set aside for display of these publications to attract more subscriber attendance at Art Basel events, as well as reviews.

Digital arts fairs

Art Basel was toying with the idea in 2013 of creating a digital art fair, possibly to supplement the existing event. Not much has eventuated in this regard, because the current form of the event seems too popular to require a digital fair as support.

However, the website features a digital catalogue for all artworks for each Art Basel event, which is also available as a tablet app, so that artworks can be referred to easily (Art Basel 2016).

Overall, digital fairs (from a participant's point of view) could mean free access to sample works if undecided about attending, uninterested or unable to attend. However, there are fewer opportunities to understand the context behind the artworks and ask questions of gallery owners or artists. Critics and curators would probably prefer broader access than a website in which to evaluate artworks. There are some financial considerations for smaller galleries, as many of these cannot afford high rental fees for the booths of highly popular events. While most have their own website, they would benefit from being promoted alongside larger galleries and also viewed by their clientele.

Conclusion

The international contemporary art fair will continue to develop and evolve as an event form as it experiences a benefit from an increasing arts discourse with new art collectors, curators and dealers from developing regions, which overlaps with the mission of biennales. With new art markets opening up, there is pressure to offer something different in terms of art experiences to this new group, which is causing the ICAFs to become more inclusive of participants without a deep knowledge of the visual arts. The social aspects of the event seem quite strong with celebrities invited and private collectors 'groomed' and congratulated in regard to their purchases. It would be difficult to replace these experiences and the educational activities with digital art sales platforms.

References

ACAS (2016) 'About', www.asiacontemporaryart.com/home/main/en/ (accessed 3 December 2016).
Art Asia Pacific (2016) 'Almanac', www.artasiapacific.com/Countries/Almanac (accessed 5 December 2016).
Art Basel (2016) 'Home', www.artbasel.com (accessed 5 December 2016).
ART HK (2012) 'About', www.hongkongartfair.com (accessed 5 December 2016).
Bagdadli, S. and Arrigoni, L. (2005) 'Strategic positioning of the Venice Biennial: Analysing the market for periodic contemporary art exhibitions', *International Journal of Arts Management*, 7(3), 22–31.
Batten, J. (2012) 'A case of mistaken identity', *South China Morning Post Magazine*, 27 May, www.scmp.com/article/1002083/case-mistaken-identity (accessed 4 December 2016).
Batten, J. (2013) 'Art Basel: A fair with little flair', *South China Morning Post*, 9 June, www.scmp.com/lifestyle/arts-culture/article/1255624/art-basel-fair-little-flair (accessed 4 December 2016).
Boyle, S., Reaiche, C., Abdullah, A. and Murad, W. (2016) 'Predicting international visitors' interest in Hong Kong arts festival', *Event Management*, 20(4), 593–605.
Chow, V. (2013) '"Tatlerisation" of Hong Kong's art scene as Kate Moss and co party', *South China Morning Post*, 24 May, www.scmp.com/lifestyle/arts-culture/

article/1245140/tatlerisation-hong-kongs-art-scene-kate-moss-and-co-party (accessed 4 December 2016).

Chow, V. (2015) 'Artists and galleries from the region share the stage with big international players at prestigious art fair that will run until March 1', *South China Morning Post*, 14 March, www.scmp.com/news/hong-kong/article/1737050/asia-gets-top-billing-hong-kongs-third-art-basel (accessed 4 December 2016).

du Cros, H. and Jolliffe, L. (2011) 'Bundling the arts for tourism to complement urban heritage experiences in Asia', *Journal of Heritage Tourism*, 6(3), 181–195.

du Cros, H. and Jolliffe, L. (2014) *The Arts and Events*, Abingdon, UK: Routledge.

du Cros, H. and Leong, S. (2011) 'A new approach to arts policy formulation that directly supports the arts and cultural identity in Hong Kong', *The Asian Conference on Arts and Humanities*, IAFOR, Osaka, Japan, 27–30 May 2011, www.iafor.org/acah_proceedings.html, 193–205.

du Preez, K. and Bailey, K. (2010) *Artistic reflection kit: A guide to assist arts organizations to reflect on artistic vibrancy and measure their artistic achievements*. Sydney: Australia Council for the Arts.

Holloway, M. (2013) 'Artistic value', *South China Morning Post*, 1 June, C2.

Kay, P. and Polonsky, M. (2010) 'Creative industries and experiences: Development, marketing and consumption', *Tourism, Culture and Communication*, 10(3), 181–186.

Lam, A. (2016) 'In pictures: Hong Kong celebrates Art Basel 2016', *South China Morning Post*, 25 March, www.scmp.com/lifestyle/arts-entertainment/article/1930554/pictures-hong-kong-celebrates-art-basel-2016 (accessed 5 December 2016).

Lau, J. (2016) 'Embracing the spotlight', *International New York Times*, 24 March, S1.

Mackellar, J. (2013) 'Participant observation at events: Theory, practice and potential', *International Journal of Event Management*, 4(1), 56–65.

Pine, J. and Gilmore, J. (1999) *The Experience Economy*, Boston: Harvard Business School Press.

Quemin, A. (2013) 'International contemporary art fairs in a "globalised" art market', *European Societies*, 15(2), 162–177.

Quinn, B. (2006) 'Problematising "festival tourism": Arts festivals and sustainable development in Ireland', *Journal of Sustainable Tourism*, 14(3), 288–306.

Ramsay, R. (2016) '19–25 March 2017 Hong Kong art week and Guangzhou', www.artgallery.nsw.gov.au/members/current-members/world-art-tours/#hong (accessed 5 December 2016).

Seno, A. (2013) 'Museums for the many is Hong Kong's new mantra', *The Art Newspaper*, 4 May, 25–26.

Sotiriadis, M. and Gursoy, D. (2016) 'Introduction', in M. Sotiriadis and D. Gursoy (eds.), *The Handbook of Managing and Marketing Tourism Experiences* (pp. xi–2), Bingley, UK: Emerald.

Tam, J. (2014) 'Art Basel Hong Kong wows "the sophisticated"', *South China Morning Post*, 19 May, www.scmp.com/news/hong-kong/article/1515156/art-basel-hong-kong-wows-sophisticated (accessed 5 December 2016).

Wang, X. (2012) 'Editorial', *South China Morning Post*, 20 May, 14.

West, S. (1995) 'National desires and regional realities in the Venice Biennale, 1895–1914', *Art History*, 18(3), 404–434.

Zaremba, A. (2012) 'Comes the time, comes the man', *Artmap Express*, 1 May, 1.

5 Couture on the catwalk

Department store fashion shows

Jennifer Laing and Warwick Frost

Introduction

Queen Elizabeth II and Prince Philip visited the USA in 1976, as part of the com-memoration of the 200th anniversary of independence from Great Britain. Bloomingdale's, an iconic US department store, took the opportunity to invite the royal couple to their premises. What did Her Majesty do during her visit? While visiting a customised boutique of American fashion, including the likes of Calvin Klein and Ralph Lauren, she requested 'a mini-fashion show of children's back-to-school clothes, worn by ten very excited young models' (Brady 1980: 11). While the fashion show was in progress, Prince Philip, at *his* request, was shown how the company's computers work. This vignette illustrates two of the key themes of this chapter. The first is the nexus between department stores and fashion shows, to which the Queen herself bore witness. The second is the gender division that has traditionally surrounded the activity of shopping in general, and fashion shows in particular.

While the English *couturière* Lady Lucy Duff Gordon, known as Lucile, is said to be have first devised the idea of the fashion show in the Edwardian era (Evans 2013; Woodhead 2007), it was the great department stores such as Selfridges and Harrods in London and Wanamaker's and Bloomingdale's in New York that used them to bring fashion to the masses. In the late 19th and early 20th centuries, these stores had a symbiotic relationship with fashion. It formed the bulwark of their revenue, particularly with respect to their female clientele, as a well-dressed woman in that era needed an extensive array of paraphernalia including corsets, petticoats, hats, gloves and stockings, with outfits often changed several times a day. The stores also provided an innovative sales and distribution channel for the textile, garment, millinery and haberdashery industries.

Women could experience the visceral pleasure of seeing and trying on clothes, but it was their attendance at in-house fashion shows that exposed them to the latest styles, with the spectacle that goes with live models, music and choreography. Fashion shows are still an integral part of the department store shopping experience, but face challenges in a world of *fast fashion*, where fashion is disposable, influenced by new media, including social media platforms and increasingly bought online in preference to physical outlets. Furthermore, in a digital world fashion businesses now have a variety of other ways to reach their customers. In this chapter, we trace the history and influence of the department store fashion show, and examine whether the reign of their catwalks is now over or has adjusted to changing times.

The genesis of department stores

The French department store or *grand magasin* originated in Paris and contributed to the city's image as a centre of style and fashion. Women in provincial areas had to be content with consulting catalogues (Rocamora 2009), but the Parisian shopper enjoyed the visceral delights of the finest wares, presented in a manner that encouraged things to be touched and were a feast for the eye. As McArthur (2013: 454) observes: 'department stores draped the physical site of shopping in glamour and decorum', while for Leach (1984: 320), they were places of 'sensuous pleasure and dreams'. Everything was conveniently in the one place and the idea of the sale or placing goods 'on special' was revolutionary. Some stores were concerned about the rise in the number of *tabbies* – the pejorative term applied to women who would hang around stores all day, trying on clothes and taking advantage of free services, but without making any purchases. Storewalkers were employed to keep an eye on this behaviour, yet some progressive stores such as Selfridges realised that it cost them more to do this than to just turn a blind eye (Lancaster 1995).

It was 'an overwhelmingly feminine world' (Steele 1988: 149), which gave women a place of empowerment away from their husbands or fathers and thus a form of haven (McArthur 2013). The French novelist Émile Zola, in his novel *The Ladies' Paradise* (*Au Bonheur des Dames*) brings to life the luxury of the 19th-century department store and its role for women in particular:

> And the mantles were here, in this sort of chapel raised to the worship of woman's beauty and grace. In the centre was a magnificent article, a velvet mantle trimmed with silver fox; on one side of it appeared a silk cloak lined with miniver, on the other a cloth cloak edged with cocks' plumes; and, last of all, some opera cloaks in white cashmere and quilted silk trimmed with swansdown or chenille. There was something for every taste, from the opera cloaks at twenty-nine francs to the velvet mantle which was marked eighteen hundred.
>
> (Zola 1883)

Chaney (1983: 29), however, takes exception to this flight of fancy, arguing that 'Zola's metaphor that a new religion of consumerism was emerging in which department stores were its temples and women the leading worshippers is misleading to the extent that it sustains the idea that female customers almost become possessed when shopping'. In fact, the opposite could be argued, in that they gained a measure of control in this new environment outside the domestic sphere. In this era, the idea of women gaining 'mastery of a language of possessions' (Chaney 1983: 29) and thus empowerment as consumers was confronting. There were concerns voiced that women shoppers, in particular the middle-class, might lose control of themselves, either through debt or shoplifting (Miller 1981; Spiekermann 1999; Tiersten 1999). Window displays at Selfridges, 'lit until midnight each night' were criticised as encouraging theft due to the 'vast piles of tantalizing merchandise freely displayed' (Woodhead 2007: 108). Department stores often downplayed this behaviour, perhaps concerned that this might reinforce perceptions that they were morally suspect places (Crossick and Jaumain 1999). Some even referred to shopping as a duty or responsibility that women should fulfil both to maintain a comfortable home life and to support national industries, such as fashion (Tiersten 1999).

The era of the grand department store coincided with a series of international exhibitions in Paris and there is a symbiotic link between the two in that 'their organisation of internal space was similar, not least because the same architects and engineers often worked on both' (Crossick and Jaumain 1999: 28). It is also suggested that the displays of the department stores might have been influenced by those of the international exhibitions (Steele 1988), with the latter prominently featuring the French fashion industry, notably its haute couture offerings. For example, the entrance gate to the 1900 Paris Exposition Universelle was topped by a statue of La Parisienne, strikingly dressed by French designer Madame Paquin (see Chapter 2). While ready-to-wear fashion was an important market for the department stores (Miller 1981), it relied on the innovations of the couture industry to set the trends and the aspirations for fashionable clothing.

Some of the more famous examples of French department stores that are still standing and trading today are Printemps (1865) and Galeries Lafayette (1896). It wasn't just the internal design and display of these stores that was novel. They also changed the urban landscape, 'where church spires and towers had once stood unchallenged' (Crossick and Jaumain 1999: 21). Their impact also extended to their innovative and lavish interiors (Crossick and Jaumain 1999). Both Printemps and Galeries Lafayette are famous for their opulent glass domes, as well as their impressive facades (Rocamora 2009). They became a form of visitor attraction and remain so today, alongside the likes of Harrods in London and Saks Fifth Avenue in New York. Their construction transformed the cityscape from a largely residential space to 'a commercial and entertainment centre surrounded by pockets of population' (Chaney 1983: 25).

The exemplar was the Bon Marché in Paris, upon which Zola's (1883) fictional store is based. It 'became the icon, an embodiment of newness and modernity, which has come to define our sense of what constituted a real department store' (Crossick and Jaumain 1999: 22). Other stores looked to it for inspiration. Selfridges in London, opened at the turn of the 20th century, dominated Oxford Street (Woodhead 2007). Its founder/owner, Gordon 'Harry' Selfridge, had worked at Marshall Field's in Chicago, which featured a stained glass cupola created by Tiffany (Lancaster 1995). Selfridge wanted an equally beautiful store, which would make a statement about his vision of the future for retail shopping. Other notable British examples of department stores with 'gallery floors, sweeping staircases and dramatic glass roofs' (Lancaster 1995: 25) included Jenners in Edinburgh and Liberty's of London. The latter's Tudor revival building was constructed in 1924 and is regarded as one of the most iconic store fronts still in existence. Yet the norm, before World War One, was 'muddled accretions to existing buildings with the inconvenience and weakness of vision that accompanied such piecemeal development' (Lancaster 1995: 22). Often the decision to upgrade to new premises was made in the aftermath of a fire (with Harrods being a notable example) rather than being the result of a deliberate business strategy (Lancaster 1995).

In the 19th and early 20th centuries, redevelopment of streets and boulevards, as well as public transport networks, provided the 'setting in which the stores' mix of theatre, architecture, fantasy and sociability could flourish' (Crossick and Jaumain 1999: 23). Department stores were often located cheek by jowl with theatres, and shopping trips might be combined with a show (Rappaport 1999). The theatrical links were often overt, with some stores supplying furnishings for stage productions, while at the turn of the 20th century, British store Fenwick's created the costumes for the popular musical *Trilby* (Lancaster 1995). Leach (1984) observes that 'the concept of *show* [our emphasis] invaded the domain of culture, whether in the shape of a theatrical show, a baby show, a show girl, a showplace or a showroom' (p. 325). People were looking to be entertained when they shopped. This is often used as an argument in contemporary times as to why online shopping will never replace the face-to-face variety.

Window displays married art and retail (Lancaster 1995; McArthur 2013), and this has continued through to modern times. The promotion of fashion lines and related accessories has often played a key part in these window fantasies. For example, in 1947, Bloomingdale's made the strategic decision to change its image towards a store that embraced the latest fashions. It commissioned American designers to create a series of ensembles that it called 'The Bloomingdale Collection'. These were displayed in the windows of the Lexington Avenue store in New York, before being given to the Costume Institute of the Metropolitan Museum of Art. They were never intended to be offered for sale to the public (Brady 1980). The windows in effect became a display case for a form of modern art.

Another way to coax spending was to create an atmosphere of *celebration* (Leach 1984). This was chiefly achieved through events, and 'the large stores excelled in their offerings of concerts, fashion shows, pageants, and extravaganzas, merging the world of shopping and that of spectacle' (Crossick and Jaumain 1999: 27–28). It was recognised that these events either enticed customers to the store, directly encouraged consumption or kept them in-store for longer, thus increasing the chance that they might spend some money (McArthur 2013). Today, we label this *destination retailing* (McArthur 2013). Some of these events were one-offs, linked to commemorations such as Jubilees or royal weddings, or exotic themes such as *The Thousand and One Nights*, used by Wanamaker's in New York in 1913 (Leach 1984). Other events were seasonal, notably Christmas celebrations, which created a 'ritualised structure for this culture of exhibition' (Crossick and Jaumain 1999: 28). The London store Roberts was said to be the first to come up with the idea of a visit to Father Christmas, creating a 'Christmas Grotto complete with Santa Claus and Cinderella' (Lancaster 1995: 24) in 1888. The level at which department stores would go to gain an advantage over the competitors is illustrated by Christmas extravaganzas in Australian stores of the

1930s, including pantomimes, fairytale gardens and a miniature circus (McArthur 2013). Live footage of the annual Macy's Thanksgiving Parade in New York, which was first staged in 1924, featured in the much-loved film *Miracle on 34th Street* (1947), leading to the event being televised nationally.

The birth of the fashion show

The genesis of the fashion show lay in the need for the French haute couture industry to sell their clothes, but also designs globally and 'evolved as much for the convenience of trade buyers as for individual clients' (Evans 2013: 11). The English designer Lucile, however, is generally credited with its invention, starting out as 'a cross between an elite party and a theatrical event held in her luxurious salon or, in the summer, its garden' (Evans 2013: 34). She used live models that were well trained in deportment and graceful movement, and they were given individual names, often of the stage variety, which added to their glamour. Interest was also encouraged by bestowing a unique name on each dress, called out by Lucile as the wearer made her appearance (Evans 2013). Invitations to these events were judiciously sent to 'a glittering mixture of guests from society and stage and even journalists' (Evans 2013: 35), to encourage press coverage and take-up of the clothes by the higher echelons. In 1909, Lucile staged *The Seven Ages of Women* in front of an audience that included Margot Asquith, the wife of the Prime Minister, two granddaughters of Queen Victoria – Queen Marie of Romania and Queen Ena of Spain – and Edward VII's mistress Lillie Langtry. Every woman who aspired to high society was there (Woodhead 2007). All the large Parisian fashion houses followed Lucile's lead by 1910 and similarly made their events invitation-only, adding to their exclusivity (Evans 2013).

Lucile understood the psychology behind watching a show and how it allowed a woman to fantasise about what she might look like in the clothes worn by a physically superb version of herself – the model. As she noted:

> When the lights are lowered to a rosy glow, and soft music is played and the mannequins parade, there is not a woman in the audience, though she may be fat and middle-aged, who is not seeing herself look at those slim, beautiful girls look in the clothes they are offering her. And that is the inevitable prelude to buying clothes.
>
> (quoted in Rappaport 1999: 192)

The movement of the clothes on a live model inspired the design process, as well as showed the clothes off to full advantage (Evans 2013). It was now beginning to be understood that clothing should look as appealing while the wearer is in motion as it does when he or she is static or seated. The pace of the show also changed over time. While Lucile's fashion shows allowed for pauses while the models changed, holding the process up, eventually the idea of a seamless show, with models frantically changing and clothes being pressed and arranged to perfection backstage (see Figure 5.1), began to hold sway (Evans 2013).

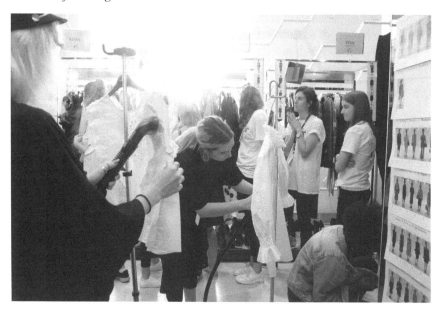

Figure 5.1 Myer Melbourne – Myer runway backstage
Source: Photo courtesy of Myer Pty Ltd/Lucas Dawson Photography

According to Weller (2013: 12), the fashion show has 'multiple value-creating moments' and she uses the example of the L'Oreal Melbourne Fashion Festival to illustrate them. Many are pertinent beyond this specific context to department store shows. They include:

1   an opportunity for event sales;
2   encouragement to purchase new clothing at the start of a season, at full price, rather than at the end of the season, when they are generally on sale;
3   accelerating the adoption of innovation through a 'trickle down' effect;
4   creating a social activity that heightens emotions, potentially affecting the way the clothes are seen and appreciated; and
5   engagement with volunteers, which may assist the fashion industry to be in touch with grassroots 'fashion moods'.

In a department store context, the show also adds to its luxury brand image, with fashion often one of the key retail markets, particularly at the high end.

The changing role of department store fashion shows

Fashion shows were adopted by department stores as a way to add colour and spectacle to the buying of clothes, through the use of live models and the theatrical devices of stages and ramps, which became known as the *catwalk* (Leach 1984).

This occurred quite early in their history, and they were used by some to build connections with France as the birthplace of luxury and fashion, through adopting the types of shows that the great fashion houses in Paris staged for foreign buyers (Evans 2013). The USA led the way here. French designers such as Poiret had been travelling to its shores for some time now, with mannequin tours or *trunk shows* used to exhibit their latest creations (Evans 2013). Local department stores now wanted a piece of the action. Leach (1984: 328) notes that 'in the early 1900s American merchants took a revolutionary step by installing the exclusive and intimate Paris fashion show in the department store, a mass consumer institution'. The first example of this is believed to be Ehrich Brothers of New York, quickly followed by Wanamaker's and Gimbels (Leach 1984). Their attraction was in part because they 'did not generally require a licence like other forms of theatrical display' (Evans 2013: 90).

By 1910, this had morphed into 'great fashion pageants ... spectacular, multimedia affairs with orchestras, models, special effects, and theatrical performances and with thousands of people in attendance' (Leach 1984: 328). There were also collective shows in Los Angeles and San Francisco involving multiple stores, known as the United Fashion Show (Evans 2013). By 1915, department store fashion shows were 'so popular that the crowds had to be dispersed by the police in small towns, where four to five thousand people might be attracted in a single afternoon' (Evans 2013: 89). These were democratic, open to the people, not just the elite of society.

The thirst for all things French led American buyers to take risks to visit Paris during World War One, just to be able to bring the latest fashions back to its waiting audience (Evans 2013). On the other side of the Atlantic, in 1913 Brown's of Chester began staging 'regular fashion shows featuring French models and gowns' (Lancaster 1995: 33). Interestingly, French department stores did not stage fashion shows until the 1920s (Evans 2013). The reason remains unclear, but perhaps they did not think they could compete or did not want to be seen to be competing with the great fashion houses.

The likes of Selfridges, however, thanks to the theatrical instincts of owner Harry Selfridge, were quick to take advantage of the potential that events, including fashion shows, offered to encourage their clientele through the front doors and keep them there for as long as possible. He 'gave his customers fun' (Woodhead 2007: 2), but the ultimate aim was to get them to spend money in the process. Societal trends, such as the vogue for the Russian Ballet, allowed the cross-over between dance and fashion to be exploited in Selfridges' window displays (Woodhead 2007) and led to a thirst for exotica and Orientalism. Fashion shows could be linked to charitable endeavours, which ensured that celebrities and the aristocracy would attend and attract press headlines. Selfridge also used a fashion show in 1926 to woo would-be investors in his store, relying on the *wow factor* as 'gorgeous models burst out of giant hat boxes on a flower-decked stage' (Woodhead 2007: 213). He wasn't however the only store-owner who leapt on this notion that fashion shows were publicity gold. Harrods staged a 'display of gowns on living models' in honour of their 1909 Diamond Jubilee (Woodhead 2007: 101). It was no coincidence that Harrods' Jubilee festival celebrations began on the day that Selfridges opened to the public for the first time (Lancaster 1995; Outka 2009). Their programme included 'grand afternoon concerts featuring the London Symphony Orchestra and the Band of the Grenadier Guards' (Lancaster 1995: 75). Competition was fierce to woo customers, with events a key part of the marketing mix. In terms of the fashion show, it was very much a strategy aimed at women. According to Evans (2013: 9) there were few examples of men's fashion shows in the 1920s and 1930s, and 'male modelling was largely a phenomenon of the late twentieth century'.

These trends spread further afield. In Australia, the Myer trading empire had begun in Bendigo in 1900 with a draper's store owned by Sidney Myer, a Russian émigré who had settled in Australia the year before (Barber 2008). This humble retail beginning morphed into a chain of emporiums, notably the premises in Bourke Street, Melbourne, established in 1911, which is still standing today and trading as Myer Melbourne. One of their innovations was the Mural Hall, opened in 1933, featuring murals, painted by Napier Waller, which showcased women, both those who achieved fame throughout history, such as Cleopatra, and those who were recognised for their achievements in sport, the arts, fashion, music and literature (Barber 2008). It was intended to be a space that could be used for events, and is described on the Victorian Heritage Register as 'a dining hall for 1000 people and a venue for fashion parades and performances' (Heritage Council Victoria 2006). It features a pair of 'mannequin stairs' [leading] down from two balconies and the change rooms to a common landing and 'a temporary catwalk or stage . . . installed at this landing level' (Heritage Council Victoria 2006). Its commissioning by Sidney Myer illustrated his ethos that 'there was more to successful retailing than selling. To [Myer] retailing was a theatrical, emotional and aesthetic experience' (Barber 2008: 67).

During the Depression, there were attempts to use parades to lift morale. Australian examples are pertinent here. Charles Lloyd Jones, then Chairman of David Jones in Australia, saw them as a way to 'stimulate business, create employment, and make our stores as happy places as possible' (quoted in O'Neill 2013: 238). Myer also embraced the colour and movement which they brought, with 'floral displays . . . an important part of the décor and ambience of the fashion parades that were, by the mid-1930s, a vital part of Myer's' (Barber 2008: 73). Norman Myer and his wife Gladys regularly travelled to the fashion capitals of the world and 'Gladys was adept at selecting what would best suit Australian conditions' (Barber 2008: 73). These latest fashions would then be reproduced in Myer's workrooms and displayed to buyers and customers in parades in the Mural Hall, before going on sale and gazumping the competition. As Barber (2008: 73) observes '[founder] Sidney Myer had always planned that his business would be the most fashionable store in Australia. Norman Myer made that vision a reality'.

Post-war developments

When World War Two ended, parades resumed. In some cases, this was used as a symbolic gesture to show that life had returned to normal and a degree of frivolity was allowed. At Selfridges, afternoon fashion shows marked the re-opening of their roof terrace, which had traditionally been used as an events space (Woodhead 2007). For others, they were used to show off the new fashions from Paris, which were a revelation to women used to rationing, with their full skirts and rich fabrics (Figure 5.2). David Jones in Sydney hosted a fashion show of Christian Dior's creations in 1948, complete with the so-called New Look (O'Neill 2013), while their rival Myer in Melbourne also brought his fashions to Australia. The parades of his clothes were an outstanding success (Barber 2008). Bloomingdale's increased its quotient of French fashions in 1959 and celebrated by hosting its own fashion show in Paris, 'for the benefit of the press, to demonstrate this expansion of the store's purchasing power' (Brady 1980: 96).

Figure 5.2 Carmen Dell'Orefici, David Jones' Parade, 1950
Source: Photo courtesy of State Library of New South Wales, Mitchell Library a2437 Online

While French fashion had the most cachet, some stores looked further afield for inspiration. David Jones staged a British Cotton Board fashion parade in 1959, complete with a guest appearance by fashion designer Hardy Amies, who had created clothes for members of the British Royal Family including the Queen. Their fashion shows also included an annual Wool Show, the annual David Jones fashion awards, which started in 1970 and numerous national promotions such as Italian Week, which featured a number of Italian-themed fashion parades, including what they claimed was 'Sydney's first all-imported high-fashion show for men' (O'Neill 2013: 141).

Another innovation in the 1950s was the in-store bridal show. In the USA, Bloomingdale's was keen to build a market amongst the New York 'career girl' and invited females working within five blocks of the department store to an 'all American' fashion show (Brady 1980). The bridal show, conceived to promote their new bridal shop, was held at night, outside normal trading hours, and was an instant success: 'Almost 2,500 ticket requests were received for a space which could hold half that number, and a repeat performance had to be staged to accommodate the rest of the interested customers' (Brady 1980: 95). Bridal shows, otherwise known as wedding fairs, have grown in popularity since then, a form of industry-themed consumer show that promotes a myriad of products and services related to weddings (Adler and Chienm 2004), including department stores' gift registries.

The fashion show was still a staple in the 1970s and 1980s, part of the experiential offering to customers. In 1974, Bloomingdale's courted the designer Valentino for an in-store boutique, and used a fashion show to mark the opening, 'at the unheard-of hour of 10:30 in the morning, though [the store's fashion director] was warned that fashionable women would never show up so early. But they did' (Brady 1980: 117). A mini-fashion show could be used by designers who wanted to put their clothes in front of store executives, while stores still produced fashion shows to introduce the new season's collection, such as Autumn/Winter or Spring/Summer (O'Neill 2013).

The importance of wowing the audience with items that were aspirational rather than affordable was understood by the organisers. One David Jones fashion parade in the 1980s was a case in point, as Australian designer George Gross remembers: 'The fashion controller came back with this couture fabric from Switzerland, madly expensive, $1500 a metre, and asked me to design a one-off garment to make an appearance at the end of the show' (quoted in O'Neill 2013: 153). They also saw a value in keeping the event exclusive and high-end, which is still largely the case today. David Jones's PR executive Skye Leckie recalls the list of invitees she would put together ('oh to be so powerful') and how people would clamour to be there, to catch up friends, drink champagne and 'a fashion show to boot . . . It was really elite' (quoted in O'Neill 2013: 216). Maggie Tabberer, former model and fashion editor of the *Australian Women's Weekly* magazine, referred to the shows as 'a big deal . . . everything was always very generously presented, always stunning, always different. It was a very superior house as far as productions and shows and fashion parades went' (quoted in O'Neill 2013: 216).

The future of department store fashion shows

While department stores are growing their online business (Knight 2017), they have not neglected in-store activities, including fashion shows. In a nod however to the changing digital environment, bloggers are often invited to comment on proceedings, which reflects trends affecting fashion shows more broadly. Carbone (2016: 14) refers to the struggle to gain a VIP seat at the Melbourne Fashion Festival, where in 2016, 'about 450 bloggers who apply for accreditation compete against 200 journalists for up to 20 front-row seats a show in this well-dressed game of musical chairs'. The Festival CEO emphasised that 'bloggers are crucial to reaching the customer' (Carbone 2016: 14). Many fashion shows are now focusing on consumers rather than buyers, with the designer Burberry a high-end example (Halzack 2016; Low 2016). New York's Fashion Week in 2016 was hailed as 'a digital attraction for everyday shoppers, rather than just a cloistered spectacle for industry insiders, with legions of people getting a peek at the shows, clothes and models via live stream or social media' (Halzack 2016). Yet, there are signs that the department stores are not hearing this message, in some cases becoming ever more exclusive in their battle for fashion retail sales.

The fashion shows staged in recent years by Myer provide an example of this tension between inclusivity and elitism. The Myer Autumn 2017 Fashion Launch was staged outside the store, in the underground car park of the University of Melbourne, a modern *brutalist*-designed space famously featured in the film *Mad Max* (1979). Such a choice symbolised two 'iconic institutions, deeply woven into the fabric of Melbourne' (Myer 2017). The autumn before, the venue was Barangaroo in Sydney, a new harbourside park, 'where Myer redefined the traditional runway experience by hosting an exclusive, intimate black-tie dinner for 120 of Australia's most influential fashion identities and celebrities' (Myer 2017). One of the celebrities who joined the 2017 catwalk was the Face of Myer, Jennifer Hawkins, a former Miss Universe (Figure 5.3). The 2017 Myer event was promoted as a theatrical experience, composed of 'two stunning fashion acts. The fashion stories were punctuated with dramatic lighting and powerful music tracks to create a remarkable experience fitting of the stunning location' (Myer 2017). The dark, moody setting of the underground car park (Figure 5.4) also tied in with the latest Myer product – the Tesla electric car – which featured in the show.

These shows are expensive to produce and stage, following trends worldwide for ever greater spectacle. One Victoria's Secret parade in 2016 was reputed to have cost $US 26 million. They may therefore fulfil a function for those designers who cannot afford to stage their own show, as they may be a more cost-effective way to display their latest creations in front of consumers and the media. Alternatively, these designers might look at group shows within a festival or fashion week, such as the Melbourne Fashion Festival (Singer 2016).

Figure 5.3 Myer Melbourne – Myer Runway 2017 – Jennifer Hawkins
Source: Photo courtesy of Myer Pty Ltd/Lucas Dawson Photography

Figure 5.4 Myer Melbourne – Myer Runway 2017 – Models in car park, University of
    Melbourne
Source: Photo courtesy of Myer Pty Ltd/Lucas Dawson Photography

This focus on the A-list guest and high-profile model can be contrasted with Myer's decision in 2016 to invite their gold and platinum customers to their Spring 2016 fashion show. According to deputy chief Daniel Bracken,

> we want to have an experiential relationship with our customers rather than just a transactional one . . . We were quite forensic about who attended and wanted to give the customers buying these brands a once in a lifetime opportunity.
>
> (quoted in Clarke 2016)

Nevertheless the VIPs were segregated from the hoi-polloi, with the former said to have 'sipped champagne and posed for cameras in a cordoned-off area, [while] customers were shown to their tiered seats where doughnuts, espresso martinis in jars and goodie bags bursting with Saint Laurent lipsticks and raw, artisan chocolate were waiting' (Clarke 2016). Not everyone was impressed, with some customers criticising the unreality of the model's physiques ('they're too skinny'), the lack of diversity and the absence of everyday brands they tend to favour ('[I] don't think they should always have a high-end fashion show'). There was giggling at some of the more extreme outfits and accessories on the catwalk, including floral crowns and floating ribbons tied to the models' wrists (Clarke 2016). It would appear that the event was not tailored to its [new] audience on this occasion.

David Jones also continues to pursue a strategy of celebrity involvement in its fashion shows. For example, in 2012, it staged a show to mark the revamping of its seventh floor and invitees included

> fashion journalists, an A to Z of thoroughbred designers and all manner of celebrities from Dannii Minogue, Delta Goodrem and Ita Buttrose to David Jones brand ambassador, Megan Gale. The company's top executives greeted guests as they arrived, while waiters offered canapés and Waterford crystal flutes filled with Veuve Cliquot.
>
> (O'Neill 2013: 102)

International model Miranda Kerr, another brand 'ambassador', was on the catwalk. This type of event contrasts with their regular store-based fashion shows, which are generally egalitarian – open to all and mostly free of charge. Perhaps they might lose some of their cachet as a result, but they provide attendees with the type of experiential offering that has traditionally been available to store customers.

The opportunities offered by social media to broaden the audience for fashion shows were not overlooked by Myer at its 2017 show. The official press release noted that

> Myer was the first department store in the world to enable the public to watch the action in full 360 degree view from home via Twitter's live video program, Periscope. The retailer provided unprecedented access to the event through its

social and digital channels with designer collections available to purchase online and in store.

(Myer 2017)

This again reflects the changing nature of fashion shows. For example, at the 2015 Melbourne Fashion Festival, '1118 looks from 68 designers were available to buy through the festival's associated e-commerce platform' (Singer 2016: 13). Consumers now expect to gain access to shows, even if just in a virtual capacity, and want instant gratification of their desire to purchase the latest clothes. There is competition from new stores such as Zara and H & M, where catwalk fashion is quickly translated into styles that are then offered at cheap prices, and discarded once considered outré. This has led to what is termed *fast fashion* (Barnes and Lea-Greenwood 2010; Laing, Williams and Frost 2014).

Another contemporary movement to affect fashion shows involves concerns over the ethics behind the manufacture of clothes, including the conditions of workers, especially in developing countries. For example, in 2011, the Melbourne Fashion Festival promoted the work of Ethical Clothing Australia (Weller 2013). Other societal concerns which might potentially affect the way that fashion shows are staged include the move towards vintage or retro clothing, thus recycling what might otherwise be thrown away, creating clothes from recyclable materials and the backlash against overly thin models (Laing, Williams and Frost 2014). Our ideas of what constitutes beauty are evolving, in what are increasingly multicultural and multiethnic communities in many parts of the world. Department stores will need to take account of these changes, which are sweeping through the fashion world more generally. Failure to do so will leave them open to criticism from a more informed and socially aware consumer base, while the ubiquity of social media platforms means that these negative views can be instantly expressed on a global or even viral scale.

Conclusion

The changing digital environment within which department stores find themselves does not seem to have altered the role of the fashion show as a staple of department stores' promotional campaigns, despite the rise of online shopping and the cost of staging an event for a live audience. The appeal of seeing a beautiful model wearing clothes and the aspirational effect that this engenders, is still strong. It is also the case that the audience for these shows is becoming broader, particularly through the aegis of social media, allowing people to take part, albeit virtually, in the event. Research is needed to explore how this alters the experience of attending fashion shows, and whether it is perceived as a less attractive alternative to being present in person.

The guest list for department store fashion shows might also need to be revisited in contemporary times. Attempts have also been made recently to invite ordinary shoppers, as opposed to just the social elite, harking back to what occurred in the past, yet press reports suggest that these moves to diversify the composition of the audience have not been entirely successful. Again, future studies might usefully explore the impact of democratising the fashion show and whether this is having a negative effect on the store's brand image, or alternatively helping it to be seen as more in tune with the times. The importance of inviting bloggers to department stores fashion shows and understanding their influence on sales and store image are other areas that warrant further research.

References

Adler, H. and Chienm, T.C. (2004) 'The wedding business: A method to boost food and beverage revenues in hotels', *Journal of Foodservice Business Research*, 7(1), 117–125.

Barber, S.M. (2008) *Your Store Myer: The Story of Australia's Leading Department Store*, Sydney: Focus.

Barnes, L. and Lea-Greenwood, G. (2010) 'Fast fashion in the retail store environment', *International Journal of Retail & Distribution Management*, 38(10), 760–772.

Brady, M. (1980) *Bloomingdale's*, New York: Harcourt Brace Jovanovich.

Carbone, S. (2016) 'Bloggers battle for front-row seats at fashion festival', *The Age*, 5 March, 14.

Chaney, D. (1983) 'The department store as a cultural form', *Theory, Culture & Society*, 1(3), 22–31.

Clarke, J. (2016) 'What "real" people thought of Myer's spring 2016 fashion show', *The Sydney Morning Herald*, 2 September, www.smh.com.au/lifestyle/fashion/what-real-people-thought-of-myers-spring-2016-fashion-show-20160825-gr1gea.html (accessed 16 February 2017).

Crossick, G. and Jaumain, S. (1999) 'The world of the department store: Distribution, culture and social change', in C. Walsh, G. Crossick and S. Jaumain (eds.), *Cathedrals of Consumption: The European Department Store 1850–1939* (pp. 1–45), Aldershot, UK and Brookfield, USA: Ashgate.

Evans, C. (2013) *The Mechanical Smile: Modernism and the First Fashion Shows in France and America, 1900–1929*, New Haven, CT and London: Yale University Press.

Halzack, S. (2016) 'For fashion fans, Instagram leads the pack', *The Age*, Green Guide, 17 March, 13.

Heritage Council Victoria (2006) 'Victorian heritage database report, Myer Melbourne (Former Myer Emporium)', *Victorian Heritage Register (VHR) H2100*, www.vhd. heritagecouncil.vic.gov.au/places/2518/download-report (accessed 10 May 2017).

Knight, E. (2017) 'Department stores move to struggle street as market takes new shape', *The Age*, 2 March, 21.

Laing, J., Williams, K. and Frost, W. (2014) 'Très chic: Setting a research agenda for fashion and design events', in K. Williams, J. Laing and W. Frost (eds.), *Fashion, Design and Events* (pp. 191–205), London and New York: Routledge.

Lancaster, B. (1995) *The Department Store: A Social History*, London and New York: Leicester University Press.

Leach, W.R. (1984) 'Transformations in a culture of consumption: Women and department stores, 1890–1925', *The Journal of American History*, 71(2), 319–342.

Low, C. (2016) 'Fashioning a festival's future is just her ticket', *The Age*, 5 March, 2.

McArthur, E. (2013) 'The role of department stores in the evolution of marketing: Primary source records from Australia', *Journal of Historical Research in Marketing*, 5(4), 449–470.

Miller, M.B. (1981) *The Bon Marché: Bourgeois Culture and the Department Store, 1869–1920*, London: George Allen & Unwin.

Myer (2017) 'Myer Autumn 2017 fashion launch', *Myer Media Release*, 16 February, 1–3.

O'Neill, H. (2013) *David Jones' 175 Years*, Sydney: NewSouth.

Outka, E. (2009) *Consuming Traditions: Modernity, Modernism, and the Commodified Authentic*, Oxford: Oxford University Press.

Rappaport, E. (1999) 'Acts of consumption: Musical comedy and the desire of exchange', in C. Walsh, G. Crossick and S. Jaumain (eds.), *Cathedrals of Consumption: The European Department Store 1850–1939* (pp. 189–207), Aldershot, UK and Brookfield, USA: Ashgate.

Rocamora, A. (2009) *Fashioning the City: Paris, Fashion and the Media*, London and New York: IB Tauris.

Singer, M. (2016) 'High fashion is high risk', *The Age*, 8 December, 13.

Spiekermann, U. (1999) 'Theft and thieves in German department stores, 1895–1930: A discourse on morality, crime and gender', in C. Walsh, G. Crossick and S. Jaumain (eds.), *Cathedrals of Consumption: The European Department Store 1850–1939* (pp. 135–159), Aldershot, UK and Brookfield, USA: Ashgate.

Steele, V. (1988) *Paris Fashion: A Cultural History*, 2nd edition, Oxford and New York: Berg.

Tiersten, L. (1999) 'Marianne in the department store: Gender and the politics of consumption in turn-of-the-century Paris', in C. Walsh, G. Crossick and S. Jaumain (eds.), *Cathedrals of Consumption: The European Department Store 1850–1939* (pp. 116–134), Aldershot, UK and Brookfield, USA: Ashgate.

Weller, S. (2013) 'Consuming the city: Public fashion festivals and the participatory economies of urban spaces in Melbourne, Australia', *Urban Studies*, 50(14), 2853–2868.

Woodhead, L. (2007) *Shopping, Seduction and Mr Selfridge*, 2012 edition, London: Profile Books.

Zola, E. (1883) *The Ladies' Paradise*, transl. Ernest Alfred Vizetelly, 1895 edition, Urbana, ILL: Project Gutenberg. Retrieved 1 June 2017, from www.gutenberg.org/files/54726/54726-h/54726-h.htm

6 Cars of futures past

Motorclassica 2016 – The Australian International Concours d' Elegance and Classic Motor Show

Gary Best

> To truly appreciate an automobile, one must have a sense of the aesthetic, an acquaintanceship with technology, a feeling for history, a liking for drama – even a sense of humor.
>
> (Kimes 1976: 6)

Showing motors

Chicago's Columbian Exposition of 1893 displayed a 'horseless carriage' but few visitors paid it much attention (Flammang and Frumkin 1998: 36). Two years later, the first British motor show: 'took place at an agricultural showground in Tunbridge Wells in 1895 with subsequent British motor exhibitions documented in 1896 and 1897' (Hayes 2016: 9–10). For most of the 20th century, many major cities offered motor shows displaying the latest vehicles in glamorous settings and, later in the century, often with women in various stages of undress (Best 2014: 50). Investment in such shows, however, could not guarantee returns for the manufacturers to defray the display costs with orders, given that for many of those attending, it may well have only been a spectator sport that offered the opportunity to gather armfuls of catalogues.

The International Organization of Motor Vehicle Manufacturers (OICA 2017) calendar lists 18 international motor shows, indicating that despite environmental challenges, displaying new automobiles as well as concept vehicles still appears to be an internationally embedded cultural practice and passion. Ten of the 2017 shows are in Europe (Barcelona, Birmingham, Brussels, Bucharest, Frankfurt, Geneva, Moscow, Sofia and Verona), three in the USA (Chicago, Detroit and New York) and then Buenos Aires, Cairo, Istanbul, Seoul and Tokyo (OICA 2017).

Another increasingly popular form of automotive display, counterpointing the motor show, is that of car clubs. At these members gather to share marque passion and debate the merits and occasional liabilities of their veteran, vintage or classic cars. What usually began informally with a few marque enthusiasts meeting to share their enthusiasm and/or the frustrations of old car ownership, in Australia and many other parts of the world as well, developed into a significant subculture of clubs, dedicated magazines and a wider awareness of, and enthusiasm for, such vehicles. There is no doubt that informal club events and swap meets draw committed enthusiasts as well as neophytes, and a public keen to be reacquainted with cars similar to those that ferried their families about in long-ago childhoods. Seven years ago in Melbourne, however, a glamorous new event premiered, consolidating and commodifying the classic and collector car milieu – enter *Motorclassica*.

Formally titled as the Australian International Concours d'Elegance and Classic Motor Show – Motorclassica has only been on Melbourne's automotive events calendar since 2010, but now is an established and popular event promoted as 'Australia's premier automotive extravaganza'. Whilst its primary focus is past and present marque prestige and exclusivity, Motorclassica is remarkably inclusive, although for visitors, a degree of automotive enthusiasm, knowledge and ownership, actual or aspirational, may be advantageous. Motorclassica is, as well, an exemplar of cultural shifts in perceptions of what constitutes a 'classic' car, with displays of glamorous as well as prosaic survivors, and also the reverse chic of patinated 'barn finds', vehicles that have been neglected, or even abandoned, but still resonate for the enthusiast.

Among the event's 2016 sponsors were Mercedes-Benz and newcomer TAG Heuer, who hosted special guest Chad McQueen, son of actor Steve McQueen (1930–80). The two other special guests were international motorsports icon Rauno Aaltonen and Australian motorsports legend Bob Holden. Other sponsors were drawn from the production, sales, auctions, enhancement, publishing, media, tourism, wine and food, and accommodation areas – approximately 75, according to Event Director Paul Mathers (interview 11 October 2016). Whilst all contributed to the event experience, it was inevitably automobility that took centre stage as it frequently has done since its earliest days. The annual consolidation of that focus continues to be a critical consideration, one that is consistent with Gupta and Vajic's emphasis on 'designing a setting in which the meaning of the experience (event) is created in a favourable way' (cited in Tattersall and Cooper 2014: 161).

Locating Motorclassica

Whilst locating events in suitable settings and structures can be a challenge, the Royal Exhibition Building (Joseph Reed, architect, 1880), in Melbourne's Carlton Gardens, provides *Motorclassica* with an extraordinary display space adjacent to the Melbourne's CBD. Freeland noted its soaring interior has 'an extravagant style of decoration' (1981: 161). The Royal Exhibition Building also indisputably evokes a cathedral-like space and, perhaps consequently, the hum of attendees tends to be muted. It is, nevertheless, difficult to establish causality between the intentions of those constructing the event experience and those attending the event without specific research methodologies. On the basis of participant observation on my two visits to Motorclassica 2016 and one to Motorclassica 2015, the most obvious cohort of those attending were males from their mid-20s to perhaps 70-plus years of age. One further assertion on the basis of that mooted cohort was the strong likelihood of individually heightened yet collectively shared attendee expectations (Crowther 2014).

The layout of the Royal Exhibition Building permits a large number of vehicles to be displayed on the ground floor, and retailers – both automotive and otherwise – to utilise the upstairs Gallery level and hopefully have more exposure to and success with prospective customers without the distraction of alluring vehicles. Motorclassica 2016's distinctive entry strategy ensuring all visitors were exposed to the retailers present was to direct them immediately upstairs to the Gallery level before encountering the vehicular displays on ground level. Whilst not being able to choose immediately between retailers and the vehicles was, for me at least, somewhat frustrating, there was no doubt sound strategic logic in routing visitors through the displays that may otherwise have been completely ignored in less exposed spaces on the ground floor. A more likely explanation was to free up as much ground floor space as possible for vehicles and event activities such as the Mercedes-Benz sponsored Main Stage. Another consideration may have been the benefit of offering a dramatic overview of not only the assembled vehicles below, thereby increasing the sense of visitor expectation, but also an opportunity to behold the architectural drama and scale of the exhibition space (Figure 6.1).

The Gallery's retail offerings were aftermarket accessories; antiques and automobilia; automotive artists and art; destinations and travel; freight; garage fitouts; insurance; lifestyle; motorcycles; publications and media; restorations and media; road safety; and watches, most of which had, not surprisingly, an automotive focus or association (Motorclassica 2016a: 40–51).

Structuring, advertising, reporting and exploring Motorclassica

Motorclassica 2016, according to Event Director Paul Mathers, is 'made up of a whole lot of different events that form the one. Each could theoretically be taken out and run as a separate event'. He observed that the 'Australian International Concours d'Elegance' is 'the hero of the show and is being pitched at the local and international audience' (Interview 11 October 2016).

Of the cars on display, the Motorclassica 2016 Automotive Concours Class listings and winners were:

> *Vintage & Veteran*: 1923 Rolls-Royce 40/50 Silver Ghost;
> *Pre-War Classic (UK & Europe)*: 1931 Rolls-Royce Phantom II;
> *Pre-War Classic (USA)*: 1936 Auburn 852;
> *Post-War Classic (Closed)*: 1956 Alfa Romeo 1900 C Super Sprint;
> *Post-War Classic (Open)*: 1959 Mercedes-Benz 190SL;
> *Modern Classic (UK & Europe)*: 1961 Volkswagen Micro Bus Deluxe 23 Window;
> *Modern Classic (USA, Australia & Japan)*: 1963 Chevrolet Corvette Z06;
> *Modern Classic (Sports and Performance under 3 litres)*: 1971 Ferrari Dino 246;
> *Modern Classic (Sports and Performance over 3 litres)*: Ferrari 512BB; and
> *Contemporary (Preservation)*: 1935 Rolls-Royce 20/25.

Figure 6.1 Motorclassica 2016, Royal Exhibition Building, Melbourne. A view from the upstairs gallery

Source: Photo courtesy of Gary Best

What is most apparent from the Concours Class listings is the continuing presence of, and awards to, the most famous and familiar automotive marques. Concessions have, however, been made that indicate the inclination, if not the necessity, to acknowledge that as distinctive vehicles age there is often an imperative for reconsideration and inclusion. The flawless 1961 Volkswagen Micro Bus Deluxe 23 Window is a modern classic, but may not generally be considered as such unless in the pristine condition as displayed, and preferably with a provenance.

British magazine *Classic and Sportscar* reported that: 'Best of Show' and 'Restoration of the Year' were awarded to an immaculate white 1969 Holden Monaro GTS. The Monaro triumphed over a very competitive and diverse field of 85 cars and motorcycles, and was described as 'faultless and a deserving winner' (Anon 2017a: 18). Two other British magazines – *Thoroughbred and Classic Cars* and *Classic & Sports Car* in their January 2017 issues also reported the highlights of Motorclassica 2016.

Octane Classic and Performance Cars quoted Event Director Mathers on the winning Monaro: 'It's an exciting decision which indicates that locally designed cars can be competitive at the same level as the world's great marques' (Dillon 2017: 40). Accompanying the article and photograph of the winning Monaro were four other photographs, the largest of which showed the spectacular interior of the Royal Exhibition Building, and another of the exterior featuring the dome with a range of 1960s Ford Cortinas displayed in sunshine as part of the Motorclassica's 2016 engagingly named 'Club Sandwich'. The 'Club Sandwich' stretched over the three days of Motorclassica 2016 and included four motorcycle clubs and 44 car clubs (Motorclassica 2016a: 37).

Thoroughbred and Classic Cars reported Motorclassica 2016 as 'Labours of love in Melbourne: Australia's most prestigious classic car show brought some exquisite restorations to light' (Anon. 2017b: 16), but neglected to mention the winning antipodean Holden Monaro GTS. T&CC only reported on an ex-Jenson Button 1978 Ferrari 512 BB, a 1952 Lancia Aurelia B20GT and a 1923 Benz 16/50 sports tourer that began as a two-seater runabout, but nothing further of the show itself.

There was also, of course, local reporting of the event. Melbourne's *Herald Sun* noted: 'Motorclassica brings extraordinary, rare, desirable and valuable collector cars and motorcycles from around Australia and the world for a three-day celebration of classic motoring' (2016: 28). *The Weekend Australian*, reported on the Theodore Bruce Motorclassica auction, and observed that 'Muscle car owners cash in on revival' (King 2016: 9). This focus was on enthusiast Jim Byrnes, who was selling his 1971 Ford Falcon GT-HO Phase III (price guide A$450,000) and hoped to buy a replica of Henry Ford's first 1896 Quadricycle, one of seven built to original specifications in 1963 to mark the centenary of the founder's birth (price guide A$34,000–44,000). Whilst the Falcon failed to sell, the Quadricycle did (hopefully to Jim), with a final bid of A$41,000. From a doctor's waiting-room, *The Senior* reported that: 'The halls of Australia's original parliament house will be lined with hundreds of exquisite cars and motorcycles for Motorclassica 2016 . . . Among them will be an 1896 Benz Velocipide – the world's first production car' (2016:

16). Finally, at 2.55 a.m. on 9 October, 2016 on Melbourne TV a late-night episode ('So Dark the Night') of *The Baron*, a 1965–66 British TV series by ITC Entertainment and starring US actor Steve Mannering as the eponymous detective (Meyers 1981) had a commercial break with an advertisement for Motorclassica 2016. Possibly the fact that, in the TV series, Mannering drove a Jensen C-V8 Mark II may have struck a chord with an enthusiast programmer.

Internationally, full-page colour advertisements for Motorclassica 2016 inviting visitors to 'Walk with the greats at Motorclassica' were in *Classic and Sports Car*, (Motorclassica 2016b) and *Octane Classic and Performance Cars*, (Motorclassica 2016c). Whilst the slogan was catchy (the artwork much less so), at Motorclassica it is more of a case of walking *amongst* the greats, as very few of the vehicles exhibited are roped off to create a barrier – security, or otherwise – between spectator and vehicle. Whilst this may not seem like an issue to most, from the owner perspective such spectator proximity could generate concern that could be partially assuaged by the belief, or hope, that the majority of visitors would respect the owner's commitment to showing their vehicles for the benefit of all Motorclassica attendees. Given the chasm between the displayed vehicles and those of perhaps the majority of visitors, Falassi's 'Ritual Structure of Events' (1987) certainly resonates here in terms of the ritual of *conspicuous display* where the most valued objects are brought out and displayed.

A counterpoint to the majority of immaculate vehicles on display was two lots in the Theodore Bruce Motorclassica 2016 Auction that were considered 'Barn finds'. Lot 9 was a 1951 Jaguar XK 120 roadster described as 'Unused for many years and with one family owner for almost 40 years'. The auction range was A$78,000–90,000 but despite its shabby charm it remained unsold. Lot 43 was a 1965 Jaguar E-Type Coupe with an auction range of $125,000–150,000 and sold for $125,000.

The 'Barn find' is, as the term suggests, a vehicle that has been neglected and/or forgotten, then unearthed to degrees of fanfare depending on rarity and potential restorability. It may have originated after the publication of Tom Cotter's *The Cobra in the Barn* (2005) but the broad use of the term can mean a pile of parts to a complete but neglected vehicle. The Motorclassica 2015 auction offered a 1912 Metz 22 (sold: A$16,875); a 1934 Packard V12 (sold: A$75,000), a 1941 Cadillac Fleetwood (sold: A$12,000) and a 1964 Bristol 408 (sold: A$12,375), each an automotive Miss Havisham, heavy with the romance of past glory.

Tour classica: Motorclassica 2016 on the road

Event Director Paul Mathers is a big fan of Tour Classica, as it shows between 60–70% of the cars and motorcycles on the roads of Melbourne and provides their owners with an opportunity to display their classics in action along a route taking in major Melbourne landmarks. The Sidney Myer Music Bowl was the starting point for the Tour Classica which then proceeded past Rod Laver Arena and Olympic Park. A turn into Punt Road and then Brunton Avenue to the Melbourne Cricket Ground was followed by a run up Spring Street past the stately Windsor Hotel and

Parliament House. The Tour then turned into Nicholson Street and made a circuit past the Royal Exhibition Building prior to entering the display spaces within Motorclassica.

An important point made by Mr Mathers was that there is a benefit for entrants completing the Tour Classica when judging time arrives, for 'if two cars or motor-cycles find themselves in equal first place in any class, additional points will be awarded to the vehicle that successfully completes the drive' (Motorclassica 2016a: 52).

Whilst there are a number of possible perspectives on the vehicles, perhaps the most significant is the means by which the past comes to life through encountering the diverse marques, their heritage and their capacity to both inspire and compel decades after their manufacture. There is, inevitably, the nostalgic impulse generated by the Motorclassica encounter, be it a perky 1958 BMW Isetta 300 (Figure 6.2) or a grand 1929 Rolls-Royce Phantom II 3-position Drophead Coupe.

A further perspective on Tour Classica is its contribution to Motorclassica 2016's overall 'eventscape', a concept that is:

> A combination of the tangible elements which shape the event environment and therefore influence the emotional responses and experiences of attendees, event staff, and other involved stakeholders.
>
> (Tattersall and Cooper 2014: 142)

Figure 6.2 A 1958 BMW Isetta 300 at Motorclassica 2016
Source: Photo courtesy of Gary Best

When considering such emotional responses and experiences, particularly in relation to attendees, one very likely, if not obvious, influence may be that of nostalgia. Whilst an uncritical response may suggest a benign construct or framework, that is not necessarily the case in all instances. Margalit (2011), for example, viewed nostalgia as distorting the reality of the past thereby permitting an idealisation of particular objects and/or experiences and reconstituting them in terms of purity and innocence. Schindler and Holbrook (2003) investigated nostalgia in terms of early experience on consumer preferences, concluding that only men show evidence of nostalgic attachment to automotive styles experiences in their youth. This also appears to be the case at certain other auto events (Best 2017) and my impression at Motorclassica 2015 and 2016 was that possibly 75% of those attending each year were males between 25 and 75.

Tour Classica 2016 was an opportunity to see a number of spectacular classics on the road while the Motorclassica 2016 display inside the Royal Exhibition Building was an Aladdin's cave of classics as far as the eye could see in all directions.

Displaying and engaging Motorclassica 2016

Lubar observed that: 'Memory is how we connect with our individual past' (1997: 15). Whilst it would be ambitious to suggest that all those attending Motorclassica 2016 critically engaged, individually or collectively, with the overall experience in terms of their individual past(s), it may be reasonable to assume that at some point in the visit either memories were recalled and/or nostalgic impulses experienced. Given that the vehicles displayed, however, were not quotidian daily drivers, the spectatorial response may have been more aligned with youthful fantasies than cherished memories of ownership.

As discussed briefly earlier, the majority of vehicles displayed are not roped off or mounted on plinths. The opportunity to inspect the vehicles from all angles is, transactionally, a spectator privilege as well as an owner's leap of faith. Belcher observed that: 'Bringing object and viewer close together is the most important function of . . . exhibitions, and the medium can achieve this in a manner which is safe for both object (in terms of security and conservation) and viewer' (1991: 38). Clearly, with Motorclassica in its seventh year, the continuing overall exhibition and individual marque display strategy is effectively communicating to its audience.

Event Director Mathers observed that the event is as much about the audience as it is about the cars. He also made the point that, being a commercial concern, it has to make money, but it is also an opportunity for those who love their cars to engage with those cars, as well as a location to explore the classic car experience. Mr Mathers also said that there has been very little negative feedback throughout the event's history, and ascribes that to the Motorclassica team aiming for optimal visitor satisfaction. The team's intent is to create in the visitor's mind a personal sense of ownership, that Motorclassica is their personal 'show of the year', and visitor feedback has confirmed that expectation. Facebook has also emerged as a critical element in the feedback loop, as has post-show data capture.

Motorclassica's display strategy is not to show the same cars year after year. Once a car has been displayed it will not be eligible for display for three years. There is also an annual celebration of different marques that have achieved milestones, and in 2016 those marques were 130 years of Mercedes-Benz, with 22 vehicles on display; 110 years of Rolls-Royce, with 18 display vehicles; and 100 years of BMW, with 13 vehicles displayed. With such lengthy heritages come long-time brand enthusiasts and consequently very active member clubs that commit fully to the Motorclassica displays as well as the aforementioned 'Club Sandwich' initiative.

Mr. Mathers also spoke at length about the history and the 'journey' of Motorclassica. He observed that in the first few years the event 'came straight out of my head'. He admitted to being a classic car enthusiast although very much at a basic level (an encouraging beginning). He has owned a Jaguar Mark II since he was 21 as well as a Triumph TR3A that was to race but he has not raced yet. He observed that his 'thing' is British cars, but he also enjoys Italian and French Art Deco designs.

His enthusiasm for developing Motorclassica was first met with patronising comments such as 'Oh, good on you – you know it will never happen', and such comments just kept on coming. His first step was to bring together advisers from the classic car movement to develop the foundations for what was to eventually become the annual 'Motorclassica' event. The first 'Motorclassica' was very successful but lost money – a lot of money, he emphasises – but his boss said 'It's such a shame that it's been such a good show, as we now will have to do it again'.

The second Motorclassica returned a profit that also covered the first year's loss, and the rest is history. The event is now run by Exhibitions and Trade Fairs Pty Ltd, but Mr Mathers observed that:

> I have no financial stake in it all but I have an emotional stake like you wouldn't believe – it is very personal to me. The passion and the people involved are a very important part of its success; it runs on passion which makes it a business model you wouldn't necessarily want to sell to someone. People are so wrapped up in it; people on the Advisory Board who have been there since the first show still want to see it grow, and call with ideas; we still argue about the same points we have been arguing about for seven years. This is the very dynamic emotional stake at the core of the success of Motorclassica. I'm 110% emotionally invested in Motorclassica and that's the kind of investment that makes it work. Personally, this is my legacy; this is what I'll tell my grandkids about. There is love behind the momentum that brings every visitor to the realized dream that has become Motorclassica.
>
> (Interview 11 October 2016)

'Meeting' a Motorclassica sponsor's guest – an authorial indulgence

TAG Heuer sponsored special guest Chad McQueen (son of actor Steve McQueen) and he appeared on stage twice on each of the three days of Motorclassica. Being a fan of the late Steve's cinematic work, particularly *The Thomas Crown Affair* (1968; directed by Norman Jewison) and *Le Mans* (1971: directed by Lee H. Katzin), I made sure of arriving early at the Main Stage in order to choose a seat with a clear view of the stage. Having suitably seated myself, leaving an empty seat to my left on the aisle, I began the 10-minute wait for activity on stage. I was aware of a group gathering to my left and a quiet male voice enquired whether he could sit for a moment. I replied 'Of course' and turned to see Chad McQueen take the seat. Well, that was quite a surprise, but as I had my copy of Matt Stone's *McQueen's Machines* (2010), which has a foreword by Chad, I wondered about whether it was appropriate or not to ask for his signature then. I decided it was not, but at that moment he got up and left with his group to go on stage, so any chance of signatures would have to wait until after his stage session ended.

Chad spoke engagingly of both himself and his father, of their mutual love of fast cars and bikes, and of growing up a Hollywood brat, so to speak. He spoke quietly, almost murmuring at times but always engaging – no bragging, no bravado – and the audience was captivated, despite the murmur of Motorclassica behind the audience.

Chad finished speaking and moved to the right of the stage where a queue had already formed. Chad moved the fans through efficiently and *was* signing books so I guessed all would be well. The guy monitoring the signing kept repeating 'Chad will have to leave soon' but then it was my turn and Chad graciously signed my book and kindly posed for a photograph as well. In that fleeting encounter, the cars, the legends, the stars and the dreams coalesced into one perfect Motorclassica moment (Figure 6.3).

Figure 6.3 Chad McQueen and Gary Best at Motorclassica 2016

Source: Photo courtesy of Gary Best

References

Anon (2017a) 'Aussie muscle fêted in Melbourne', *Classic and Sports Car*, January, 18.

Anon (2017b) 'Labours of love in Melbourne', *Thoroughbred and Classic Cars*, January, 16.

Belcher, M. (1991) *Exhibitions in Museums*, Washington, DC: Smithsonian Institution Press.

Best, G. (2014) 'Glamorous intersection: Ralph Lauren's classic cars at the Musée, and the fashioning of automotive style', in K. Williams, J. Laing and W. Frost (eds.), *Fashion, Design and Events* (pp. 44–56), London and New York: Routledge.

Best, G. (2017) 'Nostalgic automotive yearnings on the road to the museum', in M. Conlin and L. Jolliffe (eds.), *Automobile Heritage and Tourism* (pp. 23–39), London: Routledge.

Cotter, T. (2005) *The Cobra in the Barn: Great Stories of Automotive Archaeology*, Minneapolis: Motor Books/MBI Publishing.

Crowther, P. (2014) 'Strategic event creation', in L. Sharples, P. Crowther, D. May and C. Orefice (eds.), *Strategic Event Creation* (pp. 3–20), Oxford: Goodfellow.

Dillon, B. (2017) 'Motorclassica 2016: Melbourne, Australia 21–23 October', *Octane Classic and Performance Cars*, January, 40.

Falassi, A. (1987) 'Festival: Definition and morphology', in A. Falassi (ed.), *Time Out of Time: Essays on the Festival* (pp. 1–10), Albuquerque, NM: University of New Mexico Press.

Flammang, J. and Frumkin, M. (1998) *World's Greatest Auto Show: Celebrating a Century in Chicago*, Iola, WS: Krause.

Freeland, J. (1981) *Architecture in Australia: A History*, Melbourne: Penguin.

Hayes, R. (2016) *Earls Court Motor Show: An Illustrated History*, Stroud: The History Press.

Herald Sun (2016) 'What's on', Carsguide, 14 October, 28.

Kimes, B. (Ed.). (1976) *Automobile Quarterly's Great Cars and Great Marques*, New York: Bonanza Books.

King, P. (2016) 'Muscle car owners cash in on revival', *The Weekend Australian*, 22–23 October, 9.

Lubar, S. (1997) 'Exhibiting memories', in A. Henderson and A. Kaeppler (eds.), *Exhibiting Dilemmas: Issues of Representation at the Smithsonian* (pp. 15–27), Washington: Smithsonian Institution Press.

Margalit, A. (2011) 'Nostalgia', *Psychoanalytic Dialogues: The International Journal of Relational Perspectives*, 21(3), 271–280.

Meyers, R. (1981) *TV Detectives*, San Diego: A.S. Barnes.

Motorclassica (2016a) *Catalogue*, Exhibitions and Trade Fairs Pty Ltd: Melbourne.

Motorclassica (2016b) 'Walk with the greats at Motorclassica 2016', Full page advertisement, *Classic and Sports Car*, September, 48.

Motorclassica (2016c) 'Walk with the greats at Motorclassica 2016', Full page advertisement, *Octane Classic and Performance Cars*, September, 8.

OICA (The International Organization of Motor Vehicle Manufacturers) (2017) 'Calendar of auto shows', www.oica.net/category/calendar/ (accessed 23 May 2017).

Schindler, R. and Holbrook, M. (2003) 'Nostalgia for early experiences as a determinant of consumer preferences', *Psychology and Marketing*, 20(4), 275–302.

The Senior (2016) 'Event a classic for car lovers', *The Senior*, 29 September, www.thesenior.com.au/entertainment/event-a-classic-for-car-lovers/ (accessed 26 May 2017).

Stone, M. (2010) *McQueen's Machines: The Cars and Bikes of a Hollywood Icon*, Minneapolis: Motorbooks.

Tattersall, J. and Cooper, R. (2014) 'Creating the eventscape', in L. Sharples, P. Crowther, D. May and C. Orefice (eds.), *Strategic Event Creation* (pp. 141–165), Oxford: Goodfellow.

7 The symbiotic relationship between unusual venues and street food commercial events

The case of Street Feast in London

Claudia Sima and Franziska Vogt

Introduction

Street Food refers to food that is prepared, cooked or sold by vendors, not in a restaurant but on a street, in a public location, or any other location not usually associated with the preparation and consumption of food. It is a crucial element of the fabric of many cultures and countries around the world, from South America, to the Middle East, Africa and Asia. In modern-day USA, Europe and the UK it has not enjoyed the same popularity, often being perceived as cheap, unhealthy, unhygienic food, mostly sold in developing countries (Johnson 2011; Benny-Ollivierra and Badrie 2007). However, the last two decades have challenged this stereotypical image of street food. The street food landscape in the UK, for example, has experienced 'a true revolution', with London leading the charge (Johnson 2011). New trends in food and beverage consumption have been identified, such as slow travel and tourism and immersive eating (Fullagar, Markwell and Wilson 2012; Courier 2015). On the one hand, these are the direct result of strong negative emotional and behavioural reactions by some consumer groups against McDonaldisation and over-standardisation of food and society (Ritzer 2008). On the other, food and beverage or gastronomic events have become important aspects of daily life in the 21st century. Consumers are looking more and more for deep, meaningful culinary experiences in creative settings, both in their day to day life and when travelling for leisure.

This chapter presents findings from research conducted between 2013 and 2016. The aim of the research is to explore the relationships between street food, immersive eating and unusual venues and locations, with a case study on Street Feast. Street Feast started as a pop-up street food events concept combining the street food market format concept with the special events concept. The case study presents interest because it is a rare type of commercial event that successfully combines the traditional need for profit and return on investment with that of developing a sustainable business product that cares for and promotes 'local' talent, 'local' businesses and 'local' ingredients; that satisfies the individual and collective needs of a changing global clientele; adds value to the night-time economy, and gives new life and reinvents liminal spaces and places. Street Feast successfully challenges the consumer imagination and in a few short years went from fringe to mainstream, reinventing the street food concept in the process (Malin 2014; Courier 2015). It is now a popular food experience not only with Londoners, but with tourists from around the world, food enthusiasts and accidental foodies alike.

Investigating this case study helps us gain a better understanding of how and why this business concept has become so successful and potentially draws some lessons that can be applied on a larger scale to the global street food events industry. The research adopted a qualitative, inductive research design. The methods used are secondary data analysis and participant observation at Street Feast Dalston Yard, Dinerama and Hawker House. The chapter starts out by briefly introducing the concept of street food before exploring in-depth the Street Feast concept; and finishes by analysing the complex relationship between unusual and liminal spaces and places, immersive eating and the street food experience.

Street food – an ever changing landscape

Street food plays an important economic role, being consumed by millions of low and middle income consumers, as well as offering an indispensible source of income for small businesses, in particular in developing countries (Winarno and Allain 1991, Privitera and Nesci 2015). The definition of street foods was agreed upon by the Food and Agriculture Organisation of the United Nations (FAO) in the Regional Workshop on Street Foods in Asia, held in Jogjakarta, Indonesia in 1986: 'Street foods are ready-to-eat foods and beverages prepared and/or sold by vendors and hawkers especially in streets and other similar public places' (FAO 2011). Street food is commonly characterised as cheap or affordable (Tinker 1997, 2003), and to be of local or universally appealing character (Newman and Burnett 2013, Privitera and Nesci 2015). The Street Food Institute (2017) also underlines the significance of taste, availability, location and distribution: 'Typically, street food is tasty, ready-to-eat food or drink sold on the street, in a market, fair, park or other public place. It is sold by a hawker or vendor from a portable stall, cart or food truck'. All definitions appear to acknowledge and agree on the same key characteristic, the 'street' aspect. FAO set out the basic characteristics of street food, underlining its link with places and spaces not usually associated with the preparation, distribution or consumption of food and beverages. However, very little research actually exists on the impacts of these places and spaces on the food consumption experience and to what extent it facilitates immersive consumption. Most street food research focuses on health and hygiene, the economic benefits of street food, or the business side of advising sellers on how to successfully set up and run their business, arguing that food should be made available in places characterised by the flows and movement of people.

Some of the most common perceptions around street food can be summarised as:

- Types of food: popular – local or universal, or mixed (a local interpretation of international foods; or an 'international' interpretation of foods specific to a certain region). One of the main characteristics of street food is popularity. Usually vendors will focus on foods that are liked by a mass audience and therefore maximise their purchase potential. The types of food sold can be specific foods to the area and/or region or they can be foods accepted and acknowledged throughout the world (Privitera and Nesci 2015).

- Clientele, typology and motivations: busy or in a hurry; on a low income and financially challenged. The practice of selling food in the streets or in public spaces can be dated back to ancient times. Working patterns, travelling, as well as lack of cooking facilities are known as basic motivators to purchase street food (FAO 2011).
- Ingredients: basic ingredients, easily accessible on the market, usually local. However, in today's global society, the 'local' food chain has been hijacked by the international food distribution chains and ingredients from around the world can generally be found locally.
- Staff – cooks (chefs) and sellers: family, one-person business. FAO (2011) argues that the majority of street food vendors are independent, local business people. They may run the business as a one-person operation or a small family business.
- Recipes: fairly simple, personal interpretations of popular recipes.
- Menu: limited, fixed, lack of choice or diversity.
- Preparation: fast, basic utensils and preparation methods (usually fried, boiled, or steamed).
- Location and distribution: pre-cooked/ready-to-eat, and/or cooked on-site and requiring access to utilities (gas, water); pre-assembled or assembly takes place on-site; unusual venues and locations (street); flexible – the food vendor can move his/her business with the flow of people, identifying where good custom/demand may exist and maximising the potential to sell.
- Price: inexpensive, cheap, accessible and affordable. The common perception is that street food is considerably cheaper than restaurant food.
- Quality: in academic research, street food is often looked at from the perspective of food hygiene, health and safety. In less developed and developing countries, a certain degree of danger and illegality is often associated with street food. FAO (2011) warns that most street food businesses 'work without licencing' and are part of the 'informal sector'. However, in developed countries, the street food sector is usually regulated and monitored.
- Consumption: close, immediate. Street food is usually consumed close to the location where it is prepared and a short time after preparation.

Due to these characteristics, street food is often perceived as fast food because preparation is fast and some sort of standard assembly process is adopted (Winarno and Allain 1991). However, fast food is also done in a restaurant setting and overlaps with traditional, restaurant-based type of food preparation and consumption (Steyn and Labadarios 2011). New developments and trends in street food also widen the gap in perceptions between fast food and street food, especially in the UK. Perceptions of fast food in the UK have historically been negative, characterised by lack of variety or character,

> Our restaurant food was the envy of the world. But our street food? What a complete and utter embarrassment. It was either a bag of chips, a Mr Whippy, or a sausage from a rusty metal handcart pushed along by a Polish man with three fingers.
>
> (Johnson 2011: 6)

However, Johnson (2011) also comments on the quality and freshness of ingredients in today's street food, the talent and creativity of the chefs, the authenticity of the experience and the resilience of street food vendors.

Faced with tight profit margins, strict hygiene requirements and constant uncertainty over demand, many street food vendors do not stay in business for long. Quite often, these are temporary experiments rather than stable business endeavours. In spite of all these challenges, British street food vendors have embraced the uncertainty and made a spectacle out of it. The Street Food Institute (2017) argues that today's street food is 'feel-good. It's theatre. It's insanely great flavours. It's inexpensive. It's community'. Street food stalls now sell a wide range of local and international food and have gone from basic to gourmet. Their consumers are not satisfying basic human needs but are often described as foodies looking for exciting experiences and emotional triggers (Courier 2015; NCASS 2017). As a result, street food is

> revolutionizing Britain's food culture . . . It is colonising our high streets. It is reclaiming our public spaces. And it is showing us all that good food doesn't need to be stuck in a Michelin restaurant with a menu no one can understand.
>
> (Johnson 2011: 11)

Immersive consumption and immersive eating are relevant to both food and beverage tourism and events management. Immersive eating and immersive dining experiences have been identified as 'hot' trends by industry professionals (for example Strimpel 2014; Courier 2015; Duggins 2016). In academia, immersive tourist experiences are often associated with embodiment discourses and performativity or tourist performances (for example Hannam and Knox 2010); and fit in with the slow tourism movement (for example Guiver and McGrath 2016). Everett (2009), for example, argues that food often acts as a mirror into local cultures and tourists are using it more and more to 'understand' and 'experience', rather than just satisfy primitive urges. Immersive eating appears to enhance the usual consumption experience. However, more research is needed in order to understand its full potential and implications.

Immersion is defined by the Oxford dictionary as 'deep mental involvement in something' (Oxford University Press 2017). Expressions usually associated with immersive experiences range from: making use of all the senses, enabling high cognitive processes and encouraging deep outer and inner awareness. A degree of surprise, drama or theatre is usually involved to immerse the audience. Duggins (2016) argues that 'the whole restaurant's a stage in the world of immersive dining'. For example, in the 'Chambers of Flavours', a London-based immersive eating restaurant concept, instead of waiting for food to be served, participants are asked to 'hunt' for it; or food is served in unexpected settings:

> sometimes on a gondola, sometimes shoving them into a gigantic machine that looks like something from 80s kids' TV programme Bertha. In this instance, they are taking them on a tour of theatrical sets (or 'parallel dimensions'), where actors serve up a different themed course in each room.
>
> (Duggins 2016)

Bibo, a restaurant in Hong Kong, combines fact, fiction and narratives to transform the dining space into an art space and the experience of dining into a theatrical performance (Strimpel 2014). Pop-up businesses fit into the immersive experiences discourses very well. Their temporary nature is part of their appeal. They promise memorable experiences for a limited time only. Customers are encouraged to live in the moment and make rapid decisions or risk missing out. Therefore, immersive eating restaurants are no longer perceived as niche or fringe. Street food vendors are adopting these principles as well. Street Feast is an example of such a street food event concept that has embraced and capitalised on the trend.

The Street Feast concept

Street Feast is a London-based business start-up that contributed aggressively to the UK street food revolution. It started as a pop-up commercial street food market and festival back in 2012 and rapidly grew into what some describe as a 'street food market network' (Bloomfield 2016). Much like any other commercial product, Street Feast's main purpose is to yield profit for its investors and collaborators. It is designed to act as an intermediary between customers or buyers of street food and those cooking and selling street food. The Street Feast philosophy has been summarised by the business owners as:

> Since May 2012 we've been busy reviving London's abandoned car parks, builders' yards, warehouses, power stations and a 1950s market, creating a fresh way of eating, drinking and hanging out. We've breathed new life into local communities, helped launch dozens of small businesses and transformed the lives of many street food traders.
>
> (Street Feast 2015: 1)

Therefore, the business idea is based on the following principles: an exhibition of local street vendors prepare and sell their food in a controlled environment where health and safety is closely monitored; unusual venues such as abandoned warehouses, builders' yards, power stations and car parks are used to reduce rent costs and off-the-beaten-track locations in London often characterised as creative, up-and-coming, hip or cool, frequented by hipsters or trend-setters are selected.

Historically, Street Feast managed four different locations running at different times during the year, usually open 2–3 evenings per week, starting 5 p.m. to midnight, with free entry 5 p.m.-7 p.m., and a £3 entry fee past 7 p.m.:

- Dalston Yard Street Feast, in Dalston, Friday to Saturday, usually end of April to late September/early October, closed permanently in 2016.
- Dinerama, in Shoreditch, Thursday to Saturday, 'open all year round: from May – September the space is open-air, but from October the site gains a roof, carpet and heating to keep diners warm for the winter' (Timeout 2017).
- Hawker House, in Canada Water, Friday and Saturday, only during the late autumn-early spring months.
- Model Market, in Lewisham, Friday and Saturday, only during the late spring-early autumn months.

The first Street Feast had nine stalls and opened as a pop-up food market and festival in a small car park near Brick Lane (Courier 2015). A few months later, Street Feast reopened as a street food pop-up special event in Dalston (Figures 7.1 and 7.2). Two more locations were added, running at different times of the year. In 2015, a semi-permanent location in Shoreditch, Dinerama, was added (Figure 7.3). The concept has been constantly evolving with each reincarnation being more complex. Over time, Street Feast expanded to include food, alcohol and music, with areas both outdoors and indoors, covered or not depending on the venue. Street Feast is

Figure 7.1 Street Feast – Dalston – Neon
Source: Photo courtesy of Claudia Sima and Franziska Vogt

Figure 7.2 Street Feast – Dalston
Source: Photo courtesy of Claudia Sima and Franziska Vogt

Figure 7.3 Street Feast Dinerama
Source: Photo courtesy of Claudia Sima and Franziska Vogt

usually made up of a dozen or more food stalls, cocktail bars or local alcohol manufacturers, a central seating area where foodies share tables and compete for sitting
space, and some special areas. A special atmosphere is created because of the smell
of freshly cooked food, burning bonfires in Texaco marked oil barrels, and the on-
purpose run-down design of the space. Wooden tables and benches, portable toilets
and shipping containers tend to characterise the design of Street Feast sites.

Founder Dominic Cools-Lartigue argued that his inspiration came from the
street food culture outside the UK; however, the concept builds on the cultural
diversity of London, celebrating its foods and taking advantage of its potential: 'I
was fascinated by the food markets in places like Zanzibar and Barbados and
imagined what it could be like in London with all the different cultures we've got
here' (quoted in Courier 2015). He also saw that another crucial aspect that made
Street Feast successful was that of socialising:

> I started Street Feast because I was convinced that night markets, run properly
> and to the standard we do at Street Feast, would become a viable alternative
> to going to a pub or restaurant, a real evolution in how we socialise.
> (quoted in Ferguson 2016)

During our primary data collection process, we observed that strangers from
around the world ended up sharing tables and starting talking to each other at Street
Feast. Street Feast became popular largely through social media marketing and
word of mouth. A wide range of customers cross its thresholds: foodies, hipsters,
new Generation Y parents with buggies, tourists etc.

Street Feast only features local food and alcohol manufacturers and vendors. The
Street Feast brand success depends on their vendors. Malin (2014) argues that the
reason why Street Feast is so successful is because at its core it is a 'trend-based concept, bringing together the food stalls and companies that are on the pulse of London';
therefore, vendors are selected based on popularity. However, above all there are four
principles they expect from their vendors and that they use when selecting them:

- Quality: To trade with us you've got to be among the best in your field on
  the street. We're looking for amazing cooking with character and originality.
  There will always be loads of great burgers, barbecue, tacos and pizza on
  the menu at Street Feast – but what's new? Maybe now's a good time to
  start thinking outside the bun.
- Consistency: The most successful street food traders do one thing really
  well. Street food is about getting the most out of a small number of quality
  ingredients; your 400th street meal of the night should be as good as the
  first. If your crew can't learn your menu in a couple of hours, it's too com-
  plicated. We know it can be difficult when you're stretched across a number
  of sites, managing different staff and staying on top of red tape. This year
  we'll be a lot more forthcoming with help and feedback, enabling you to
  keep more customers happy more of the time.

- Magic: We want to work with people who make their customers feel special. When people buy their food from you it should come quick, quick, quick, but also with bags of energy and charisma.
- Professionalism: Be on time, be clean, don't get drunk. If you're sick or hungover, don't come in. That goes for your staff too please.

(Street Feast 2015: 1)

Street Feast vendors are actively encouraged to: develop menus and foods that have character; be original and creative; use ingredients smartly; streamline and simplify cooking and assembly processes but without having an impact on food quality and provide good service quality at all times. Sobriety and seriousness are also required from all business partners. The requirements are strict and the selection process demanding. Vendors are encouraged to be food artists and innovators. Only a few vendors get to exhibit their skill each weekend, and usually they rotate. Each night offers a different set of vendors and therefore a different, unique event experience.

Their main selling points to traders are the spirit of community and fun, but with a profit:

- Community: Street Feast is an open network of great traders, brilliant bartenders, hospitable hosts and visionary owners. If you are cordial, punctual and willing to pitch in, you'll fit in fine.
- Fun: Trading with us is a hard graft but it can also be very profitable, rewarding and fun.

(Street Feast 2015: 2)

Street Feast offers a range of benefits to members, from marketing to counselling; all delivered in a light but professional tone:

- Fair pitch fees.
- A huge footfall of hungry customers.
- An opportunity to be your own boss and make good money.
- Great marketing and exposure for your business/brand.
- Help with finding staff.
- Regular coaching and feedback.
- Drop-in surgery sessions to help you improve your food, recruit better staff, become more profitable, grow your business, open a restaurant and anything/ everything else in-between.
- Free resources. Starting off in street food is a daunting task but you're not on your own. We've been around the block a few times. All our sites have market directors onsite who know how to wire a plug, put out a fire and jump start a '74 Citroen H Van with a tin can and a piece of string.
- A professional and enjoyable working environment and unbeatable vibes.

(Street Feast 2015: 2)

After four years of using the space, Dalston Yard was closed in 2016. The area is being redeveloped:

> Last weekend, Street Feast in Dalston Yard held its last ever foodie (and let's face it, boozy) sessions as it closed for the summer. But the sad news is that the famous street-food peddlers won't be returning to their original Dalston setting next summer (where they've been stationed for the last four years), as the site – like many of our favourite nightlife spots of late – is being transformed into flats.
>
> (Richards 2016)

Although the event no longer fits into the classic definition of pop-up businesses because for the last four years it has followed a fairly stable schedule, in many ways it is reinventing the concept of pop-ups. Each reincarnation is different and each evening is different. As previously argued, due to the rotation of exhibitors, each event is a unique performance. But Street Feast is also the embodiment of what is cool and trendy in an ever changing London. When it started, Dalston was perceived as an off-the-beaten track area in London, run-down and in need of investment. Four years later it is experiencing unprecedented regeneration and gentrification. The fact that Street Feast had to relocate from Dalston Yard to make room for new developments is an example of how fast things change and how temporary businesses and experiences actually are.

In addition, in 2015, Street Feast was sold to London Union:

> The momentum attracted the interests of investors, notably Leon founder Henry Dimbleby, who is leading the development of a permanent space for Street Feast. He set up London Union, and earlier this year the new company acquired Street Feast with Cools-Lartigue remaining a minority shareholder.
>
> (Courier 2015)

The plan is

> to create a single, enormous, street food market "like the Boqueria in Barcelona" . . . By 2020 the pair plan to have at least a dozen local markets in London, a large permanent site and several markets abroad. They will target North America and are discussing plans for Berlin.
>
> (Luckhurst 2015)

The permanent venues as well as the expansion plans are the result of the success of the business concept and the growing demand.

Although it is losing some of the original characteristics, the essence of Street Feast remains local talent and unusual venues: 'The markets will be a resource for communities across the capital and the funding model echoes that philosophy. It's part of our approach,' says Downey. 'We have community traders and we're taking buildings that are derelict in areas that are underserved by food options. It helps to have a big group of enthusiastic investors' (quoted in Luckhurst 2015). In addition, the 'people power' element and constant innovation mentality is also visible in the funding approach for the new developments:

The permanent market is being financed partly through crowdfunding. The pair are looking for 700 people to make a minimum contribution of £5,000, aiming to raise £3.5 million in total. This would make it the biggest food and hospitality crowdfund ever.

(Luckhurst 2015)

In five years, Street Feast went from a one-off pop-up food market event to a recurring street food festival, to a network of street food special commercial events, to an expanding street food empire. It has done this by relying on local talent, clear business principles, unusual locations and venues and a loyal, expanding clientele. In the process, it has changed perceptions of street food and increased its popularity.

The symbiotic relationship

Slow travel and immersive eating suggest a different food experience, one in which the consumer chooses quality over quantity (Fullagar et al. 2012). As Table 7.1 summarises, Street Feast still maintains some of the classic characteristics of street food; however, its biggest innovation is bringing together multiple street vendors

Table 7.1 Comparison between classic perceptions of street food and the Street Feast concept

Characteristic	Classic perceptions of street food in the UK	Perceptions of Street Feast's street food
Types of food	Popular – local or universal; or mixed	Innovative; experimental
Clientele, typology and motivations	Busy or in a hurry; low income and financially challenged	Slow consumption; social; diverse clientele (cosmopolitan, foodies etc.)
Ingredients	Basic ingredients, easily accessible on the market, usually local	Basic and/or limited range of ingredients, easily accessible on the market, usually local
Staff	Family, one-person business	Family, one-person business
Recipes:	Fairly simple, personal interpretations of popular recipes	Innovative; Experimental
Menu:	Limited, fixed, lack of choice or diversity	Limited, fixed, lack of diversity from each vendor, but rich diversity due to the Street Feast street market event approach
Preparation	Fast, basic	Fast, basic
Price	Inexpensive, cheap, accessible, and affordable	Accessible; mixed opinions
Quality	Unhealthy, unhygienic, unregulated and unmonitored.	Healthy, hygienic, regulated, monitored
Consumption	Close, immediate	Close, immediate

under one brand and as a result offering a diverse range of street foods. Street Feast also successfully manages perceptions of hygiene through a very clear vendor recruitment policy. It replaced 'boring' with innovation and creativity. As a result it attracted a diverse and loyal clientele. Street Feast proved that street food doesn't have to be cheap and people are willing to pay for perceived value.

However, the two characteristics that form the foundation of Street Feast are actually classic street food characteristics: 'local' talent has always been an essential characteristic of street food; also, the 'street' and 'public' element. Street Feast Hawker House, in Canada Water, is based in a modern storage facility and Dinerama is set in a former bullion truck depot in Shoreditch. Over the years Street Feast used a wide range of unusual venues. In the events industry, the venue and location are highly important; they are representative of the event's message and personality. Street Feast chooses the venues on purpose to generate immersive experiences. Cool, edgy, eccentric, exotic, tasty are words usually used to describe the Street Feast experience and the choice of venues directly influences these perceptions: 'Set in a former bullion truck depot in Shoreditch, . . . the look on the ground floor [of Dinerama] is somewhere between a yard and a warehouse' (Timeout 2017).

Conclusion

Street Feast identified immersive eating trends and opportunities in the marketplace early on and started one of the most successful business ventures in London. Street Feast challenges the meanings of street food by fostering a symbiotic relationship between unusual venues and street food with the purpose of stimulating immersive eating experiences. The growing numbers of event attendees is proof that the event concept has value. It can be argued that street food commercial events such as Street Feast are the counterbalance to a globalised, fast-paced food society; however, with Street Feast expanding, it remains to be seen if they can keep their initial business concept and if they end up losing 'the local' in favour of 'the global'.

References

Benny-Ollivierra, C. and Badrie, N. (2007) 'Hygienic practices by vendors of the street food "doubles" and public perceptions of vending practices in Trinidad, West Indies', *Journal of Food Safety*, 27(1), 66–81.
Bloomfield, R. (2016) 'From old street to Dalston: Street Feast boss Jonathan Downey has scaled the London ladder to become a property millionaire within 20 years', *Homes & Property*, www.homesandproperty.co.uk/property-news/from-old-street-to-dalston-how-street-feast-boss-jonathan-downey-has-scaled-the-london-ladder-to-a106411.html (accessed 3 January 2017).
Courier (2015) 'Secret cinema and Street Feast: The new impresarios', *Courier*, www.courierpaper.com/cover-story/secret-cinema-street-feast-new-impresarios/ (accessed 5 April 2016).

Duggins, A. (2016) 'The whole restaurant's a stage in the world of immersive dining', *The Guardian*, www.theguardian.com/lifeandstyle/wordofmouth/2016/may/31/the-whole-restaurants-a-stage-in-the-world-of-immersive-dining (accessed 3 January 2017).

Everett, S. (2009) 'Beyond the visual gaze? The pursuit of an embodied experience through food tourism', *Tourist Studies*, 8(3), 337–358.

FAO (2011) *Selling street and snack foods*, Food and Agriculture Organisation of the United Nations, www.fao.org/docrep/015/i2474e/i2474e00.pdf (accessed 5 June 2016).

Ferguson, J. (2016) 'Street Feast owner talks Casa Havana: Bringing a taste of Cuba to London', *The Mirror*, www.mirror.co.uk/lifestyle/going-out/street-feast-owner-talks-casa-8654649 (accessed 6 September 2016).

Fullagar, S., Markwell, K. and Wilson, E. (Eds.) (2012) *Slow Tourism: Experiences and Mobilities*, Bristol: Channel View.

Guiver, J. and McGrath, P. (2016) *Slow Tourism: Exploring the Discourses*, www.clok.uclan.ac.uk/14084/1/Slow%20tourism-%20exploring%20the%20Discourses.pdf (accessed 3 January 2017).

Hannam, K. and Knox, D. (2010) *Understanding Tourism: A Critical Introduction*, London: Sage.

Johnson, R. (2011) *Street Food Revolution: Inspiring New Recipes and Stories from the New Food Heroes*, London: Kyle Books.

Luckhurst, P. (2015) 'What Street Feast did next: Henry Dimbleby and Jonathan Downey on crowdfunding', *Evening Standard*, www.standard.co.uk/goingout/restaurants/what-street-feast-did-next-henry-dimbleby-and-jonathan-downey-on-crowdfunding-london-union-and-a3102566.html (accessed 13 June 2016).

Malin, A. (2014) 'Meet the man behind the fairground', *About Time Magazine*, www.about-timemagazine.co.uk/life/meet-the-man-behind-the-fairground/ (accessed 6 April 2016).

NCASS (2017) *What is street food? NCASS – The Nationwide Caterers Association*, www.streetfood.org.uk/what-is-street-food.html (accessed 12 January 2017).

Newman, L.L. and Burnett, K. (2013) 'Street food and vibrant urban spaces: Lessons from Portland, Oregon', *Local Environment: The International Journal of Justice and Sustainability*, 18(2), 233–248.

Privitera, D. and Nesci, F.S. (2015) 'Globalization vs. local: The role of street food in the urban food system', *Procedia Economics and Finance*, 22, 716–722.

Richards, L. (2016) 'Street Feast Dalston Yard has closed to make room for more housing', *TimeOut*, www.timeout.com/london/blog/street-feast-dalston-yard-has-closed-to-make-room-for-more-housing-092716 (accessed 2 January 2017).

Ritzer, G. (2008) *The McDonaldisation of Society 5*, London: Pine Forge/Sage.

Steyn, N.P. and Labadarios, D. (2011) 'Street foods and fast foods: How much do South Africans of different ethnic groups consume?', *Ethnicity & Disease*, 21, 462–466.

Street Feast (2015) 'What we do', www.streetfeast.com (accessed 2 January 2017).

Street Food Institute (2017) 'What is street food?', www.streetfoodinstitute.org/what-is-street-food/ (accessed 2 January 2017).

Strimpel, Z. (2014) 'Immersive eating: Restaurant exudes faction mentality', *LS: N Global*, www.lsnglobal.com/briefing/article/16185/immersive-eating-restaurant-exudes-faction-mentality (accessed 5 May 2017).

Timeout (2017) 'Dinerama', *TimeOut*, www.timeout.com/london/restaurants/dinerama (accessed 29 January 2017).

Tinker, I. (1997) *Street Foods: Urban Food and Employment in Developing Countries*, Cary, NC: Oxford University Press.

Tinker, I. (2003) 'Street foods: Traditional microenterprise in a modernizing world', *International Journal of Politics, Culture, and Society*, 16(3), 331–349.

Winarno, F.G. and Allain, A. (1991) 'Street foods in developing countries: Lessons from Asia', *Food, Nutrition and Agriculture 1*, www.fao.org/docrep/u3550t/u3550t08. htm#street%20foods%20in%20developing%20countries:%20lessons%20from%20asia (accessed 5 May 2017).

8 Narrowing the gap between paddock and plate

The Real Food Festival, Australia

Trudie Walters

Introduction

Food events and food festivals have become popular in recent years, capitalising on the burgeoning interest in all things 'foodie' (Getz and Robinson 2014). They are often used as a means of differentiating smaller rural areas to drive tourism and regional development in an increasingly crowded marketplace (Barrie 2008; Getz, Robinson, Andersson and Vujicic 2014; Hall 2005; Kalkstein-Silkes, Cai and Lehto 2008). As such, much of the existing research is tourism-centric and focuses on the motives, perceptions and profile of those who attend food festivals, and the economic impacts of such events (see for example Axelsen and Swan 2010; Çela, Knowles-Lankford and Lankford 2007; Robinson and Getz 2014).

While there has been some work on producers' participation in farmers' markets or agri-tourism (see for example Che, Veeck and Veeck 2005; Griffin and Frongillo 2003), the food producers participating in food festivals have been largely overlooked in the literature to date. For this group of stakeholders, there is a more fundamental motivation at work: generating business. This may particularly be the case for smaller, boutique or artisanal food producers wanting to engage and educate food consumers with an interest or passion for the local food movement. This chapter examines the value of a local food festival from the perspective of local food producers, through a case study of the Real Food Festival on the Sunshine Coast in Queensland, Australia. A series of in-depth interviews with food stallholders sheds light on a variety of ways in which they use the Real Food Festival as a medium for achieving their business aspirations.

The real food festival

The Sunshine Coast is approximately one hour drive north of Brisbane city, on the east coast of Australia, and for decades has been a popular domestic tourist destination (Gration 2014). The rural Sunshine Coast hinterland is about a 30-minute drive inland from the coast and is home to a number of small historic townships; Maleny is the largest with a population of around 3,500 (Australian Bureau of Statistics 2013). Small-scale dairy farming and fruit orchards have been the agricultural mainstay of the local hinterland communities over the last century, although there have been significant challenges to the former industry in recent years (Sunshine Coast Council 2016; Green 2010). Deregulation, drought, increasing bureaucracy and compliance costs coupled with falling prices for producers meant that many farmers in the region were struggling to maintain a viable business and remain on the land (de Rijke 2012; Keith 2012). In addition, in 2006 the controversial Traveston Dam project in the Mary Valley (part of which lies in the Sunshine Coast hinterland) was mooted by the Queensland State Government amidst strong opposition by the local community. Many farms that had been in the same family for generations were subsequently sold to the government, only to be put up for sale again in a staged release after the project was refused approval by the federal government in 2009, causing financial and social disruption for the Mary Valley community for nearly a decade (Courtney 2015).

Against this backdrop, the Real Food Festival was established in Maleny in 2011 to celebrate and support Sunshine Coast hinterland local farmers and food producers in this difficult time, and demonstrate that they were valued by the community (Gilmore 2011; Gration 2014). The Festival sought to provide an outlet for the farmers to sell their produce while at the same time educating the public about the importance of local food producers. Initially a single-day event, the organisers decided to stage it over a weekend from its second year. In addition to the market stalls of primary producers, there were also food wholesalers, food retailers, those selling value-added food products, a diverse programme of speakers (topics ranged from permaculture to nutrition), cooking demonstrations and activities for children (Figure 8.1).

Figure 8.1 The Real Food Festival 2015
Source: Photo courtesy of Trudie Walters

There were just over 4000 attendees and 84 stallholders in the first year, increasing to over 8800 and close to 100 respectively by 2014. Nearly three quarters of attendees were from the Sunshine Coast and approximately one quarter were from the greater Queensland region including many from Brisbane (Gration 2014; Real Food Festivals 2015). However, after five years of successfully staging the Real Food Festival, the organisers announced in early 2016 to the disappointment of many that the event would 'take a break' that year, with the format of future events yet to be decided (Moffat 2016).

Narrowing the gap between paddock and plate: stallholders' perspectives

The 11 participants interviewed for this study included primary producers (PP), value-adders (VA), wholesalers (W), chefs (C) and retailers (R) who had stalls and/ or were sponsors or speakers at the Real Food Festival over the period 2011–15. All were small-scale owner-operated businesses, mirroring the business environment in Australia where some 90% of businesses have an annual turnover of less than AUD$1 million and fewer than 20 staff (McKerchar, Hodgson and Walpole 2009). The majority were based in the Sunshine Coast hinterland, with just two from outside this area but still within the wider Sunshine Coast region. A number of the participants had attended the Real Food Festival every year, some had attended on a more irregular basis, and a few attended for the first time in 2015. Interviews ranged from 25 to 90 minutes and were audio-recorded for later transcription. Five major themes were identified relating to their experiences and business motives for attending the festival: opportunistic business launch; deliberate marketing strategy; generating awareness and exposure; collaboration and collective marketing; and building and supporting community.

Opportunistic business launch

Perhaps surprisingly, two of the new food producers revealed a spontaneous, unplanned approach to participating in the Real Food Festival, rather than utilising it as part of a deliberate strategy to launch their business. The timing of the Real Food Festival provided them with an opportunity to launch their business which they took advantage of – despite an initial degree of unpreparedness:

> I said to my wife, 'Well, if we're going to find out whether this thing's going to work or not, we need to launch it at the Real Food Festival.' And she said, 'Oh well, next year'll be good', and I said, 'No no, the one in ten days time!' [laughs] . . . basically two weeks before the Real Food Festival we didn't have a trailer, we didn't have a Safe Food licence, we didn't have a marquee, we had no marketing material, and I just had an idea! And ten days later I'd pulled it all together, and we had an amazing response at that Real Food Festival, that really launched it for us . . . And at that point we didn't actually have a plan, it was just, 'If this works we've got to take the next step'.
>
> (PP1)

The Real Food Festival, the timing, coincided with our launch! [*Interviewer: was it just coincidence or did you time it like that?*] Yeah, the website was good to go, everything was good to go, and it was a girlfriend of mine in town, she said, 'You should go in the Real Food Festival!' and I said, 'Well we don't have meat to sell' and she's like, 'That doesn't matter!'

(PP3)

Despite being aware of the event, neither producer had considered attending until they saw the marketing or someone suggested that it might be a good idea. In both cases the Real Food Festival proved a successful vehicle for launching their food-producing business despite having little (or no) actual product available for sale at their stalls. In addition to securing pre-orders for their product during the festival, these business owners were able to generate databases of nearly two hundred customers who were interested in their product and signed up to receive e-news-letters or other forms of marketing.

Such an ad hoc approach to the launch of a new business venture certainly seems to support the finding of Stokes (1997) that the owners of small businesses tend to place a low priority on marketing. However, it also suggests that the Real Food Festival provided an opportunity for entrepreneurial marketing – that is, thinking outside conventional marketing techniques by starting with an idea for an innovative product and then trying to find a market for it (Stokes 2000). Both of the new food producers were able to 'test' the market and have meaningful dialogues with customers, indicating a more informal approach to market research.

Deliberate marketing strategy

In contrast to the new businesses, those that had been established for a number of years used the Real Food Festival in a more considered and deliberate manner, with evidence that they viewed it as part of a broader (and more conventional) marketing strategy aimed at a particular market segment (Stokes 1997):

The Real Food Festival was very appealing to us, because of its location, because of the profile of the attendees at that market, at that event were really exactly the demographic we were looking to match with . . . households inter-ested in knowing their food source, who buy regularly from independent grocers and markets . . . fifty percent of those customers were visiting from Brisbane, and that also matched with our, that's our target profile within our café and retail shop. So we were able to invite visitors, the customers at the Real Food Festival we could actually tell them 'look, our shop is open today til 5pm'.

(PP/R6)

For the majority of the established businesses, the decision to attend the Real Food Festival was part of a calculated strategy that included attendance at a small number of other food events in Queensland aimed at similar target markets that also provided good value for money:

> Last year we did [the Real Food Festival] ourselves, I guess cos we wanted to more participate in the whole event . . . I think outside of that box of that festival what we've also tried to do is try to participate in other food-based events.
>
> (W/R4)

Interestingly, for one food retailer who sponsored the Real Food Festival, business dropped off during the festival, but they took a longer-term view of the benefits of participation:

> Our sales drop . . . because everyone's going there, to buy their stuff, right, but that's ok, we know that everyone knows that you can get it here [at our shop] anyway, so we know that the Food Festival does a great job in raising awareness of what's local, and then they'll come back to us for the other 51 weeks of the year to buy it with us, so our sales go like that [makes a dipping motion with his hand] during the Festival, but after that they [makes a rising motion].
>
> (R1)

One business, in addition to their core business of value-added food products, also ran gourmet food tours which were carefully planned around the timing of the Real Food Festival each year so they could attend. While staff or family members were capable of running the stall on their behalf if necessary, the owners believed that the Real Food Festival was sufficiently important that they be there in person to tell the story of their business.

Generating awareness and exposure

For nearly every interviewee, awareness and exposure were significant motives for participation in the Real Food Festival, although the focus of the awareness and exposure differed between participants:

> It raises awareness of local products, Sunshine Coast products, and we sell a lot of those products.
>
> (R1)

> The Real Food Festival is about exposing people to new products and giving them some knowledge of it. It's not so much about [them] taking home two hundred dollars worth of [product].
>
> (PP1)

I should say that the economic return was not why we were there, it was about exposure – we're here, this is [the farm], this is what we do, and to that extent we made some good contacts.

(PP2)

The big thing is the exposure for your business . . . So to me, yes it's about the sales, this is me personally, it IS about the sales but it's also about telling people about [my other business elements], and to me very important is telling people about my [gourmet food tours]. If I get one couple from a food festival that go on my [gourmet food tour] it's worth every cent to me. It's the exposure, it's big exposure, you're being exposed to thousands of people.

(PP7)

Some of the interviewees (generally but not always the owners of newer businesses) valued the business exposure gained through participation at the Real Food Festival over sales of product on the day, as they recognised that it was only through raising awareness of their business that long-term economic viability would be possible. Again, this finding highlights the stallholders' preference for entrepreneurial marketing techniques such as word-of-mouth and informal networks (Stokes 2000) and suggests that they appreciated the Real Food Festival as a platform for achieving this. This contrasts with some other studies, where economic return through product sales was the strongest motivation for participating in food events such as farmers' markets (Griffin and Frongillo 2003). This may relate to differences in the underlying focus of the events; a weekly or monthly farmers' market may essentially function as a 'direct-to-customer retail' space where continuity of both suppliers and attendees is important (Hall, Mitchell, Scott and Sharples 2008), whereas an annual food festival may function more as a combination of education and entertainment, often incorporating a tourism or destination branding element (Lee and Arcodia 2011; Sharples and Lyons 2008).

Collaboration and collective marketing

In addition to businesses benefitting from participating in the Real Food Festival individually, there was value through collaboration and collective marketing. Some businesses actively collaborated with others to showcase their product to best advantage:

For a couple of years I brought up a guy that did mushrooms. So what he'd do is he had half a dozen dishes, and one he'd cook up [with my product]. So people would want to try [my product] so I'd say, 'Yeah, go and see X and buy a plate of mushrooms . . . and that was really good . . . it got the message out there. Where you could have a local product, a known local product, working together, people would [makes a gesture that people liked it and would buy].

(PP5)

Other elements of the festival programme, such as guest speakers and celebrity chef cooking demonstrations, provided different opportunities to collaborate and promote one's products:

> [attendees are] also being exposed to some new foods, and I think in particular in this year they were being exposed at a greater rate to talks which gave them probably the insight that [we] gave them in eight hours of talking they were able to get by having a producer up on stage with, say, a chef and actually discussing their product.
>
> (PP1)

Research on small-scale agri-tourism operators in Michigan, USA, has highlighted the importance of collaboration, although the collaboration centred on information sharing and referrals to other farmers/agri-tourism providers (Che et al. 2005). Likewise, vendors at farmers' markets in upstate New York also collaborated, aiming to maintain the integrity and pricing of their products (Griffin and Frongillo 2003). This contrasts with the Real Food Festival where, as illustrated above, some producers worked as a team with other producers or with end-users such as chefs to showcase complementary products and educate attendees how to use them, thereby adding value to both products – and to the Festival itself.

Some interviewees articulated a more holistic view of collaboration; they viewed the Real Food Festival as a platform for the collective marketing of the destination, with broader messages being disseminated about the Sunshine Coast hinterland as a food destination:

> I think the Food Festival is more about promoting the region than about promoting individual food products . . . it's telling the story that Maleny or the hinterland is a food destination, there's ALL of these products, it's not about any one, it's all about the collective.
>
> (W/R4)

Again this was reminiscent of the Michigan agri-tourism study, which found that when operators worked collectively the region strengthened its reputation for agri-tourism; the diversity of product offered heightened the destination's attractiveness for visitors (Che et al. 2005). In the case of the Real Food Festival, it was a serendipitous (but important) spin-off for the participants rather than a deliberate coming-together to market the destination in a cohesive and strategic manner. Nevertheless, it is argued that the Festival showcased a critical mass of local food producers to the attendees, helping to facilitate the development of a place-based identity for the Sunshine Coast – and the hinterland in particular (Che et al. 2005; Lee and Arcodia 2011). This notion of collective marketing of the destination leads into the final theme, that of building and supporting community through the Real Food Festival.

Building and supporting community

The Real Food Festival, while helping the stallholders to achieve their business goals, also had broader social outcomes which were significant for the interviewees. As noted by many researchers, festivals and events contribute to building and supporting communities – particularly where the community collectively organises the event, or comes together to create or reinforce a strong shared-place identity (see for example Derrett 2003; Jaeger and Mykletun 2013; Luonila and Johansson 2015). While the Real Food Festival is not a community-initiated or organised event, interviewees nevertheless identified a strong sense of community as both a motivation and a benefit of attending.

The concept of community was delineated in different ways by different stakeholders. For some interviewees it was a geographic sense of community; participating in the festival allowed them to support the local Maleny and hinterland community of which they were a part, a way of 'giving back' and helping to ensure the economic and social viability of the community. Interestingly, for this retailer (R1) fostering a greater sense of community through involvement in the Festival also helped them to achieve their business aspirations. Being local residents and actively supporting local producers was an important part of their business strategy that helped to differentiate them from the larger-scale non-locally owned competition within the broader region:

> It was a fit for us . . . local, it's local, we know [the organiser], she's a mate, she shops here all the time, she's helped us out, helped introduce us to local suppliers, so we wanted to support her . . . plus it's about locals supporting locals, which is what we're about.
>
> (R1)

Some linked the notion of building and supporting community with their business in a different way, noting that local businesses were the lifeblood of the community and that the economic benefits of the Real Food Festival accrued more widely – their own participation in the Festival indirectly helped to ensure the viability of other businesses in the town, which then kept the community as a whole viable:

> People didn't just spend their money at the festival, I'm sure they went to restaurants and I'm sure they went to the shops, for the economy I think it's fantastic . . . again, it's exposure. A lot of people see the place . . . at the end of the day . . . if you're not economically viable then you're going to go under . . . and your community revolves around your businesses, and if they, if they go under, then you've got a problem in the town.
>
> (PP7)

For others, the sense of community was defined psycho-socially rather than geographically – it revolved around other stallholders and festival attendees who shared similar values surrounding food production and consumption. It was about forming and maintaining relationships within the local food community:

We were up there and there was a lot of my suppliers up there which was great.
(PP/R2)

It was great for us just touching base with a lot of like-minded people . . . a lot of interesting people that want to do what we're doing, on a bigger scale, with a lot more animals, which is what we'd like to do as well, so yeah it was great talking to them.

(PP3)

This resonates with Griffin and Frongillo's (2003) study, where the farmers high-lighted the importance of social interaction at the farmers' markets; they mentioned both the customers' appreciation of their product which further affirmed their value as farmers, and a sense of shared identity and community with other farmers. Taking it further, for one chef the Real Food Festival not only provided the ability to build and extend his social network, it also deepened his understanding of food:

For me personally . . . from a personal experience point of view, and for my own development as a chef and as a person, it's invaluable, I really love it. I've got friends all over the countryside now! . . . the more I see how things are grown, the better I understand food.

(C1)

Through discussions with the community of food producers present at the Real Food Festival he was able to co-create knowledge around food which in turn enriched his chef practice, certainly an intangible but valuable motivation for, and outcome of, participation.

Conclusion

This chapter has provided insights into why local food producers (including pri-mary producers, wholesalers, retailers, value-adders and chefs) participated in the Real Food Festival, a local food event on the Sunshine Coast in Queensland, Australia. In addition to the (perhaps expected) economic returns, the participants articulated a far broader range of motivations which were generally more impor-tant than solely focusing on the fiscal benefits of product sales on the day. Two primary producers capitalised on the opportunity that the Real Food Festival pro-vided for them to launch their business to market, despite being somewhat unpre-pared for the event. Interestingly, while they both knew about the Festival, neither had considered it as an option until they either saw it being marketed or someone suggested it to them as a suitable vehicle for a business launch. Others, whose businesses were more established, used the Real Food Festival as part of their overall marketing strategy to target their specific demographic in order to expand their customer base. Generating awareness and exposure for the business, for new products or for the region was seen as an important driver of participation for many local food producers. Collaboration and collective marketing enabled further ben-efits for the businesses and the region; this was manifested through enhanced attractiveness of both the food products to consumers and the Sunshine Coast hinterland as a food destination to visitors. Finally, participation in the Real Food Festival was seeing as being fundamental to contributing to a sense of community, whether geographically bounded or psycho-socially grounded. The local food-producer businesses considered that participation in the event fostered a sense of community, be it the Sunshine Coast hinterland community or the gathering of a like-minded 'food' community. For one participant, the fostering of a sense of community helped them to achieve their business goals.

This study has therefore revealed a more nuanced understanding of how participants used this food event to further their business aspirations, and in doing so contributes to the somewhat limited literature in this area. Much of the research to date has focused on event and festival attendees, visitors and/or local residents (for example Axelsen and Swan 2010; Robinson and Getz 2014), social, cultural or economic impacts of events (Çela et al. 2007; Derrett 2003), or the use of events in destination branding (Barrie 2008; Kalkstein-Silkes et al. 2008; Lee and Arcodia 2011). This chapter has provided an insight into the perspective of a different stakeholder group, the stallholders themselves, and finds a multi-faceted set of motivations that may be sought and achieved. Given that many of the stallholders in the current study indicated that they also participate in farmers' markets, an interesting avenue for future research is to investigate how they use these different types of events to achieve business goals and aspirations. For example are the motivations for participation in farmers' markets and food festivals similar, do they perceive and use them in complementary ways, or are they seeking to achieve different objectives? Research is also needed to establish whether similar motivations are found amongst food producer stallholders participating in different types of community events (sporting, cultural, music) or indeed in other cultural contexts. These findings may also prove useful to event planners seeking to understand the deeper motivations and provide more meaningful beneficial outcomes for their stallholders beyond the most obvious economic drivers of participation.

References

Australian Bureau of Statistics (2013) *2011 Census QuickStats – Maleny*, www.censusdata. abs.gov.au/census_services/getproduct/census/2011/quickstat/SSC30999?opendocumen t&navpos=220 (accessed 10 April 2016).

Axelsen, M. and Swan, T. (2010) 'Designing festival experiences to influence visitor perceptions: The case of a wine and food festival', *Journal of Travel Research*, 49(4), 436–450.

Barrie, W. (2008) 'Case study on the use of Scottish food events in promoting Scottish tourism and food', in C.M. Hall and L. Sharples (eds.), *Food and Wine Festival and Events Around the World: Development, Management and Markets* (pp. 78–84), Oxford and Burlington, MA: Elsevier/Butterworth-Heinemann.

Çela, A., Knowles-Lankford, J. and Lankford, S. (2007) 'Local food festivals in Northeast Iowa communities: A visitor and economic impact study', *Managing Leisure*, 12(2/3), 171–186.

Che, D., Veeck, A. and Veeck, G. (2005) 'Sustaining production and strengthening the agritourism product: Linkages among Michigan agritourism destinations', *Agriculture and Human Values*, 22(2), 225–234.

Courtney, P. (2015) 'Mary Valley revival: Last of properties sold during Traveston dam project back in private hands', *ABC News*, www.abc.net.au/news/2015-04-19/mary-valley-revival-last-of-properties-sold-back-in-private-hand/6402514 (accessed 3 May 2016).

de Rijke, K. (2012) 'The symbolic politics of belonging and community in peri-urban environmental disputes: The Traveston Crossing Dam in Queensland, Australia', *Oceania*, 82(3), 278–293.

Derrett, R. (2003) 'Making sense of how festivals demonstrate a community's sense of place', *Event Management*, 8, 49–58.

Getz, D. and Robinson, R.N.S. (2014) 'Foodies and food events', *Scandinavian Journal of Hospitality and Tourism*, 14(3), 315–330.

Getz, D., Robinson, R.N.S., Andersson, T. and Vujicic, S. (2014) *Foodies and Food Tourism*, Oxford: Goodfellow.

Gilmore, M. (2011) 'Hinterland to host real food festival', *Hinterland Times*, 9 April, www.hinterlandtimes.com.au/2011/04/09/hinterland-to-host-real-food-festival/ (accessed 15 April 2016).

Gration, D. (2014) 'Food events in the Sunshine Coast, Australia: Paddock to patisserie and back', in D. Getz, R.N.S. Robinson, T. Andersson and S. Vujicic (eds.), *Foodies and Food Tourism* (pp. 159–168), Oxford: Goodfellow.

Green, E. (2010) *Maleny: An Alternative History*, Maleny, QLD: Elaine Green.

Griffin, M.R. and Frongillo, E.A. (2003) 'Experiences and perspectives of farmers from Upstate New York farmers' markets', *Agriculture and Human Values*, 20(2), 189–203.

Hall, C.M. (2005) 'Rural wine and food tourism cluster and network development', in D. Hall, I. Kirkpatrick and M. Mitchell (eds.), *Rural Tourism and Sustainable Business* (pp. 149–164), Clevedon: Channel View.

Hall, C.M., Mitchell, R., Scott, D. and Sharples, L. (2008) 'The authentic market experience of farmers' markets', in C.M. Hall and L. Sharples (eds.), *Food and Wine Festival and Events Around the World: Development, Management and Markets* (pp. 197–231), Oxford and Burlington, MA: Elsevier/Butterworth-Heinemann.

Jaeger, K. and Mykletun, R.J. (2013) 'Festivals, identities and belonging', *Event Management*, 17, 213–226.

Kalkstein-Silkes, C., Cai, L.A. and Lehto, X.Y. (2008) 'Conceptualising festival-based culinary tourism in rural destinations', in C.M. Hall and L. Sharples (eds.), *Food and Wine Festival and Events Around the World: Development, Management and Markets* (pp. 66–77), Oxford and Burlington, MA: Elsevier/Butterworth-Heinemann.

Keith, S. (2012) 'Coles, Woolworths, and the local', *Locale: The Australasian-Pacific Journal of Regional Food Studies*, 2, 47–81.

Lee, I. and Arcodia, C. (2011) 'The role of regional food festivals for destination branding', *International Journal of Tourism Research*, 13(4), 355–367.

Luonila, M. and Johansson, T. (2015) 'The role of festivals and events in the regional development of cities: Cases of two Finnish cities', *Event Management*, 19, 211–226.

McKerchar, M., Hodgson, H. and Walpole, M. (2009) 'Understanding Australian small businesses and the drivers of compliance costs: A grounded theory approach', *Australian Tax Forum*, 24(2), 151–178.

Moffat, N. (2016) 'Don't give up on real food festival: Farmers', *Sunshine Coast Daily*, 11 February, www.sunshinecoastdaily.com.au/news/hinterland-needs-the-real-food-festival-farmers/2928688/ (accessed 12 February 2016).

Real Food Festivals (2015) *2014 Post-Festival Report*, www.realfoodfestivals.com.au/wp-content/uploads/2014/12/2014-RFF-Post-Festival-Report-small.pdf (accessed 19 September 2015).

Robinson, R.N.S. and Getz, D. (2014) 'Profiling potential food tourists: An Australian study', *British Food Journal*, 116(4), 690–706.

Sharples, L. and Lyons, H. (2008) 'Ludlow Marches Food and Drink Festival', in C.M. Hall and L. Sharples (eds.), *Food and Wine Festival and Events Around the World: Development, Management and Markets* (pp. 101–112), Oxford and Burlington, MA: Elsevier/Butterworth-Heinemann.

Stokes, D.R. (1997) 'A lesson in entrepreneurial marketing from the public sector', *Marketing Education Review*, 7(3), 47–55.

Stokes, D.R. (2000) 'Putting entrepreneurship into marketing: The processes of entrepreneurial marketing', *Journal of Research in Marketing and Entrepreneurship*, 2(1), 1–16.

Sunshine Coast Council (2016) *Blackall Range (Montville/Flaxton/Mapleton)*, www.library.sunshinecoast.qld.gov.au/Heritage/History-by-Locality/Town-Histories/Blackall-Range (accessed 1 December 2016).

9 The Noodle Grand Prix as a regional food industrial heritage festival

A Japanese case study

Sangkyun Kim, Eerang Park and Bokyung Kang

Introduction

Public fascination with culinary and gourmet culture and food tourism has a long history in Japan. It is loosely rooted in the *meibutsu* Japanese culture, in which famous things (for example, regional signature dishes or food) are associated with a local place and culture (Tussyadiah 2005). For example, the Japanese perceive and associate Kagawa, Gunma, and Akita Prefectures with Sanuki udon, Mizusawa udon and Inaniwa udon respectively, as the three most nationally recognised udon noodle production regions. This is in line with the assumption that food production and consumption is associated with historical, social, cultural and ecological values of particular geographic areas and their specific gastronomic and culinary heritage and culture (Everett and Aitchison 2008; Hjalager and Richards 2002; Long and Labadi 2010; Mak, Lumbers and Eves 2012).

The obsession with their noodle culture and tradition is a social and cultural phenomenon in Japan, noodles being thus described as 'a staple of Japanese cuisine and food culture' (Kim 2015: 91). This is demonstrated by the udon noodle tourism phenomenon as well as noodle-themed museums such as Shin-Yokohama Ramen Museum in Yokohama and Gion Udon Museum in Kyoto (Jones 2011; Kim and Ellis 2015; Kim and Iwashita 2016). The Japanese national udon championship, the so-called U-1 Grand Prix, is also worth noting.

Although there are no accurate historical dates, it is said that the Japanese noodle culture was already flourishing by the 10th century since its introduction from China in the 8th century (Kushner 2012; Okada 1993). The Japanese udon noodle is considered to be the oldest noodle from a variety of Japanese noodles commonly known as soba, somen and ramen. The udon noodle became a nationwide hit in the 17th century, and it remains an important part of contemporary Japanese society's daily food production and consumption. Udon is a thick white noodle made of white wheat flour, water and salt, which creates a cream-coloured, soft and elastic texture, and glossy appearance. It is served in a flavourful soup (e.g. sardine) or just with seasonings, with various toppings including fresh egg, seafood or vegetable tempura, though there are many regional variations and preferences (Kim and Ellis 2015).

While the distinctive scent of Japan's food tradition and culture continues, 'Bii-kyu (B-rank) gourmet' has become a buzzword in Japan in recent years.

It refers to casual and inexpensive but tasty dishes that are not traditionally seen as gourmet food. Ramen noodles, yakisoba fried noodles, gyoza fried dumplings and takoyaki octopus balls exemplify this social and cultural trend. Such a contemporary trendy sub-food culture has resulted in the sudden proliferation of local, regional and national competitions for B-rank gourmet dishes. The winners of such competitions often experience a nationwide boom in their popularity (Kim 2015; Kim and Ellis 2015).

However, most of these events are one-off or temporary events and merely focus on entertaining the commercial values of fashionable consumable food items, in this case B-rank gourmet, reflecting contemporary social and cultural trends and changes. Those newly invented food-themed festivals and events tend to neglect the historical and geographical contexts in which they occur and thus lack (local) identity and uniqueness in terms of their geographic context, and authenticity and liminality in terms of their historical context (Ma and Lew 2012).

Using an exploratory case study method, the research context of the current chapter is the 'Men-1 Grand Prix' festival, known as the 'Tatebayashi Noodle Grand Prix' in English, held in Gunma Prefecture, which is situated at the centre of the Japanese archipelago approximately 130 kilometres northwest of Tokyo. Unlike the aforementioned B-rank gourmet competitions and similar events, the 'Men-1 Grand Prix' is a very recently developed authentic regional food festival that encapsulates the history, heritage, culture and identity of the regional food production industries associated with wheat flour, soy sauce and udon noodles. This unique regional food festival is not only an important showcase for regional economic redevelopment and regeneration but also plays a vital role in re-affirming regional food industrial heritage and identity. Above all, active collaboration between agriculture, commerce and the food and tourism industries is the centrepiece of this food festival development with the support of regional and local governments and communities (Kim 2015).

As a diverse range of events and festivals can be conceptualised as industrial events, this chapter focuses on a regional noodle grand prix festival rooted in the regional agriculture and food industrial heritage of Tatebayashi, Japan. The chapter helps to address the current paucity of research on how food-themed festivals and events appear to be rare within the context of food heritage in general and food industrial heritage in particular. Thus, it aims to examine and discuss the positive role that the Tatebayashi Men-1 Grand Prix plays in generating active collaboration and alliances amongst various regional industries as well as in (re)constructing and sustaining regional and local traditions and identities.

The importance of innovation and creativity in creating a competitive edge for peripheral regions that have experienced economic decline, such as the city of Tatebayashi, is also discussed. Its positive impacts and subsequent lessons for other cities and regions, particularly many developing countries, which may wish to consider utilising their food (industrial) heritage in order to attract domestic (and international) visitors and as a way of marketing their country, will be presented.

Research methodology and data

The chapter attempts to thematically review and evaluate existing data sources, mainly from two leading Japanese language national daily newspaper archives – the Mainichi newspaper archive, MAISAKU (www.dbs.g-search.or.jp/WMAI/IPCU/WMAI_ipcu_menu.html) and the Yomiuri newspaper archive, YOMIDASU (www.database.yomiuri.co.jp/rekishikan/), which are often used for text mining and analytics. 'Men-1 Grand Prix' was used as a searching keyword during the period 2011–16. Relevant academic journal articles and informal conversations with some local enterprises were also included to provide richer research contexts and thus help to explore the past and current trends and patterns (Jennings 2010).

The data searching generated 21 relevant newspaper articles, which became the base of the research data. Examples and discussions are therefore contextualised within Men-1 Grand Prix-related backgrounds, plans, objectives and strategies, activities and outcomes reported by the above newspaper articles. The following sections will include: (1) the emergence and success of Men-1 Grand Prix; (2) the new food industrial heritage-themed tourism attractions and package tour programme; (3) the promotion of Tatebayashi through new innovative noodle menus and stories; and (4) Menkoi girls as a cultural ambassador of Tatebayashi promoting regional produce.

Emergence and success of the Tatebayashi Men-1 Grand Prix

The city of Tatebayashi in Gunma Prefecture has a long historical and geographical association with wheat flour (the Nisshin Flour Milling Inc.) and soy sauce (the Shoda Shoyu Company) production; excellent conditions for udon noodle production and associated businesses, such as udon noodle eateries (for example, Harada noodle, Hanayama udon shop, Tatebayashi udon shop). Noodle-related small- and medium-sized family enterprises (SMEs) had flourished in this region, until there was a wide-scale economic downturn associated with a significant decline in the region's agriculture and food production industries (Kim 2015). It was inevitable that the region would need to transform itself through socio-economic redevelopment to survive and Tatebayashi decided to capitalise on its food industrial heritage.

While Sanuki udon in Kagawa Prefecture initiated its aggressive tourism campaign and marketing (for example, udon taxi, udon passport, udon map, and souvenir merchandise) at the governmental level (Jones 2011; Kim and Ellis 2015), the campaign in Tatebayashi was relatively small-scale at the local business and community level. It was initiated by the Tatebayashi Udon Society which initially consisted of 47 local noodle SMEs, including udon shops and flour milling factories. Its first campaign started in May 1994, when its motto of 'Udon Heartland Tatebayashi' was enthusiastically established. Banners announcing the city of Men (meaning 'noodle' in Japanese) were hung in the train station and city hall. This also led to the production of the very first udon map, featuring the locations of members' udon shops.

Despite the above initiative, the noodle-related industry in Tatebayashi was in a position where it was extremely difficult to develop alternative activities that would give them a competitive edge. This was because udon noodles in Tatebayashi were not as well recognised nationally, despite their regional fame and recognition, compared to the three most recognised udon noodle regions in Japan, namely Sanuki udon in Kagawa, Inaniwa udon in Akita, and Mizusawa udon in Gunma (Kim and Ellis 2015; Yomiuri Shimbun 2016e).

In 2011, the city of Tatebayashi decided to host a new food festival called Men-1 Grand Prix to enhance its competitiveness against the aforementioned noodle regions. Community-based regional socio-economic redevelopment and regeneration was at the core of this initiative, creating collaboration amongst various stakeholders including the Tatebayashi Udon Society, the Tatebayashi Chamber of Commerce and Industry, the city council of Tatebayashi, Gunma Prefecture, and the local residents of Tatebayashi (Mainichi Shimbun 2016a). The three key objectives of Men-1 Grand Prix are presented as follows:

> The first is to (re)capitalise on the city's udon noodle heritage as a potential tourism attraction and enhance the image of Tatebayashi as "Udon Heartland", which is grounded in both the history and geography of the region. The second is to develop new regional signature noodle dishes through active collaboration between agriculture, commerce, food and tourism industries. The third is to retain and sustain the cultural identity of the region that has a strong historical and geographical association with udon noodle production.
>
> (Kim 2015: 439–440)

The first event was held on the 25th of September 2011 and involved 57 noodle shops (27 Udon shops, 17 Yakisoba shops, nine Ramen shops, three Somen shops, and one Pasta shop). The second Noodle Grand Prix took place on 14 October, 2012. At this second event, there were 55 noodle shops from Gunma (36 shops), Tochigi (14 shops), Ibaraki (one shop), and Saitama (four shops) Prefectures involved. Six noodle shops of national renown were also invited as special guests – Fujinomiya yakisoba (fried noodles sprinkled with small pieces of meat and fish powder) from Fujinomiya City, Shizuoka Prefecture, Toyama Black soy-sauce ramen from Toyama City, Ishikawa Prefecture, Nozawa miso ramen from Aizu city, Fukushima Prefecture, Soki soba from Nago city, Okinawa Prefecture, and Meat Bukkake Udon from Sanuki city, Kagawa Prefecture. Out of 61 noodle dishes, udon noodle dishes were served by 23 shops, followed by fried noodles dishes by 17 shops, ramen by 15 shops, soba by five shops, and pasta by one shop (Men-1 Grand Prix Official Homepage 2016). Alongside these noodle dishes, visitors were able to enjoy live stage performances and a speed-eating contest of Kamatama udon (boiled hot udon noodles topped with a soft boiled egg and soy sauce).

As demonstrated in Table 9.1, the Tatebayashi Men-1 Grand Prix has already become the most important festival in Gunma Prefecture's tourism and events calendar and has steadily increased its visitor numbers every year since 2011, with the

Table 9.1 Summary of Men-1 Grand Prix Performance for 2011–15

Year	Number of event days	Participating noodle shops	Number of visitors
2011	1	57	55000
2012	1	61	60000
2013	2	60	80000
2014*	2	47	65000
2015	2	60	85000

*Note: Day One in 2014 attracted only 10,000 visitors due to rainfall, while 55,000 visited on the second day.

exception of the year 2014, when the visitor numbers dropped due to poor weather conditions on the first day of the festival. The popularity and success of the festival is also confirmed by the fact that what began as a one-day event has, since 2013, become a two-day event, following repeated requests by visitors who stated that one day was not long enough to taste the many different noodles on offer. Both Yomiuri and Mainichi newspapers highlight that the event is the largest national food festival in Japan that is solely focused on noodles (Mainichi Shimbun 2016c; Yomiuri Shimbun 2016b, 2016c), given that approximately 60 noodle shops from all over Japan have participated in this competition every year since 2011. Visitors cast their vote with the chopsticks that they used to eat the noodle dishes.

New food industrial heritage-themed tourist attractions and package tour programme

The city of Tatebayashi and the wider Gunma Prefecture also supported initiatives by two historical regional food companies, Shoda Shoyu (a soy sauce brewing company) and Nisshin Seifun (a flour milling company), to open cultural museums in the Shoda Memorial Museum and Nisshin Milling Museum as new tourism attractions that are themed around soy sauce and wheat flour respectively and that showcase the history and development of the regional food industrial heritage and culture. This initiative is particularly welcomed by Hjalager and Richards (2002), who posit that distinctive local food heritage is increasingly becoming a valuable source of new tourism products with significant potential for promoting regional community development.

As such, the government's aim was to purposely promote the region's food and tourism industries by taking an integral role in the development of new tourism precincts and possibly re-imagined destination attributes, alongside the Men-1 Grand Prix (interview with a regional government officer 2012). Indeed it demonstrates the strong cooperative and collaborative partnerships amongst various stakeholders such as local government and local or regional food production companies. From the perspective of local businesses, the museums provide a showcase for their long-standing desire to preserve their traditions and heritage, and their wish to contribute to the cultural enlightenment of local communities in the name of corporate social responsibility (Nisshin Seifun 2016).

Shoda Shoyu Company has been brewing soy sauce in Tatebayashi since its establishment in 1873. The Shoda family's old shop, originally built in 1853, was renamed the Shoda Memorial Museum and was opened to the public in 2014 (interview with the Shoda Memorial Museum 2016). As shown in Figure 9.1, the Shoda Memorial Museum is only open on weekends and exhibits numerous displays of articles associated with the history of the Shoda family and the company, including the Shoda family tree dating back 300 years, the brewing equipment used at the beginning of its operations, and posters from the 1920s (Shoda Shoyu 2016). Although it offers free admission, it doesn't attract many casual visitors, but focuses on a range of school field trips targeted at different age groups, ranging from primary schools to high schools (interview with the Shoda Memorial Museum 2016).

The Nisshin Milling Museum was opened to the public in November 2012 following the success of the second Men-1 Grand Prix. It charges 200 Japanese yen (about US$2) for admission and is open Tuesdays to Sundays between 10:00 a.m. and 4:30 p.m. The Japan External Trade Organisation (JETRP) promotes it as a new industrial tourist attraction. The Nisshin Milling Museum consists of the main building and new building. The main building introduces the history of Nisshin Seifun over the past 100 years, whereas the new building provides a variety of user-friendly interpretation tools to allow visitors to experience and understand modern milling technology (Nisshin Seifun 2016).

Figure 9.1 Shoda Shoyu uniform in the Meiji period at the Shoda Museum
Source: Photo courtesy of Bokyung Kang

In 2016, the Tobu Travel Company jointly developed a new package tour programme in alliance with Men-1 Grand Prix, Nisshin Milling Museum, Shoda Memorial Museum, Tatebayashi udon shop, and Tobu Railway (TOBUSEN in Japanese). The package tour programme costs 5,800 Japanese yen for adults and 4,800 Japanese yen for concession tickets, and includes a return train ticket on a special express train 'Ryumou Round-trip' from Tokyo Akasaka Station to Gunma Tatebayashi Station, a noodle token worth 900 Japanese yen for the Men-1 Grand Prix festival, adult admission to the Shoda Memorial Museum and the Nisshin Milling Museum, and assorted souvenirs such as a pack of Nisshin dry pasta noodles, a Tatebayashi fresh udon set and a Gunman mascot key holder.

Promoting Tatebayashi through new innovative noodle menus and stories

The Tatebayashi Men-1 Grand Prix ultimately aims to promote innovation and creativity in the development of new noodle menus rooted in regional stories and produce. In 2011, the fourth-generation proprietor of Harada noodle shop, established in 1916 in Itakura, a neighbouring town of Tatebayashi, won the first Grand Prix with a newly invented 'Kyuri hiyashijiru udon', a cold udon noodle coined from a regional tradition in which regional vegetable farmers would often eat chilled cucumber miso soup as a snack whilst on their breaks. In 2016, the Harada noodle shop also invented another cold udon noodle 'Itakurajiru no mori udon' served with cold vegetable soup (See Figure 9.2).

Figure 9.2 Itakurajiru no mori Udon of Harada Udon Shop served in plastic container at 2016 Tatebayashi Men-1 Grand Prix

Source: Photo courtesy of Bokyung Kang

This innovative marriage of basic, humble indigenous regional snacks and fresh Tatebayashi udon noodles immediately became an authentic regional signature udon dish. The Harada noodle shop explained that they could not possibly make such a fresh udon noodle dish without using fresh cucumber grown in Tatebayashi due to their ideal weather conditions for cucumber production (Mainichi Shimbun 2016b). Indeed, 'Kyuri hiyashijiru udon' is made of two key regional products – 100% Tatebayashi-grown wheat flours and fresh Tatebayashi cucumbers (Yomiuri Shimbun 2016a), which is evidence of active collaborative alliances for example, between vegetable grower and udon maker in this case. This success story has led to the generation of at least two positive (promotional) effects for the city of Tatebayashi, that is, it not only re-affirmed its status as 'Udon Heartland Tatebayashi' but also generated awareness of the high quality vegetables produced in Tatebayashi. In fact, Tatebayashi is famous for the high quality of its green vegetables production (for example, cucumbers, leeks, scallions, and spring onions) alongside wheat production.

In 2012, the Harada noodle shop's 'Kyuri hiyashijiru udon' won for the second time in a row. The runner-up was 'Shio Ramen' from Tatebayashi. 'Bunbuku Chagama Curry Tsuke Kamatama udon' by Hanayama Udon came third. The Hanayama Udon was established in 1894, and has a long history of 120 years. This special udon dish was invented by utilising three local signature resources: Tatebayahsi udon noodles, Morinji (a temple associated with the Bunbuku Chagama fairy tale), and soy sauce made by the Shoda Shoyu Company. 'Bunbuku Chagama' (The Wonderful Tea-Kettle in English) is a very famous Japanese fairy tale about a tea-kettle that sprouted a head and tail like a badger or a raccoon dog (*Nyctereutes procyonoides*) and made the tinker who bought it very rich; it was a source of good fortune. Bunbuku in Japanese has two meanings; one is the sound of boiling water and the other is the distribution of fortune. It is said that the raccoon dog turned into an ordinary kettle and was venerated as a precious treasure, and worshipped as a saint at the Morinji temple. Thus, there are 20 raccoon dog statues along the path to the temple. There are also 13 picture cards depicting the story along the road from Morinji railway station to the temple.

The fifth-generation proprietor of Hanayama udon shop in Tatebayashi, who previously came third in the festival in 2012, won the Grand Prix for the best new udon pasta in 2015 (Yomiuri Shimbun 2016g; Mainichi Shimbun 2016d). It is worth noting that the Hanayama udon shop also won the first Japanese national udon championship held in Tokyo in August 2013, which attracted over 1 million visitors (Udon Museum Foundation 2016). Such unusual and innovative noodle dishes and their stories have increased awareness of the Tatebayashi Men-1 Grand Prix amongst a broader and more diverse audience, with the aid of modern media coverage such as online newspapers and Social Networking Sites (SNSs) such as Facebook. Although the impact of media coverage on place marketing and promotion is not within the scope of this chapter, the media play a crucial role in not only shaping tourist motivations and visitation patterns, but also in creating new touristic places (Butler 1990; Urry 1994).

Menkoi girls: the cultural ambassador of Tatebayashi

To celebrate the inaugural Men-1 Grand Prix, a girl band was set up consisting of 14 females from primary school-age through to university students, who were attending a private calligraphy school in Tatebayashi. Participation was voluntary and the band supported local community members. In 2013, the band was named 'Menkoi Girls', which means 'girls loving noodles' in Japanese, and began its official role as the cultural ambassador of Tatebayashi and the Tatebayashi Chamber of Commerce and Industry, promoting Men-1 Grand Prix, Tatebayashi udon noodles and home-grown vegetables (Kanazawa 2016; Yomiuri Shimbun 2016d). In the same year, 'Menkoi Girls' released its debut song and album called 'Cucumber chorus' to allay cucumber growers' concerns about a sharp fall in cucumber prices. Their CD is available from Amazon, as well as at the Men-1 Grand Prix.

It is documented that 'Menkoi Girls' played a crucial role in animating the event among already loyal supporters. The band also collaborated with regional restaurants to perform an elaborate Christmas dinner show and sold all of their 250 tickets costing 10,000 Japanese yen each (Yomiuri Shimbun 2016f). Figure 9.3 shows the 'Menkoi Girls' posing for their fans, Men-1 Grand Prix visitors and the media.

Figure 9.3 Menkoi Girls at Men-1 Grand Prix
Source: Photo courtesy of Bokyung Kang

Discussion and conclusion

Industrial events tend to be broad and inclusive in their coverage as they merge many different events, including exhibitions, trade shows, new product and brand launches, farmers' markets, food and wine festivals and World Expos. The current chapter identifies how food-themed festivals and events appear to be rare within the context of food heritage in general and food industrial heritage in particular. The Tatebayashi Men-1 Grand Prix in Japan is a regional community development and socio-economic regeneration campaign with a specific focus on sustaining its regional food industrial heritage and rejuvenating its stagnant regional economy that is associated with two key historical regional industries, namely agriculture and food production, including noodle eateries and restaurants.

In the context of Men-1 Grand Prix, tradition and modernity or heritage and innovation and creativity, seemingly contradictory terms, are symbiotic. This is supported by the objectives of this industrial event, which were to encourage the participating noodle shops to be innovative and explore hybridity as they developed new noodle dishes, whilst also sustaining and retaining their food heritage. Likewise, local noodle shops incorporated their local and regional stories and resources into new product development. 'Kyuri hiyashijiru udon' of Harada noodle shop, and 'Bunbuku Chagama Curry Tsuke Kamatama udon' and 'udon pasta' of Hanayama udon shop exemplify this.

This is indeed the role industrial events play in shaping future innovations and developments of relevant businesses through the initiative and introduction of new products and knowledge diffusion (Lampel and Meyer 2008). There has also been increased attention given to the role that the creative sectors can play in the transformation of rural and peripheral regions in the context of tourism and event or festival development (Long and Morpeth 2016), which is closely related to the case of Men-1 Grand Prix in Japan. This reflects the fact that the constantly changing cultural and social practices in contemporary Japanese society constitute a threat to traditional food production and consumption (for example, fresh handmade udon noodles made from local produce). It is also affected by constantly modified food market interests and demands (Cheung 2013), which therefore requires an innovative and creative way of reinterpreting regional food industrial heritage and its symbolic meaning. In this regard, the Men-1 Grand Prix initiative, given its popularity and continuity, considers the external threats mentioned above as an opportunity to redevelop the city's image in which tradition and heritage co-exist with innovation and creativity, resulting in the city of Tatebayashi having an advanced competitive edge in an increasingly crowded marketplace of regional food festivals and events.

Furthermore, it is evident that strong cooperative and collaborative actions and alliances between local communities and relevant stakeholders (for example, regional food production companies, travel agencies, local and regional governments, transportation and regional tourist attractions) were the centrepiece of the event, which is essential for such a regional community event given that the objectives of multiple stakeholders are often in conflict, especially in a region where the status of tradition and heritage can create a stubborn mind-set that is very inflexible and extremely suspicious of innovative approaches (Spilková and Fialová 2013). The sincere support of the local community, exemplified by the 'Menkoi Girls', played an important role in cultivating local patriotism and community pride, and educating people about the sustainability of cultural heritage rooted in the region (Kim 2015).

Industrial heritage or industry history sites as value generators in a post-industrial economy, and their transformation into industrial heritage tourism attractions, have been well documented (Fu, Kim and Zhou 2015; Hospers 2002; Jonsen-Verbeke 1999; Kerstetter, Confer and Bricker 1998). The potential for industrial heritage, and the cultural events and/or mega-events associated with it, to be a means of showcasing the city and accelerating the process of urban renewal in post-industrial cities such as Manchester, has been noted (Carlsen and Taylor 2003). Thus, industrial heritage-themed events are not a new phenomenon. However, as mentioned earlier, there has been a paucity of research specifically examining regional food and food industrial heritage, and their associated festivals, in the Asian context. This chapter contributes to filling this gap in the literature.

From a festival or event tourism perspective, the Tatebayashi Men-1 Grand Prix is a hybrid industrial event whose theme is regional food heritage, but that combines local heritage with the modern leisure festival (Ma and Lew 2012). This means that the uniqueness, identity and authenticity of the event is deeply rooted in the region's long historical and geographical association with udon noodle production heritage, whilst being innovative enough to create the liminality generated by unusual new menus, storytelling and voting method, which were fun for the visitors. This is somewhat similar to agricultural industry-related tourism and events that give visitors the opportunity to witness the quality and uniqueness of the food products being produced in the region (Che 2006). Yet, Kim (2015) argues that the Tatebayashi Men-1 Grand Prix is different from many other contemporary food-themed festivals that lack tangible and intangible values that are embedded in the locality due to the introduction of de-contextualised commercial festive products.

Thus, this chapter concludes that regional or local food (industrial) heritage and cultural assets can become a powerful means of creating industrial events, and can thus generate a new sense of place, leading to place making. This is even more promising given that there exists a growing recognition among researchers and practitioners of the increasingly close relationships between traditional food products, intangible heritage and regional or local identities, which are all linked to particular geographic areas and attributes and their specific food production industries (Hashimoto and Telfer 2008). These are all key precursors of successful food-related industrial events.

References

Butler, R. (1990) 'The influence of the media in shaping international tourist patterns', *Tourism Recreation Research*, 15(2), 46–53.
Carlsen, J. and Taylor, A. (2003) 'Mega-events and urban renewal: The case of the Manchester 2002 Commonwealth Games', *Event Management*, 8(1), 15–22.

Che, D. (2006) 'Select Michigan: Local food production, food safety, culinary heritage, and branding in Michigan agritourism', *Tourism Review International*, 9, 349–363.

Cheung, S.C.H. (2013) 'From foodways to intangible heritage: A case study of Chinese culinary resource, retail and recipe in Hong Kong', *International Journal of Heritage Studies*, 19(4), 353–364.

Everett, S. and Aitchison, C. (2008) 'The role of food tourism in sustaining regional identity: A case study of Cornwall, South West England', *Journal of Sustainable Tourism*, 16(2), 150–167.

Fu, Y., Kim, S. and Zhou, T. (2015) 'Staging the "authenticity" of intangible heritage from the production perspective: The case of the craftsmanship museum cluster in Hangzhou, China', *Journal of Tourism and Cultural Change*, 13(4), 285–300.

Hashimoto, A. and Telfer, D.J. (2008) 'From sake to sea urchin: Food and drink festivals and regional identity in Japan', in C.M. Hall and L. Sharples (eds.), *Food and Wine Festivals and Events Around the World* (pp. 249–278), Oxford: Elsevier.

Hjalager, A. and Richards, G. (Eds.). (2002) *Tourism and Gastronomy*, London: Routledge.

Hospers, G. (2002) 'Industrial heritage tourism and regional restructuring in the European Union', *European Planning Studies*, 10(3), 397–404.

Jennings, G. (2010) *Tourism Research*, 2nd edition, Milton, Queensland: Wiley.

Jones, T. (2011) 'The udon economy: Food and tourism in Kagawa Prefecture', *International Christian University (ICU) Comparative Culture*, 43, 29–72.

Jonsen-Verbeke, M. (1999) 'Industrial heritage: A nexus for sustainable tourism development', *Tourism Geographies*, 1(1), 70–85.

Kanazawa, M. (2016) 'Syodo Papomansu: Ongaku to dance wo majie Hirou Menkoi Girls ni Chi-mu meisyou henkou Tatebayashi no machi PR wo kaisi' [Calligraphy performance: 'Menkoi Girls' starting the Tatebayashi PR with dancing and music], *Mainichi Online*, www.dbs.g-search.or.jp/WMAI/IPCU/WMAI_ipcu_menu.html (accessed 10 September 2016).

Kerstetter, D., Confer, J. and Bricker, K. (1998) 'Industrial heritage attractions: Types and tourists', *Journal of Travel & Tourism Marketing*, 7(2), 91–104.

Kim, S. (2015) 'Understanding the historical and geographical contexts of food festival tourism development: The case of the Tatebayashi Noodle Grand Prix in Japan', *Tourism Planning & Development*, 12(4), 433–446.

Kim, S. and Ellis, A. (2015) 'Noodle production and consumption: From agriculture to food tourism in Japan', *Tourism Geographies*, 17(1), 151–167.

Kim, S. and Iwashita, C. (2016) 'Cooking identity and food tourism: The case of Japanese udon noodles', *Tourism Recreation Research*, 41(1), 89–100.

Kushner, B. (2012) *Slurp! A Social and Culinary History of Ramen: Japan's Favorite Noodle Soup*, Leiden: Global Oriental.

Lampel, J. and Meyer, A.D. (2008) 'Field-configuring events as structuring mechanisms: How conferences, ceremonies, and trade shows constitute new technologies, industries, and markets', *Journal of Management Studies*, 45(6), 1025–1035.

Long, C. and Labadi, S. (2010) 'Introduction', in S. Labadi and C. Long (eds.), *Heritage and Globalisation* (pp. 1–16), New York: Routledge.

Long, P. and Morpeth, N.D. (Eds.). (2016) *Tourism and the Creative Industries: Theories, Polices and Practice*, Oxford: Routledge.

Ma, L. and Lew, A.A. (2012) 'Historical and geographical context in festival tourism development', *Journal of Heritage Tourism*, 7(1), 13–31.

Mainichi Shimbun (2016a) 'Men-1 Granpuri Tatebayashi de Raigetsu 25niti, 28niti Gurume Syutten' [Men-1 Grand Prix held on 25 September with 58 noodle restaurants

competing], *Mainichi Online*, www.dbs.g-search.or.jp/WMAI/IPCU/WMAI_ipcu_
menu.html (accessed 14 October 2016).

Mainichi Shimbun (2016b) 'Men-1 Granpuri: Hiyashijiru Udon ga Guranpuri Tatebayashi-
gunma' [Cold miso udon winning the first Men-1 Grand Prix], *Mainichi Online*, www.
dbs.g-search.or.jp/WMAI/IPCU/WMAI_ipcu_menu.html (accessed 14 October 2016).

Mainichi Shimbun (2016c) 'Men-1 Granpuri Tatebayashi de 5,6Nichi Kaisai Tasaina
Menyu, Ken Naigai 60Ten' [Men-1 Grand Prix on 5th and 6th in Tatebayashi with 61
noodle restaurants], *Mainichi Online*, www.dbs.g-search.or.jp/WMAI/IPCU/WMAI_
ipcu_menu.html (accessed 14 October 2016).

Mainichi Shimbun (2016d) 'Men-1 Granpuri Tatebayashi Zyousou yakisoba san I Hou-
monnsya Ouen' [Zyousou yakisoba receiving the third prize at Men-1 Grand Prix with
visitors' support], *Mainichi Online*, www.dbs.g-search.or.jp/WMAI/IPCU/WMAI_
ipcu_menu.html (accessed 14 October 2016).

Mak, A.H.N., Lumbers, M. and Eves, A. (2012) 'Globalisation and food consumption in
tourism', *Annals of Tourism Research*, 39(1), 171–196.

Men-1 Grand Prix Official Homepage (2016) www.t-cci.jp/men1 (accessed 10 September
2016).

Nisshin Seifun (2016) www.nisshin.com/english/environment/ (accessed 10 September
2016).

Okada, T. (1993) *Komugiko no shokubunkashi* [Food Culture History of Flour], Tokyo:
Asakurashoten.

Shoda Shoyu (2016) www.shoda.co.jp/en/index.html (accessed 10 September 2016).

Spilková, J. and Fialová, D. (2013) 'Culinary tourism packages and regional brands in
Czechia', *Tourism Geographies*, 15(2), 177–197.

Tussyadiah, I.P. (2005) 'A gourmet trip: One direction of domestic tourism in Japan', *Tourism Review International*, 9(3), 281–291.

Udon Museum Foundation (2016) www.udon.mu/ (accessed 10 September 2016).

Urry, J. (1994) 'Cultural change and contemporary tourism', *Leisure Studies*, 13,
233–238.

Yomiuri Shimbun (2016a) 'Kanto no 57ten Syuuketu Men-1 Guranpuri Gunma' [Competi-
tion amongst 57 noodle shops in Kanto area], *Yomiuri Online*, www.database.yomiuri.
co.jp/rekishikan/ (accessed 14 October 2016).

Yomiuri Shimbun (2016b) 'Men-1 Granpuri Tatebayashi ni 61Ten ga Syuuketu Gunma' [61
noodle restaurants getting together at the Tatebayashi Men-1 Grand Prix], *Yomiuri
Online*, www.database.yomiuri.co.jp/rekishikan/ (accessed 14 October 2016).

Yomiuri Shimbun (2016c) 'Syoku no Aki Konnyaku Oonabe Men-1 Granpuri Gunma'
[Devil's tongue jelly stew noodle at Men 1 Grand Prix in Gunma in autumn], *Yomiuri
Online*, www.database.yomiuri.co.jp/rekishikan/ (accessed 14 October 2016).

Yomiuri Shimbun (2016d) 'Kaite Odotte Tatebayashi PR: Menkoigirls audition' [Calligra-
phy dance team Menkoi Girls' new member audition], *Yomiuri Online*, www.database.
yomiuri.co.jp/rekishikan/ (accessed 14 October 2016).

Yomiuri Shimbun (2016e) 'Hunsyoku NOW: Udon Tasai Zenkoku he Hassin' [Flour-based
noodle NOW: Variety udon show for all parts of the country], *Yomiuri Online*, www.
database.yomiuri.co.jp/rekishikan/ (accessed 14 October 2016).

Yomiuri Shimbun (2016f) 'Gunma gentei' [Gunma test], *Yomiuri Online*, www.database.
yomiuri.co.jp/rekishikan/ (accessed 14 October 2016).

Yomiuri Shimbun (2016g) 'Jimoto Udon Ten Pasuta V Tatebayasi Men-1 ni 8Man 5000nin
Gunma' [A local udon pasta winning the Men-1 Grand Prix and attracting 85,000 visi-
tors], *Yomiuri Online*, www.database.yomiuri.co.jp/rekishikan/ (accessed 14 October
2016).

10 Saudi food events as multi-purpose products

Emad Monshi

Introduction

In the last 15 years, the number of Saudi food events has grown from zero to 62 ongoing events around the Kingdom (see Table 10.1). Despite the Saudi Commission for Tourism and National Heritage (SCTNH) helping to stage and promote most events from their early days, the commercial aspect of such events outweighs the tourism and social impacts. Saudi Arabia does not have a tourist visa, and most food events' visitors are locals. Therefore, the current goals of staging and growing the number of Saudi food events are to promote local products, businesses and the agriculture industry, and to diversify the national economy away from oil dependency. This chapter shows that 90% of Saudi food events are farmers' markets due to their design, despite being called food festivals.

Event design

Food events may be classified as food festivals if their design includes festivity elements targeting a wide spectrum of potential visitors, or farmers' markets if their main objective is supporting farmers or beekeepers to sell their products to potential buyers. The main idea of festivity is to provide an event's visitors with an out of ordinary time (Falassi 1987). Festivity is associated with fun, to be enjoyed by locals as well as visitors. Nevertheless, 'festivity is a key element to producing better experiences at community festivals and enhanced by increasing attendee participation from that of being a spectator, physically and emotionally involved, to ultimately being collaboratively creative' (Staley 2014: 29). Accordingly, a festivity element is a cornerstone for festivals to celebrate special occasions (Arcodia and Whitford 2006), including harvest seasons of certain agriculture products. A definition of farmers' markets that grasps their core elements is 'recurrent markets at fixed locations where farm products are sold by farmers themselves [. . .] at a true farmers' market some, if not all, of the vendors must be producers who sell their own products' (Brown 2001: 658). While the majority of farmers' markets definitions include five common elements: types and freshness of food, regularity of operation, event location, and determinants of participation (AAF 2015; BCAFM 2011; VFMA 2011), only a few definitions have embraced the festivity element (CFMA 2006; Jolliffe 2008).

Table 10.1 Saudi food events by provinces

No.	Event	No.	Event
Makkah Province (17–1 events)		*Alqassim Province – Cont. (14–3 events)*	
1	Mango festival in Alqunfuthah	36	Qoot festival for packed dates in Alqassim
2	Honey festival in Alardiyat province		
3	Almamool Almakkai Market	37	Grapes festival in Alqassim
4	Figs and berries festival in Taif	38	Ghee and sheep festival
5	Almonds festival in Taif	39	Exhibition of dates and food Alqassim
6	Taif rose festival	40	Alhnaini festival – Onizah
7	Honey festival in Taif	41	Strawberry festival – Albkaryah
8	Taif pomegranate festival	42	Algat date festival*
9	Grape festival in Taif	43	Shagra date festival*
10	Global food festival in Taif	44	Mathnab date festival*
11	Food festival in Masharef	*Eastern Province (5 events)*	
12	International Coffee Week – Jeddah	45	Alahsa festival of palm and dates
13	Taste Week Festival – Jeddah	46	Marketing Alahsa manufacturer dates festival
14	Saudi food, hotels and hospitality exhibition		
		47	Palm trees and dates festival in Aljubail
15	Foodex Saudi		
16	Nakahat – Int. exhibition for tea, coffee and chocolate	48	Alaseda festival (local dish)
		49	Taste Week Festival – Dammam
17	Fruit festival*	*Asir Province (5 events)*	
Riyadh Province (13–1 events)		50	Honey festival in Rijal Almaa
18	Jania festival for palm trees and dates in Riyadh	51	Honey festival in Ahad Almajarda
		52	Sifri Bisha festival (dates)
19	Alkharj date festival	53	Grapes festival in Balgaran
20	Watermelon festival in Riyadh	54	Wheat festival in Balasmeer
21	Watermelon festival in Wadi Aldawasir	*Jazan Province (4 events)*	
22	Watermelon festival in Sajer	55	Alhareed festival (fish)
23	Dairy festival in Alkharj	56	Mango and tropical fruits festival
24	Global cuisine festival	57	Honey festival – Aledabi
25	Taste Week Festival – Riyadh	58	Coffee beans festival
26	Singaporean food festival in Riyadh	*Aljouf Province (3 events)*	
27	Int. coffee and chocolate exhibition	59	Olive festival in Aljouf
28	Food Festival	60	Aljouf dates festival
29	Food and handicraft festival	61	Ghee and honey festival
30	Almajma'a date festival*	*Albaha Province (3 events)*	
Alqassim Province (14–3 events)		62	International honey festival – Albaha
31	Buraidah date festival	63	Pomegranate festival – Alqura
32	Onizah date festival	64	Banana and Kadi festival – Almekhwa
33	Riyadh Alkhabra date festival	*Almadinah Province (5–2 events)*	
34	Albkairia date festival	65	Saudi taste festival
35	Kulaijah festival in Buraidah		

No.	Event	No.	Event
Almadinah Province – Cont. (5–2 events)		*Najran Province – Cont. (2 events)*	
66	Dates festival in Alola	71	Bees and beekeepers festival
67	Citrus festival in Alola	*Hail Province (3–2 event)*	
68	Alais dates festival*	72	Kulaijah festival in Hail
69	Almadinah Almonorah dates and food industries festival*	73	Dates and grapes festival*
		74	Hail tourism and agriculture festival*
Najran Province (2 events)		*Tabouk Province (1 event)*	
70	Najran national festival for citrus and agriculture investment	75	Fruit and roses festival
		Northern Borders Province (0 event)	

Source: adapted from (Monshi and Scott 2017)
* Events that do not exist anymore.

Based on definitions of event design (Brown 2010; Getz 2012), less than 10% of Saudi food events may be characterised as truly food festivals (a subset of festival and cultural celebrations), while the rest are farmers' markets (a subset of industrial events). These food events send mixed signals by labelling themselves as festivals, while failing to include festivity elements in their event design. Most Saudi food events ignore the importance of event design principles, through the following problems. First, they select or build venues that do not match the scale of their events. Second, they disperse their visitors' focus by including unrelated side events to their main themes. Third, they stage events at city centres far away from the agricultural or natural environment. Fourth, they schedule long formal activities at the beginning of their events (Alfifi 2010; Alobaid 2016; ArabNews 2012; WAS 2011). These conclusions were based on analysing thousands of Arabic newspaper articles, videos and images on Facebook, Twitter, Instagram, Youtube and Snapchat, for the last five years (2013–17). The analysis depends on detecting festivity elements on main and side events at Saudi food events. Therefore, farmers' markets are playing four non-tourism roles, while food festivals with festivity elements have the potential of attracting local visitors and one-day travellers, as well as tourists.

Purposes of Saudi food events

The Kingdom of Saudi Arabia is one of the hidden or least explored tourism destinations from around the world. Developing food events helps enhance destination appeal through achieving five main objectives: changing the Kingdom's image, enhancing local communities' pride and government organisations' roles, increasing channels of outlets, and for the few well-designed events, attracting tourists is the fifth purpose.

Changing the Kingdom's image

The Kingdom is well-known for hosting the holy mosque in Makkah, and the huge crude oil reserves in its Eastern Province. Due to many factors, such as having no strategy to attract foreign tourists (including no tourist visa), the image of Saudi Arabia as a tourism destination is simply a country blessed with gold oil reserves that lie underneath yellow sands. However, the tourism industry in general and food events in particular are image changers. With 62 annual food events being staged at 12 out of 13 Saudi provinces (Table 10.1), the Kingdom is flourishing with a wide spectrum of colours generated by 13 different groups of food events (see Table 10.2). Giving destinations a colourful image is a common practice, as Rotterdam has used events to replace a harbour-city image with a colourful cultural and leisure city image (Richards and Palmer 2010), and rural towns in North America proclaim themselves as the capital of certain food types to attract visitors (Hall and Gossling 2016). However, as the majority of Saudi food events attract local visitors and national media coverage, they do not qualify as major events. Therefore, the role they play in changing provinces' and the Kingdom's image is limited. Such events can send clear messages to local and regional media that Saudi Arabia is a large garden with many fruit baskets, rather than a predominantly arid desert.

Based on Saudi's topography and local communities' expertise, different products are nurtured, harvested, packed in suitable packaging and finally motivate organisers to stage food events. A few regions, provinces and cities are successful in positioning themselves based on their food events: the Southern Region (Asir, Albaha and Jazan Provinces) for honey, Alqassim province as the capital of dates in the region, Riyadh Province as the watermelon destination, Aljouf Province for olives, Tabuok Province for fruits, and Taif city for roses (see Table 10.1). Such branding is achieved by staging several events for the same products in one certain geographical location and/or due to the selection of reflective logos for SCTNH branches for each province. As unique cultural identities of destinations with food production capabilities are usually rooted in agriculture (Everett and Aitchison 2008; Kim 2016; Ma and Lew 2012), staging food events can support branding of destinations as food tourism. However, this concentration of similar events at one location may come with a price. For date events, competition is a challenge as there are 19 different date events around the Kingdom, especially the ones staged in Alqassim province. This province, in particular, has eight ongoing date events and three other date events that failed to keep going, most likely due to high competition. To overcome such challenges, the Buraidah Date Festival developed its event design by increasing the area of its main event, adding several side events related to dates and local culture, focused on traditional marketing as well as social media (for example, using local and regional celebrities to send live snapchat videos) and operating the festival with local volunteers to enrich visitors' and tourists' experiences.

Enhancing local communities' pride

Staging successful and popular food events gave Saudi citizens in each province a pride at national and regional levels. Citizens from Alqassim Province, for example, are proud of being farmers and producers of dates, and that their province is

Table 10.2 Saudi food events by products

19 Date Events

Buraidah date festival	Alkharj date festival	Sifri Bisha festival (dates)	Onizah date festival
Riyadh Alkhabra date festival	Albkairia date festival	Alhnaini festival – Onizah	Alahsa festival of palm and dates
Palm trees and dates festival in Aljubail	Aljouf dates festival	Dates festival in Alola	Kulaijah festival in Buraidah
Alaseda festival	Qoot festival for packed dates in Alqassim	Kulaijah festival in Hail	Marketing Alahsa manufacturer dates festival
Almamool Almakkai Market	Exhibition of dates and food Alqassim	Jania festival for palm trees and dates in Riyadh	

8 Honey Events

Honey festival in Rijal Almaa	Honey festival in Alardiyat province	Honey festival in Ahad Almajarda	Bees and beekeeper's festival
Honey festival	International honey festival	Honey festival in Taif	Ghee and honey festival*

8 Taste Events

Global cuisine festival	Taste Week Festival (3 cities)	Saudi taste festival	Global food festival in Taif
Foodex Saudi	Saudi food, hotels and hospitality exhibition	Tea, coffee and chocolate exhibition	Singaporean food festival in Riyadh

5 Fruit and Roses Events

Figs and berries festival in Taif	Taif rose festival	Banana and Kadi festival	Fruit and roses festival
Mango and tropical fruits festival*			

3 Grapes Events / **3 Watermelon Events** / **3 Coffee Events**

Grapes festival in Balgaran	Grape festival in Taif	Watermelon festival in Riyadh	Watermelon festival in Sajer	Coffee beans festival	Int. coffee and chocolate exhibition
Grapes festival in Alqassim		Watermelon festival in Wadi Aldawasir		International Coffee Week	

2 Citrus Events / **2 Mango Events**

Najran national festival for citrus and agriculture investment	Citrus festival in Alola	Mango festival in Alqunfuthah	Mango and tropical fruits festival

2 Pomegranate Events / **2 Ghee Events**

Taif pomegranate festival	Pomegranate festival	Ghee and honey festival*	Ghee and sheep festival

2 Food Events

Food festival (2 cities)	Food and handicraft festival

6 Single Products Events (no common products)

Wheat festival in Balasmeer	Almonds festival in Taif	Alhareed festival (fish)	Olive festival in Aljouf	Dairy festival in Alkharj	Strawberry festival

* An event placed at two different groups.

the capital of date festivals in the Gulf Corporation Council (GCC) region. Benckendorff and Pearce (2012) used Maslow's (1954) hierarchy of needs to identify the basic physiological needs motivating visitors to attend events; such needs motivate organisers as well to stage food events. Staging events associated with Islamic culture and local agriculture-identity can satisfy organisers' top three layers of Maslow's (1954) psychology theory: love/belonging, esteem and self-actualization. Pride and psychological needs are associated with certain types of food rooted in Islamic culture.

Dates of palm trees were mentioned more than any other fruits in the Holy Quran, and references of the palm tree are found in chapters Maryam, Qaf, Alshuara and Alnahl of the Holy Quran. In chapter Maryam (verse 25), God provided Maryam, Prophet Isa's mother, with fresh dates when she was experiencing discomfort and pain during the final stages of her pregnancy, as God said: 'Shake the trunk of the palm toward you and fresh, ripe dates will drop down onto you'. In Hadiths narrated by the companions of Prophet Mohammed, dates were linked as a symbol with Islam, Muslims and as one of the blessings that would be offered in Paradise. In the statement narrated by Ibn Umar: 'The Prophet said there is a tree among the trees which is similar to a Muslim [in goodness], and that is the date palm tree' (AlBukhari 2010), and in another Hadith, the Messenger said: "Ajwah dates are from heaven and it cures from magic' (Ben Hanbal 2008). Ajwah is one of the exceptional varieties of dates grown in Almadinah province. Ironically, there are no date events in Almadinah city, where the closest date event has just returned in 2017 after interruption and was staged 300 kilometres to the north as the Dates Festival in Alola.

The Prophet stressed the significance of dates as a source of nutrition and sustenance in several Hadiths. The Prophet taught his disciples that the date is an antidote to poison and an effective defence against black magic: 'Whoever eats seven dates of Ajwah in the morning will not be hurt by poison or sorcery on that day' (AlBukhari 2010). The Prophet said: 'If you break your fast, break it with dates, if you don't have it, break it with water as it is purifying' (Abu Dawood 2009). On the basis of these Hadiths, Muslims insist on breaking their fasts with dates throughout the month of Ramadan. Nevertheless, dates are a common ingredient in the Muslim diet as the Prophet said: 'People in a house without dates are in a state of hunger' (Abu Dawood 2009).

From historical and political points of view, dates and dairy products are part of the Saudi national food security. During the political tension between the Kingdom and Western countries and the oil-embargo in the 1970s, former King Faisal bin Abdulaziz was proud to be a Bedouin, who used to live in tents with only dates and water for food. Long before that, the Kingdom choose to use the figure of a palm tree as part of its national symbol (two crossing swords protecting one palm tree in the middle), which has been adapted by the Saudi Vision 2030, the SCTNH and General Authority for Entertainment. To support palm trees, the Ministry of Agriculture and Water legislated protective policies, and research centres at Saudi universities developed scientific research. Therefore, association with the prophetic foods or national security represents a major role for Saudi food events as they give their organisers great pride.

Enlighten government organisations' roles

After its establishment in 2000, the SCTNH started speeding up prospecting and maintaining archaeological and heritage sites, acquiring the responsibility of the hotel sector and supporting the development of the event tourism sector. While archaeology, heritage and hotel sectors take a long time for a society to reap their fruits, events tourism is to some extent easier to develop, represents an important motivator for the tourism industry (Getz and Page 2016) and attract, significant media attention. As part of their design, major Saudi event tourism usually attracts provinces' governors, the president of the SCTNH or representatives of them to the ribbon-cutting ceremony. In addition, food events attract farmers, employees and volunteers, potential buyers as visitors, government officials and media reporters, which enhance the image of all involved stakeholders. This political side of event tourism is extremely important to attract local communities' support and financial and non-financial government support, which sustains the financial and social sustainability objectives of these events (Richards and Palmer 2010).

Opening ceremonies are important elements in designing all types of events. In comparison with business and sport events, festivals usually have smaller opening ceremonies. Food festivals usually avoid large ceremonies as they are staged at outdoor locations, which are not suitable to host large formal ceremonies. While Alhareed festival's core values are to celebrate the fishing season for parrotfish (the why of an event is being staged?), targeting local community (who is an event being staged for?), to compete in fishing (what will happen at an event?), and to highlight a certain environmental phenomena and fishing culture in a festivity atmosphere (what an event designer wants and how to achieve it?), the actual event design invests annually in the opening ceremony and its fancy temporary settings (Alfifi 2010; WAS 2011). Such a ceremony does not meet the event's core values and design principles requirements, leading the media to focus on the ceremony more by using headlines such as *The Bullet of the Governer's of Jazan Province Announcing the Start of Alhareed Festival* (Alfifi 2010; WAS 2011). All event aspects should be related to the event design core values to maximise an event audience's engagement (Getz and Page 2016) and let them leave the event with clear images related to the phenomena. Therefore, while opening ceremonies at Saudi food events are important to attract attention and support of several stakeholders, many of them reduce the events' design quality and profitability margins, and divert media attention.

Increasing numbers of outlets

Before the development of the Olive Festival in Aljouf, farmers of olives and manufacturers of related products depended heavily on traditional retail outlets in Aljouf province to sell their harvest. They faced challenges in crossing their province borders and the Saudi borders to export their products to national, regional and global markets. Food events not only provided farmers with new outlet channels, but also better ones as events attracted government officials and a large number of visitors over a short period of time at the beginning or during harvest seasons. Food events help reduce storage costs, renting costs, transportation costs, insurance costs and exporting costs, which allowed farmers and food manufacturers to reduce overall costs, and consumers to buy fresh products. Nevertheless, by placing all the harvest of one agricultural product and related products at one location, the level of competitions was raised, quality was highlighted and improved, and eventually customers' needs were satisfied. In addition to traditional food events, some organisers such as the Jizan Mango Festival and Onizah Date Festival invented online systems to export their products across their host provinces and across the Saudi borders.

Buraidah Date Festival, for example, grew the size of its main event – the auction site (ArabNews 2012; Alobaid 2016) to maximise its commercial capacity. From an agriculture perspective, the festival motivated Alqassim farmers to import Ajwah date seeds from Almadinah province, implant them in Buraidah, harvest their dates and sell them at the festival to add a new outlet. From a marketing perspective, the festival developed a short high quality promotional video, launched an Arabic hashtag on social media translated 'our dates are gold', and a 360° online viewing experience to attract visitors and tourists. From a human resources perspective, the festival is operated by local Saudi citizens from Alqassim province and creates more than 3,000 jobs/year, which maintains its unique local heritage related to dates and makes it a tourism attraction. All these initiatives helped the festival in reaching a new sales record of about SR 2.4 billion in 2016, attracting local, regional and global media attention, and regional tourists from other Saudi provinces and GCC countries, and eventually maximised its economic, social and environmental impacts. Other innovations developed by Saudi food events include implementing a health committee (the Olive Festival in Aljouf and Onizah Dates Festival) to raise the quality of exhibited produce and food products and to price quality products and/or exclude poor quality products that do not meet certain standards. Other events developed attractive websites (Roses and Fruits Festival in Tabouk), or an integrated social media marketing strategy (Foodex Saudi) and motivated the establishment of a factory to help in packing and storing the tons of dates being harvested every year in Asir province (Sifri Bisha Festival).

Attracting tourists

By analysing Saudi food event designs, 90% of the events represent platforms to sell food products to potential buyers, and 10% implemented festivity elements to attract visitors and tourists. Farmers' markets used most of their floor plans as open markets, while festivals included entertainment, recreational and educational areas. While farmers' markets locations are suitable for farmers and manufacturers to exchange goods and money with consumers, festivals' venues are more attractive to visitors as well as tourists. Festivals were successful in attracting local residents, visitors and tourists, who were visiting events for their festivity atmospheres and social interactions. They enable farmers to display their harvest tools and traditional and modern agriculture techniques, food manufacturers to show their manufacturing processes, and/or local chefs to demonstrate their cooking recipes. Festivals' core values are smartly activated to add value for their visitors and tourists to enrich their experiences. As implementing festivity elements outside main venues are common practices by organisers (Chalip 2006), Buraidah Date Festival developed many side events that match the main theme of the festival including the Palms Shadows Festival (educational and entertainment event), a night carnival for families and children, 36 date auctions (business and entertainment events) and a photography competition for professional photographers (competitive event). Including Buraidah Date Festival, as the best food festival in the Kingdom, Taif Rose Festival and Strawberry Festival are two other clear examples of the importance of food festivals over farmers' markets.

In comparison to farmers' markets, food festivals bring money from outside their host destination by increasing the demand on the transportation industry, increasing occupancy rates at hospitality operations and demand on all services and products offered by the retail industry including souvenirs. Nevertheless, destinations that brand themselves using food tourism events can attract food tourists all year round (Taylor and Kneafsey 2016). Therefore, food festivals support their host destinations to have a culinary image (role number 1), enhance residents' pride (role number 2), support government organisations' roles (role number 3), increase the number of outlets (role number 4) and attract visitors and tourists (role number 5). Understanding the appropriate event classification can help in predicting their potential economic, social and environmental impacts, future development and future existence. Nevertheless, it can support event evaluation and understanding factors that led to the closures of 13 Saudi food events.

Conclusion and recommendations

While Buraidah Date Festival and five other food festivals include festivity elements and platforms to sell agricultural products, the other 56 Saudi food events are farmers' markets despite being labelled as festivals. Farmers' markets support farmers, the agriculture industry and/or local communities rather than attracting visitors and tourists. Food festivals can attract more visitors, higher revenues for farmers, better funding and sponsorship deals, and therefore offer better chances to survive competition and other challenges. Festivals have stronger positive impacts on host destination image, and are more sustainable in terms of economic impacts, social impacts and environmental impact. Festivals provide organisers with suitable platforms to add events and activities that increase food products sales, engage local communities and support environmental projects. Nevertheless, food festivals can advance the Kingdom's rank on the Travel and Tourism Competitiveness Index (Saudi Arabia ranked 64th) by playing a major role in overcoming regional competition (United Arab Emirates ranked 24th and Qatar ranked 43rd) (World Economic Forum 2015).

Despite including festivity elements, some festivals can only attract one-day-trip visitors from other provinces as they are staged at remote destinations with limited accommodations opportunities (Strawberry Festival and Grape Festival).

Nevertheless, most food events have no clear linkages with other tourism attractions and poor collaborations with other event organisers, tourism operators and entertainment organisations, which increase their challenges in attracting visitors and tourists. Transforming farmers' markets into food festivals to attract a wide spectrum of visitors and tourists requires the inclusion of festivity elements (for example, fruit harvest, honey making, food processing, entertainment and/or educational events) that match the main event's theme. Nevertheless, conducting market orientation, choosing suitable venues and developing innovations helps in satisfying visitors and tourists needs, meeting their expectations and gaining their loyalty. Investigating success factors of ongoing events and failure factors of fading events are also important actions to develop existing events and Saudi Arabia as an emerging tourism destination. Collaborations between major government organisations and research centres including the Ministry of Environment, Water and Agriculture, Saudi Commission for Tourism and National Heritage (SCTNH), General Authority for Entertainment and the Tourism Information and Research Centre are essential to achieve micro and macro objectives.

References

Abu Dawood, S.i.A. (2009) *Sunan Abi Dawood*, Damascus, Syria: Alresalah Alalmiah.

Alberta Agriculture and Forestry (AAF) (2015) 'Alberta approved farmers' market program guidelines', www1.agric.gov.ab.ca/$department/deptdocs.nsf/all/apa2577 (accessed 12 December 2016).

AlBukhari, M.I. (2010) *Sahih AlBukhari*, Cairo, Egypt: Dar Bin Hazm.

Alfifi, S. (2010) 'Governor of Jazan participates with Farasan people in Alhareed fishing', *Fifa*, 9 April, www.faifaonline.net/faifa/news-action-show-id-5093.htm (accessed 10 November 2016).

Alobaid, A. (2016) 'KSA: $61 Million Revenues of Buraidah Dates Festival', *Asharq Al-Awsat*, 19 August, www.english.aawsat.com/2016/08/article55356736/ksa-61-million-revenues-buraidah-dates-festival (accessed 10 January 2017).

ArabNews. (2012) 'World's largest dates festival opens in Buraidah', *Arab News*, 3 September, www.arabnews.com/world%E2%80%99s-largest-dates-festival-opens-buraidah (accessed 10 January 2017).

Arcodia, C. and Whitford, M. (2006) 'Festival attendance and the development of social capital', *Journal of Convention and Event Tourism*, 8(2), 1–18.

BC Association of Farmers' Markets (BCAFM) (2011) 'About the BCAFM', www.bcfarmersmarket.org/about-bcfma (accessed 12 December 2016).

Benckendorff, P. and Pearce, P. (2012) 'The psychology of events', in S. Page and J. Connell (eds.), *Routledge Handbook of Events* (pp. 165–185), London: Routledge.

Ben Hanbal, A. (2008) *Almusnad*, Beruit, Lebanon: Dar Alkotob Alilmiyah.

Brown, A. (2001) 'Counting farmers markets', *Geographical Review*, 91, 655–674.

Brown, S. (2010) *Event Design: Creating and Staging the Event Experience* (vol. 2), Adelaide: Visible Management.

California Farmers' Market Association (CFMA) (2006) *California Farmers' Market Association Roles and Regulations for Certified Farmers' Markets*, Walnut Creek, USA: California Farmers' Market Association.

Chalip, L. (2006) 'Towards social leverage of sport events', *Journal of Sport and Tourism*, 11(2), 109–127.

Everett, S. and Aitchison, C. (2008) 'The role of food tourism in sustaining regional identity: A case study of Cornwall, South West England', *Journal of Sustainable Tourism*, 16(2), 150–167.

Falassi, A. (1987) *Time Out of Time: Essays on the Festival*, Albuquerque: University of New Mexico Press.

Getz, D. (2012) *Event Studies: Theory, Research and Policy for Planned Events*, New York: Routledge.

Getz, D. and Page, S.J. (2016) 'Progress and prospects for event tourism research', *Tourism Management*, 52, 593–631.

Hall, C.M. and Gossling, S. (2016) 'From food tourism and regional development to food, tourism and regional development', in C.M. Hall and S. Gossling (eds.), *Food Tourism and Regional Development: Networks, Products and Trajectories* (pp. 3–57), New York: Routledge.

Jolliffe, L. (2008) 'Connecting farmers' markets and tourists in New Brunswick, Canada', in C. M. Hall and L. Sharples (eds.), *Food and Wine Festivals and Events Around the World* (pp. 232–248), Oxford, UK: Elsevier.

Kim, S. (2016) 'Regional development and Japanese obsession with noodles: The udon noodle tourism phenomenon in Japan', in C.M. Hall and S. Gossling (eds.), *Food Tourism and Regional Development: Networks, Products and Trajectories* (pp. 135–144), New York: Routledge.

Ma, L. and Lew, A.A. (2012) 'Historical and geographical context in festival tourism development', *Journal of Heritage Tourism*, 7(1), 13–31.

Maslow, A. (1954) *Motivation and Personality*, New York: Harper and Row.

Monshi, E. and Scott, N. (2017) 'Developing event tourism in Saudi Arabia: Opportunities and challenges', in H. Almahrazi, A. Hafidth and N. Scott (eds.), *Tourism in the Arab World: An Industry Perspective* (pp. 33–55), Bristol: Channel View.

Richards, G. and Palmer, R. (2010) *Eventful Cities: Cultural Management and Urban Revitalisation*, Oxford: Butterworth-Heinemann.

Staley, E. (2014) *Musical Festival Management: An Exploration of Sustainable Events and Business Models*, (Master Degree), American University, Washington, DC.

Taylor, E. and Kneafsey, M. (2016) 'Food tourism and place identity in the development of Jamaica's rural culture economy', in C.M. Hall and S. Gossling (eds.), *Food Tourism and Regional Development: Networks, Products and Trajectories* (pp. 177–189), New York: Routledge.

Victorian Farmers' Market Association (VFMA) (2011) 'Victorian farmers' market association', www.vfma.org.au/Main/About (accessed 12 December 2016).

WAS (2011) 'Jazan governor launches development projects worth of SR170 million in Farasan', *Aleqtisadiah*, 28 April, www.aleqt.com/2011/04/28/article_532189.html (accessed 11 January 2017).

World Economic Forum (2015) *The Travel and Tourism Competitiveness Report*, www3.weforum.org/docs/TT15/WEF_Global_Travel&Tourism_Report_2015.pdf (accessed 17 May 2017).

11 Craft beer festivals

The craft brewers' experience of getting beer to market in the USA and UK

Alison Dunn and Gerry Kregor

Introduction

Miller (2011) argues that beer has played a key role in social-cultural celebrations and events since ancient times. He highlights the role of beer in, for example, ancient Egyptian rituals and in Scandinavian folklore. The origins of the world's largest beer festival, Oktoberfest are more recent. A successful community celebration of a royal wedding in 1810 became an annual festival which now hosts over six million visitors in September in Munich (Cann 2015).

Beer has, over the centuries, grown from a local product that underpinned social and cultural events to a mass-produced commodity controlled by a small number of international conglomerates. These conglomerates exerted such control of the beer market, it led Porter (1980) to predict that the drive towards greater consolidation could not be challenged (Carroll and Swaminathan 2000). Porter (1980) did not foresee the rise of the craft beer movement which reversed the decline in the number of breweries across much of the world.

Drawing on interviews with craft brewers from the West Coast of the USA and from the UK, this chapter analyses how craft brewers have used festivals as a component of a three-part business strategy to circumvent barriers to distribution and to build brand awareness.

Reaction to consolidation

The website of the US Brewers Association – the 'passionate voice for craft brewers' (Brewers Association 2016) – includes statistics on the history of beer production in that country since 1873. The statistics reveal a history of sustained concentration and industrialisation of beer manufacturers throughout the 20th century, with the number of breweries in the USA falling from 4131 in 1873 to 110 in 1985, as large brewers acquired and merged with competitors (Warner 2010). An additional feature of brewery consolidation was the creation of international beer brands and their collection into marketing-driven multinational conglomerates.

Carroll and Swaminathan (2000) contend that resource partitioning theory suggests that industries that consolidate allow space at the margins for small-scale specialist producers to emerge. In the USA, the UK and Australia (among others), consolidation in the beer industry ensured the market was dominated by mass-produced and mass-marketed bland beers (Bockway 2013). In the USA the growth in demand for imported beers, which were regarded as having more flavour than leading US brands, was the first indicator that some consumers were seeking alternatives to the brand leaders (Nelson 2005). Home-brewing, legalised in the USA in 1978, exploded as an alternative to commercial offerings (Ogle 2006). Home-brewing, many argue, led to brewing on a small commercial scale, first known as micro-brewing, then craft brewing (Elzinga, Horton Tremblay and Tremblay 2015). The Brewers Association statistics demonstrate that from 1986 the declining trend in US brewery numbers was overturned. The number of independent breweries started to escalate – from 124 in 1986 to 4269 by 2015 (Brewers Association 2016) – as craft breweries emerged.

In the UK, the move away from local beers towards global brands, prompted the rise of an alternative beer segment, that of cask-conditioned Real Ale. Special interest associations emerged to support the burgeoning segment, such as the consumer organisation the Campaign for Real Ale (CAMRA). Discontent with the quality of mass-produced beer is exemplified by the opening paragraph of the History of CAMRA on the organisation's website:

> CAMRA was formed in March 1971 by four men from the north-west who were disillusioned by the domination of the UK beer market by a handful of companies pushing products of low flavour and overall quality onto the consumer.
>
> (CAMRA 2016)

The Real Ale Brewers in the UK and the craft brewers in the USA, Canada, Australia and elsewhere faced barriers to get their beer to market. The mega-brewers had crowded out the market with massive production, control of distribution networks, domination of retail shelf-space and international mass advertising. The new small-scale brewers found it difficult to secure distributors and access retail shelf-space and even faced obstacles to communicating with consumers that their beer existed (Dunn and Wickham 2016). The small-scale and local reach of craft brewers meant they had to develop alternative strategies to get their beer to market. Three main strategies were adopted. First, if they faced barriers in getting their beer to consumers they invited the consumers to their beer. Brewery tours and tasting rooms attracted consumers looking for beer with flavour where they could sample beers at their freshest and meet the people who made it. The second technique involved taking beers to festivals, markets and community events. This technique built brand awareness as large numbers of consumers were reached in one area at the same time. The third tactic was to build a craft beer culture, largely through social media, to encourage loyalty amongst consumers by making them feel that they were part of something special (Dunn and Kregor 2014).

In order to showcase real ale to consumers, CAMRA established the forerunner to the Great British Beer Festival (GBBF) in 1975, the name GBBF being coined in 1977 (de Castella 2007). CAMRA currently runs 260 annual regional competitions that feed into the GBBF (CAMRA 2016). In the USA, the Brewers Association emulated the GBBF and established the Great American Beer Festival (GABF) in 1982. 'Great' craft beer festivals have proliferated around the world. The Great Canadian Beer Festival and the Great Japan Beer Festival are annual events as are the Great Kiwi and the Great Australian Beer Festivals. As craft beer festivals have formed a major aspect of craft brewery business strategies, craft brewers were interviewed to explore their experiences with festival participation.

Method

Data for this chapter were drawn from in-depth interviews with craft brewers to explore their supply-side perspective on experiences of building brand awareness and distribution channels for their beer. Interviews were conducted in the USA in California in 2010 and Washington and Oregon in 2014 and in the UK, specifically, North Yorkshire and Scotland in 2012 (Figures 11.1 and 11.2). An exploratory approach was adopted to investigate how and why craft brewers use festival participation to build brand awareness and get their beer to market. Alonso and Liu (2010) recommend an exploratory approach for topics that have received limited research interrogation. Charters and Menival (2011) advocated the use of semi-structured interviews to ensure a degree of continuity between subjects and to offer flexibility to allow additional ideas to be collected.

Figure 11.1 National festivals such as the Great American Beer Festival attract hundreds of brewers and thousands of visitors

Source: Photo courtesy of Brewers Association

Figure 11.2 Beer festivals allow attendees to meet the brewer and learn more about their product

Source: Photo courtesy of William Murphy CC BY-SA 2.0

In total 22 semi-structured interviews with owners or managers of craft brewer-ies were conducted; seven in California, nine in the UK and six in Oregon and Washington. Each study location contained large numbers of breweries which were filtered by the use of three study criteria:

1   the brewery was a craft brewery (as defined by the Brewers Association or CAMRA)
2   the brewery attracted visitors, and
3   the brewery was accessible to the researchers during the study period.

A profile of the 22 participating breweries is presented in Table 11.1.

Two main themes emerged from the interviews, one on festival participation and the other on the related topic of craft beer competitions. These two themes will structure the discussion of the results of the interviews, with an exploration of the benefits and shortcomings of participation in both.

Breweries in the study

Table 11.1 outlines the size and location of each brewery and allocates a code number that will be used to attribute quotes to the individual brewer, to satisfy confidentiality requirements. Each brewer is sequentially numbered (B1-B22) and

Table 11.1 Participating brewery profile

Brewer No.	Location	Date Opened	Capacity	Staff	Tourism Facilities
B1C	Los Angeles	Feb 2010	12 Barrel	3 family + 1	Tasting Bar; Tours; Events
B2C	San Diego	1996	50 Barrel	> 40	Tasting Bar; Tours; Events
B3C	San Diego	July 2010	1.5 Barrel	Owner + 1	Tasting Bar; Tours
B4C	San Diego	1996	2 x 120 Barrel	< 340	Tasting Bar; Tours; Events; Garden; Restaurant
B5C	San Diego	May 2006	n/a	28	Tasting Bar; Tours
B6C	San Diego	2002	12 Barrel	2 Brewery; 18 Restaurant	Tasting bar; Bar; Restaurant
B7C	Central California	1996	60 Barrel	< 40	Tasting Bar; Tours, Events
B8Y	North Yorkshire	Sept 2003	5 Barrel	3	Tasting Bar; Tours; Event brewing
B9Y	North Yorkshire	1984	n/a	n/a	Bar; Tours
B10Y	North Yorkshire	1991	30,000 Barrel/pa	9	Tasting Bar; Tours
B11S	Scotland	1996	Visitor centre 5 Barrel. Brewery 20 Barrel	3	Visitor Centre, tours, events
B12S	Scotland	1997	20 Barrel	Small team	Small Tours; Shop
B13S	Scotland	2007	36,500 Hectolitres pa	Brewery 45 Retail 100	Tours
B14S	Scotland	1997	120 Barrel	13	Tasting Bar; Tours
B15S	Scotland	2003	10 Barrel	0	Tours
B16S	Scotland	2005	10 Barrel	2 Partners + 1	Tours; Events
B17W	Seattle	Oct 2013	1 Barrel	Owner + 1 part-time	Tasting Bar; Tours
B18W	Seattle	Jan 2013	10 Barrel	2 partners + 2 sales/bar	Tasting Bar; Tours; Events
B19W	Seattle	Nov 2007	35–40 Barrel/day	Owner + 16	Tasting Bar; Tours
B20O	Portland	1993	4 Barrel	Owner + 1 brewing, 16 sales/bar	Restaurant
B21O	Portland	April 2012	15 Barrel	2 partners + 4 brewing, 2 sales/bar	Tasting Bar; Tours
B22O	Portland	May 2010	Brewpub 3.5 Bar. Brewery 30 Barrel	35 in total	Brewpub & Tasting Bar

their location identified with a suffix; C for California, Y for Yorkshire, S for Scotland, W for Washington and O for Oregon.

Craft beer festivals as marketing

All the brewers interviewed demonstrated a reluctance to pay commercial media for advertising. Word-of-mouth marketing was favoured across the three locations and timeframes. Many brewers hinted that they expected the 'beer to do the talking' (B6C). By that they meant that their consumers would taste and like the beer that had been brewed to the best of the brewers' ability, then spread the word to their friends directly or via social media which was referred to by a Californian brewer 'as word of mouth on steroids' (B2C). Brewers in the UK also preferred word-of-mouth marketing to advertising. One brewer commented 'our main technique is word of mouth. We do not advertise locally. We don't do anything to promote the business which is bizarre and yet the business goes on' (B11S).

Festival participation was viewed by all the brewers as part of their marketing strategies. Most viewed festivals as an effective method of building brand awareness or as many said 'gaining exposure'. A Californian brewer related 'we are new to the game, festivals are hard work but they do gain you recognition' (B1C). All of the feedback from Californian interviewees on festival participation was positive. One brewer was particularly enthusiastic about festivals; he responded, 'Absolutely, next to social media that would be the next largest thing that we do' (B7C). Educating consumers about craft beer was a feature of the Californian interviews. As Brewer B2C said 'I'd get in there and try to educate the people. I'd have them taste our beer and I'd tell the story. Talk about how our beers were different from the mass-produced stuff.'

A further aspect of events that featured strongly was a willingness to support or give back to their local communities. The biggest brewery in the study donated $1m to local charities following anniversary celebrations in 2010. They regularly donate approximately $.75 m worth of beer annually to charity events and their interviewee took the view that 'It is so important for a business not to just reside in the community but to be a part of it if you want to be successful' (B4C). The third-largest Californian brewer studied was also enthusiastic, saying:

> Oh, I love festivals . . . as many as we can. Beer is a good way for any charity to raise money so we have always donated. Right from the start we had people coming, saying "It would be really great if you could donate a keg to our fund raiser, you can come and pour the beer and talk to people". So although it's a good way to give money to charity for a lot of different causes it's a way for us to promote without any real advertising budget except for a small amount of beer. It's a great way to expose yourself to more people.
>
> (B2C)

However, donating to charities was also problematic for many breweries in all three locations. Mega-brewers have a history of donating large quantities of beer to charity events; they too find it an effective promotional strategy but this creates competition in the 'giving space' for smaller brewers. Laws exist to facilitate donations, 'in California, breweries can legally donate beer to non-profit organisations if they are a certain classification' (B4C). But as one brewer stated, 'the big brewers spill more in a month than I make in a year' (B3C). Most of the small brewers were inundated with requests for donations they could not satisfy. In the UK brewers were faced with a similar situation as one respondent noted:

> We do get requests for donations of beer. So we decided to pick one charity to aim our efforts at and we use it to deflect other requests from charities. We do support other charities over and above the RNLI [Royal National Lifeboat Institute], but you have to draw the line somewhere.
>
> (B14S)

Brewers interviewed in the UK did report some differences to their US counterparts. Although CAMRA organises a suite of local beer festivals, the interviewees talked mainly about combined food and drink festivals, whereas in the USA they discussed craft beer festivals specifically. Participation in UK food and drink events was facilitated through local food and drink associations. Three examples mentioned were Delicious Yorkshire, Tayside Food Forum and Stirling Tastes Good, in addition to regular food and drink festivals in larger cities.

An additional point of difference mentioned by UK brewers concerned the use of wholesalers to organise craft brewers' presence at beer festivals. The brewery supplies the wholesaler, who ensured the beers were represented at festivals. One of the interviewees commented that 'We sometimes get awards from festivals that we didn't know we were in' (B14S). UK respondents discussed craft beer festivals and competitions simultaneously. In both rounds of interviews in the USA, festivals and competitions were discussed separately. Major national festivals do run competitions such as the Champion Beer of Britain at the GBBF and the gold, silver and bronze medals awarded at the GABF.

A prominent feature of the UK festival scene was that beers were invited to participate in festivals where they would be judged and be showcased to the public. For example, a UK brewer made this point when asked about festival participation:

> Yes [we participate in festivals] but you don't sell your beer to festivals. It is a bit like the Good Beer Guide, it is essential because you cannot buy your way in. You are selected and your beers go forward to competitions because people drink them.
>
> (B11S)

At the time of the interviews in the UK, CAMRA, the consumer association, and the Society of Independent Brewers (SIBA), which represents craft brewers, were in dispute. Where there had been one suite of competitions run jointly by the two associations, two separate contests were developing. SIBA now organises a range of regional competitions with their national competition 'BeerX' held annually in March. This event is more of a trade show for business insiders, leaving the CAMRA-organised GBBF to cater to craft beer consumers.

Washington and Oregon craft brewers interviewed in 2014 expressed a more strategic approach to festival participation, with one brewery targeting events only in the brewery's key markets:

> Yes we do we try to do big events. Since we are small, we try to get the most bang for our buck. We distribute beer in 6 states and two provinces. We try to visit those places during their 'Craft Beer Weeks'.
>
> (B21O)

In the Californian interviews (2010), only the two biggest brewers alluded to a targeted approach to events. They had identified Los Angeles as 'just going to take off' (B2C). Only one of the UK brewers reported being involved in festivals in locations where the brewery had an established market. He stated 'we went to a festival in Copenhagen last month. Scandinavia is a huge market for us' (B13S).

In addition to a more targeted approach, brewers in Portland and Seattle were more critical of the benefits of craft beer festivals. The smallest brewer remarked that for his business 'it makes no sense to do a festival more than an hour from here' (B17W). One of the more established brewers commented 'Being in the event never made a huge difference. I never saw an increase in sales after the event' (B20O).

A Seattle brewer gave a detailed response:

> Festivals are a necessary evil. I don't find them all that great for marketing. Most people drink too much, don't remember what they drank. It's not a win for me. I'm there so they see my name, my banner. I'm there but if they had my IPA they also had 12 other IPAs. It's brand recognition at best. I do them because there is a lot of them, but I say yes to about a third. If it's small or in an area where we don't sell a lot of product I usually say no.
>
> (B19W)

Brewer 19W's view was echoed by Brewer 18W who replied to being asked about festival participation with:

> Yep, but we are trying to pare back. From a brewery perspective, it's not an attractive proposition. For one, the beers at festivals tend to be weird. They are really high in alcohol or contain really weird ingredients. It doesn't take long for participants to become intoxicated, which can be hard to deal with. If we had staff that were out-reach sales staff we'd do more. It's not that good an experience!
>
> (B18W)

Those responses raise the issue of festival attendees' behaviour. Elzinga et al. (2015) suggested when craft beer festivals emerged they surprised local officials as they did not end in brawls. The idea that large groups of people would gather to drink beer implied to some observers that their motivation would be to get intoxicated. Elzinga et al. (2015: 249) cite Charles Papazian who established the GABF. Papazian expressed the opinion that craft beer drinkers "got happy not stupid", and more recently reasserted this view:

> When we started, we poured full mug servings – 8-ounce pours of unlimited servings. That wasn't relevant as to what we were trying to convey, so that was abandoned in the early years. We wanted it to be more education and a beer tasting festival – not beer drinking.
>
> (Noel 2016)

The brewers interviewed in 2010 emphasised the educational role of craft beer festivals and those interviewed in 2014 were notably more critical of festivals. As craft brewing grew and accounted for a bigger proportion of the market, the need to educate consumers about craft beer styles diminished. In addition, criticism of the utility of festivals by the later interviewees may allude to a maturation or saturation of the festivals market, leading to a decline in the role of festivals as an effective vehicle for building brand awareness.

Criticism of beer festivals as an aid to brand awareness brings into focus the comparison of festival participation as compared to other forms of promotion such as social media. All the brewers we talked to in the USA had embraced social media. UK brewers appeared a little behind, with many of them only starting to develop social media strategies. Sam Calagione, owner of the hugely successful and pioneering brewery Dogfish Head in Delaware, believes the brewery's social media are more effective than festival participation:

> Even if I'm standing behind the Dogfish booth at the Great American Beer Festival and there are over one hundred people lined up to talk to me about our beer, my work is not nearly as effective as the work Mariah does in her online outreach . . . she has personally built our Facebook community to the point where today, when we announce in that world that our spring seasonal Aprihop beer is hitting the shelves around the country, over 100,000 people will get that message.
>
> (Calagione 2011: 121)

Craft beer competitions

Calagione's view of craft beer festival participation being less effective than social media did not stretch to winning competitions. He confirmed that winning the largest and most prestigious competitions (including gold at the GABF and silver in the World Beer Cup) can reinvigorate sales of a beer which was previously the brewery's 'lowest-volume-year-round product' (Calagione 2011: 172).

Competition success was seen by most of the brewers in the study as a boon, although some of the smaller brewers were wary of the extent to which winning a title could disrupt their business. In the UK, one brewer stated 'If you won the national championship there would be no way you can keep up with demand. The company would quadruple in size almost instantly and that involves all sorts of considerations, especially money.' (B16S)

Another UK brewer reported that he entered a competition run by a large UK supermarket:

> CAMRA is a genuine competition. If you can win Best Beer of Britain it will change your life like it did for Harviestoun. It changes the whole dynamic of your business. We won the supermarket beer challenge. What we were doing was like a lifestyle business, but that turned it into something that keeps you needing to feed the beast. You have to ramp up from a small business to a large business. We had to grow from a five barrel to a 20 barrel system.
>
> (B11S)

Craft beer competitions in the USA and UK are often organised in association with craft beer festivals and competitions often 'build' through club, regional, state and national levels (Figures 11.3 and 11.4). Some competitions are determined by a popular vote but judging of the competitions at the higher levels is a serious business. The competitions are structured in categories or styles, there is a defined rubric for judging and the judges are selected from a pool of experienced or qualified persons.

Figure 11.3 At larger festivals beer judging is highly organised and rigorous
Source: Photo courtesy of Brewers Association

Figure 11.4 Beer judging requires meticulous documentation
Source: Photo courtesy of Brewers Association

Recognition as a beer judge may come through being a professional brewer or beer journalist/blogger or through certification under one of the beer judge training schemes. It is not uncommon to have one or two 'celebrity' judges such as chefs, winemakers, artisan food producers or media personalities.

Becoming a certified beer judge generally requires passing of a theory exam and a practical exam. This grants a provisional status and allows verified accumulation of experience and continuing professional development until a 'recognised' status is achieved and then on up the ranks until recognition as a 'master'. The Beer Judge Certification Program (BJCP) in the USA (and internationally) and The National Guild of Wine and Beer Judges (NGWBJ) in the UK are the two major schemes.

The aim of beer competitions is to provide feedback to brewers on the technical merit and general appeal of their beers, to allow them to calibrate their own approach to brewing and to improve their beers. Experienced beer judges bring the industry knowledge, experience and vocabulary necessary to provide meaningful feedback on the beers tasted. Winning major beer competitions can significantly influence a beer's perception by the public and thus its popularity and sales.

American competitions are generally judged to BJCP guidelines, in which there are currently 34 categories with over 100 recognised styles defined by aroma, appearance, flavour, mouthfeel, alcoholic strength and characteristic ingredients. Beers are judged on their technical merits, trueness to style and overall drinking pleasure. Points are awarded for each characteristic and then added for a final result. The NGWBJ system is similar. Medals may be awarded based on points. It is common to re-enter each category winner into a grand champion or 'best of show' taste-off.

The bigger brewers in the study entered an extensive range of competitions. The biggest US brewer interviewed entered 300 competitions per year (B4C). In response to a question about publicity generated by competition success, another of the bigger Californian craft brewers stated:

> Yes, especially the most recent award which is the best award you can get [World Beer Cup]. It really steps it up. We got a lot of attention from a lot of press. It gets you exposure you couldn't afford otherwise. We can't afford to do a full campaign newspaper or radio advertising. Winning [an] award like this – it's free advertising.
>
> (B2C)

However, not all of the bigger craft brewers were enamoured by winning competitions. The second-largest craft brewer in California responded 'We won the World Beer Cup three times, big deal. It seems like the most amazing thing in the world but the reality is a lot of people don't understand what that means' (B7C). He believed competitions were 'good for the industry but not so much for consumers. It doesn't translate into sales.' Smaller brewers held similar views. The smallest Californian brewer interviewed said about competition entry:

> I never felt the need to enter competitions. As a home brewer, validation came from friends who liked the beer. In two months we've sold almost 200 two litre growlers and dozens of refills. Winning a medal might be better but this suits me now. My validation comes from retail sales.
>
> (B3C)

Brewers in the Pacific Northwest were also more cautious. The smallest brewer said of competitions:

> The GABF is the big one and the World Beer Cup are not worth doing as there's so much competition. I've faith in our beer, it is above average in terms of quality, but going up against 100s of other beers; it is a crap shoot. It's not entirely objective, there is variability in the judging. Putting beer on a vertical scale is not realistic, it's not how you experience beer. Winning a medal is good, it can bring attention, so I do try from time to time in case we get lucky but it's expensive. The GABF is hundreds of dollars.
>
> (B17W)

Another Seattle brewer stated:

> I do [enter competitions] but I'm very selective. I don't like paying much to enter my beer in competitions. If it's over $50 I won't do it. I have never entered the GABF but there are a handful of free ones I enter every year.

I think they can be good for marketing, but it's not necessary. At least in Seattle, the consumer doesn't care about that information. They just want to have their friend recommend a beer. They don't care if you win a gold medal, that means someone said it was good, but "What does my tongue say" . . . that's what matters.

(B19W)

One of the established brewers from Portland was quite cynical about competitions; he recounted:

I'm really not interested in what the judges think about my beers, I'm more interested in what the people think. I won the GABF once 17 years ago. Who am I trying to impress with my medals? Nowadays there are so many breweries that have won medals it's getting less and less impactful. We don't do coupons, we don't do happy hour, we are just looking for regular people and there is enough people [that] we don't have to win competitions.

(B20O)

A more positive response came for another of the Portland brewers who said that competitions:

are not vital to our business. It is good for professional development and it is good for employee pride when we win medals. It is fun to see how your beer stacks up. It is more of an internal morale booster than a business strategy. But that said, at the GABF last week we won the gold medal for IPA and that is one that carries a lot of weight. Our IPA keg sales doubled last week. But that medal is the only one that can do that for your beer business. Our beer gets better because we can learn from being judged and make better beer. Improving our beer is part of the value proposition of our brand.

(B22O)

One of the UK brewers echoed the views expressed by some of the US brewers when he said 'It is nice to have awards, we won Champion Beer of Scotland a while back but it didn't seem to make any difference from a commercial point of view. We didn't see an increase in sales' (B14S). A second UK brewer who discussed festivals and competitions simultaneously stated:

So, you have CAMRA who do the Great British Beer Festival and you have SIBA. Both awards routes are very important to us; that definitely gets brand awareness going. One of our beers won Supreme Champion Beer at the GBBF in 2009 which was massive for us, for our little brewery in the North.

(B12S)

The interviewee of the largest UK brewery in the study alluded to competitions, particularly regional competitions, as being important when the business was trying to break into the market: 'In the early days we entered regional CAMRA festivals and SIBA and supermarket competitions. We've entered the World Beer Cup the last few years and won stuff there' (B13S). His comments indicate that as their brand matured the need for local competition success lessened and international competitions became more important.

Conclusion

All the brewers interviewed confirmed that participation in craft beer festivals aided their marketing strategies. Brewers who entered the market at an earlier point, particularly in the 1990s, relied more heavily on taking their beers to festivals so they could educate consumers about their new styles of craft beer. Brewers entering the market more recently did not mention educational motivations and were more likely to emphasise some shortcomings of festival participation.

A cross-over between festivals and competition entry was revealed. This was especially evident in interviews with UK craft brewers. The fact that the national public festivals awarded prestigious titles helps explain the intersection between the two types of events. Attitudes to competitions mirrored those of festival participation. Competitions were viewed as essential in the early period of craft beer development but became vehicles for brand recognition only latterly.

By 2016 craft beer had out grown its niche status. Del Buono (2015: 32) suggests that due to 'the introduction of new products [and] the ease with which brewers are joining the industry', competition in the segment is on the rise. Craft brewers are now less worried about educating consumers and more focused on standing out from the competition with craft beer festivals becoming viewed as less valuable in this process. All but the most prestigious craft beer festivals and competitions may have out-lived their usefulness, culminating in an uncertain future for festivals as a support mechanism in the value chain of craft beer.

References

Alonso, A. and Liu, Y. (2010) 'Wine tourism development in emerging Western Australian regions', *International Journal of Contemporary Hospitality Management*, 22(2), 245–262.

Bockway, C. (2013) 'Wine country beer: Craft beer history', www.winecountrybeer.com/winecountrybeer/History.html (accessed 12 January 2014).

Brewers Association (2016) 'Number of breweries', www.brewersassociation.org/statistics/number-of-breweries/ (accessed 20 November 2016).

CAMRA (2016) 'The history of CAMRA', www.camra.org.uk/key-events-in-camra-s-history (accessed 22 November 2016).

Cann, C. (2015) 'On our radar', *Travel Trade Gazette UK & Ireland*, 61. UBM Information Ltd, 8 October, http://content.yudu.com/A3x765/TTG-08-10-15/resources/index.htm?referrerUrl= (accessed 15 March 2017).

Carroll, G. and Swaminathan, A. (2000) 'Why the microbrewery movement? Organisation dynamics of resource partitioning in the US brewing industry', *American Journal of Sociology*, 106(3), 715–762.

Calagione, S. (2011) *Brewing Up a Business: Adventures in Beer*, New Jersey: Wiley.

Charters, S. and Menival, D. (2011) 'Wine tourism in Champagne', *Journal of Hospitality and Tourism Research*, 35(1), 102–118.

De Castella, T. (2007) 'Here for the beer', *New Statesman*, 44–45, 13 September, http://www.newstatesman.com/travel/2007/09/real-ale-britain-beer-industry (accessed 14 March 2017).

Del Buono, A. (2015) 'Crafting the American culture', *Beverage Industry*, 30–38, 1 November, https://www.highbeam.com/doc/1G1-446734489.html (accessed 15 March 2017).

Dunn, A. and Kregor, G. (2014) 'Making love in a canoe no longer? Tourism and the emergence of the craft-beer movement in California', *Cauthe Conference*, Brisbane: University of Queensland.

Dunn, A. and Wickham, M. (2016) 'Craft-brewery tourism best practices: A research agenda', *Annals of Tourism Research*, 56(1), 140–142.

Elzinga, K., Horton Tremblay, C. and Tremblay, V. (2015) 'Craft-beer in the United States: History, numbers and geography', *Journal of Wine Economics*, 10(3), 242–274.

Miller, N. (2011) 'Festivals of ales throughout the ages', *Brew and Brewer*, Summer 2011, 32–35.

Nelson, J. (2005) 'Beer advertising and marketing update', *Review of Industrial Organisations*, 26, 269–306.

Noel, J. (2016) 'Chicago craft beer insiders dish on Great American Beer Fest', *Chicago Tribune*, www.chicagotribune.com/dining/drink/beer/ct-great-american-beer-festival-chicago-brewers-20161010-story.html (accessed 20 November 2016).

Ogle, M. (2006) *Ambitious Brew: The Story of American Beer*, Orlando: Harcourt.

Porter, M. (1980) *Competitive Strategy Techniques for Analyzing Industries and Competitors*, New York: Free Press.

Warner, A. (2010) 'The evolution of the American brewing industry', *Journal of Business Case Studies*, 6(6), 31–46.

12 Supporting the industry or just consuming leisure? The case of industrial festivals and events in Jeonju, South Korea

Eerang Park and Sangkyun Kim

Introduction

The number of festivals and events in South Korea (hereafter Korea) has doubled since 1995 when the Korean local authority system was re-established, while the continuous development of festivals and tourism products featuring local identity and culture has become a major strategy used by many local governments to gain a competitive edge (Kim 2001). This has been further accelerated by a recent Korean national tourism policy that aims to achieve three key objectives by 2018, which are: (1) to host 17 million foreign tourists each year, (2) to create 300,000 tourism industry jobs and (3) to reach a figure of 230 million domestic tourists annually (Shim 2011). The tourism and events industry is now one of the most important sectors in the Korean economy (Kim and Nam 2015).

The tremendous increase in the number of festivals and events in Korea cannot, therefore, be fully understood without taking into account the aforementioned government policy for tourism to be the engine of an improved national economy (MCST 2013). In particular, the promotion of domestic tourism through festival and event tourism development is considered one of the major factors in the drive to have 230 million domestic tourists by 2018. As such, the very strong emphasis on tourism in the political and cultural economy of regional and local festivals in Korea has led to an unprecedented, rapid growth of the events industry. However, the subsequent intense competition has often resulted in falling profitability and the demise of many newly developed festivals and events.

In this process, distinctive local cultural and natural features are often deemed to be at the centre of event design and development, but there has been ongoing controversy and criticism over the lack of local identity and originality in events and festivals in the Korean context (Chang 2000; Yang 2002). This is not a new phenomenon, as Ma and Lew (2012) highlight that a major reason for the great number of failures of contemporary festivals in China lies in either the de-contextualisation or mis-contextualisation of the festivals. Similar issues have also been found elsewhere around the world in the discourse of over-commercialisation or commodification and the loss of local authenticity in the context of festivals and events (see for example, Smith and Forrest 2006).

Thus, the sustainability of regional festivals and events depends on the successful promotion of local identity driven by well-coordinated local resources

(Backman, Backman, Uysal and Sunshine 1995). The quality and uniqueness of a festival are of great importance in the development of successful festival and event tourism (Gursoy, Kim and Uysal 2004). The locality is central to increasing awareness of the region and the event(s) among event attendees, as well as in both attendees and local communities being able to create a sense of attachment (Lee, Kyle and Scott 2012). In summary, the long-term success of festivals is only achievable when they can 'strengthen their sense of local identity for residents, remain unique in some way, embody liminal experiences for participants, and soften the tension between commodification and cultural authenticity' (Ma and Lew 2012: 28).

Having acknowledged the above, this chapter aims to introduce and examine how local industrial heritage-themed cultural festivals deeply rooted in the regional culture and tradition play a crucial role in fostering the relevant industries and sustaining the industrial heritage in the region by creating a more sustainable environment in which a place's historical geography and sense of local identity and authenticity is maintained in the face of tourism and industrial event development and the commodification of their culture. Intangible heritage associated with music and sound, traditional paper production and craftsmanship, and local fermented food culture and products will be the main focus of this chapter within the context of local industrial heritage cultural festivals, not from the economic development perspective, but rather from geographical, cultural and historical perspectives.

The focus of this chapter is Jeonju, the capital of Jeonbuk Province and a second-tier city in Korea, which is situated approximately 200 kilometres southeast of Seoul. Known as one of Korea's oldest cities, Jeonju was once seen as representative of the country's arts, cuisine, customs and the traditional paper industry. It therefore has a variety of nicknames, such as the primary creative city in Korea, the gourmet capital of Korea, and the capital of Korean gastronomy and cuisine. More recently, Jeonju has become known for the Cittaslow ('slow city') status of Jeonju Hanok Village, which was accredited in 2010 because of its 700 traditional Korean houses (Hanok) and various cultural heritage features. The leisure features of this traditional Korean village include its traditional landscape, historic buildings and shrine, and traditional food and crafts. Since its Cittaslow accreditation in 2010, Jeonju has experienced remarkable growth in tourism, with approximately 5.9 million tourists visiting in 2014, and the rapid growth of tourism facilities, including an annual growth of 75.3% in the food and beverage sector and 64.2% in the accommodation sector (Park 2016).

The research context: festive events in Jeonju, Korea

In the early 1960s, Korea entered the modern era and experienced rapid economic development due to the Korean government's Economic Development Master Plan (1962–96) along with a National (Land) Development Master Plan (1963 – current). During the substantial development period of the 1970s, the master plans focused on the establishment of the economic infrastructure, and thus, massive land developments, including highways, new industrial complexes and estates, and multi-purpose dam constructions, were carried out, particularly in the East and Southeast of Korea. In the 1980s, the focus shifted to a balance between national development and national welfare, with the priority being the rapid industrialisation of both Southeast and Southwest Korea.

Despite the above efforts, Jeonju, located in the Southwest of Korea, was often neglected by the development plan, which failed to bring major projects to the city. As a consequence, it remained as a relatively less developed region compared to other second-tier cities in Korea. This uneven distribution of the National Development Master Plan has meant that Jeonju has remained a less industrialised city, but is more culturally protected and has kept its regional and local identity and traditions through food, culture and the arts.

However, Jeonju has also experienced a rapid modernisation process which has meant that once-flourishing traditional small-scale industries based on regional food, culture and the arts (for example, *hanji*, traditional Korean paper) have struggled to survive. Jeonju has recently made a great effort to revitalise these traditional industries by means of festivals and events. As Table 12.1 exhibits, there are currently eight annual events taking place in Jeonju, which can be grouped into three major categories of regional industrial heritage: (1) traditional paper production: Jeonju Hanji Cultural Festival rooted in the long history of the traditional paper production industry and craftsmanship; (2) film, music and arts production: Jeonju International Film Festival rooted in the local film-making industry, which was in decline and already faded out from local residents' memory; Jeonju International Sori Festival (*sori* refers to traditional music and sounds); Jeonju Daesasup Game (folk arts, literature and martial arts competitions), and Jeonju Dano Festival (traditional seasonal customs); and (3) local food production: International Fermented Food Expo, Jeonju Bibimbap Festival (*bibimbap* is a traditional signature dish of this region) and Jeonju Peach Festival.

It is evident that regardless of their different themes, the vast majority of these events are characterised as industrial heritage (both tangible and intangible) events. Although their formats and styles are much like that of the community festival or contemporary art or cultural festival, the traditional and historic value of the

Table 12.1 Annual industrial and cultural festivals and events in Jeonju

Category	Event title	Host season	History
Traditional paper production	• Jeonju Hanji Cultural Festival	May	since 1996
Film, music and arts production	• Jeonju Daesasup Game	May-June	since 1975
	• Jeonju Dano Festival	June	since 1959
	• Jeonju International Film Festival	April-May	since 2000
	• Jeonju International Sori Festival	September – October	since 2001
Local food production	• Jeonju Peach Festival	July	since 1999
	• International Fermented Food Expo	October	since 2003
	• Jeonju Bibimbap Festival	October	since 2007

region's industrial heritage is central to the themes and development of these events. In particular, intangible heritage as demonstrated by individual creativity, skill and craftsmanship (arts, folk, martial arts, traditional paper and food) is noticeable in all but the Jeonju Dano Festival. Intangible heritage and regional or local identities associated with traditional food are inherent assets that the city can utilise to develop its creative industries; this is a global trend in economic development and regional (re)development (Hashimoto and Telfer 2008; Kim and Iwashita 2016; see also Chapter 9).

With one exception, these events have been ongoing for more than 10 years; the second category in particular, 'arts, folk and martial arts', has a very long history. Events in Jeonju can be viewed as exemplary in terms of sustainable event development and practices, given their successful reinterpretation and redevelopment of industrial and intangible heritage. Despite the collective feature of the locality and the uniqueness of local culture shared by the festivals and events in Jeonju, limited attention has been paid to events in Jeonju from the historical and heritage perspective. The potential, value and meaning of cultural and industrial heritage events and festivals has not been sufficiently discussed; thus, this chapter will look closely at three distinctive industrial events in Jeonju (the Hanji Cultural Festival, the International Sori Festival, and the International Fermented Food Expo) and attempt to shed light on the value and meaning of these events in terms of their rootedness in the traditions and culture of Jeonju along with the aim proposed previously.

Case studies have been selected from each of the categories in Table 12.1 and the themes are all attributed to the authentic Korean style, the so-called *Han* style, which the central Korean government has incorporated into its national policy since the mid-2000s to promote traditional Korean culture more globally. It includes six themes that represent the origin of Korean culture: Hangeul (Korean alphabet), Hansik (Korean food), Hanbok (traditional Korean costume), Hanok (traditional Korean houses), Hanji (traditional Korean paper) and Hansori (Korean music and sound). The *Han* style, a symbolic national brand of Korea, is used to promote the cultural experiences of Korean tourism through a modern interpretation of the six themes or categories mentioned above. This strategy seeks to generate economic opportunities from the familiarisation and industrialisation of traditional Korean cultural assets. Jeonju features strong *Han*-style industries including food, housing, traditional paper production and music, and the selected three events clearly demonstrate the *Han*-style of rich locality and identity.

The Jeonju Hanji cultural festival

Hanji, the Korean traditional paper made from the bark of mulberry trees, was being actively produced until the 1970s when demand for it dramatically decreased. The *hanji* production industry was then in decline until the early 2000s (Kim 2009). *Hanji* can be dyed into a variety of colours or made into ancient scripts. The history of *hanji* goes back a thousand years, and the most modern manufacturing methods used date back 500 years. *Hanji* combines a unique manufacturing method (craftsmanship) that has been handed down through the generations with the great resource of mulberry bark, creating a product that is tougher and more durable than modern paper. *Hanji* is an exceptional cultural asset in Jeonju, not only for its uniqueness, but also for its versatility; it can be used to make commodities ranging from basic stationery such as notebooks, living commodities like lamps and plates, and even wearable items such as socks and neckties. The texture of the mulberry fibre and the array of coloured dyes available are also visually appealing; its artistic merit is recognised by both craftsmen and contemporary artists.

Hanji produced in Jeonju has long been acknowledged as having the best quality, and indeed Jeonju is known as the cultural origin of *hanji* art. The province currently produces approximately 70% of *hanji* in Korea in its well-established paper production industry. Alongside the central government's *Han*-style strategy, the city of Jeonju decided to establish the foundation of the cultural heritage industry, and *hanji* was one of the main areas that was developed as a result (Jeonju Hanji Cultural Festival 2016). In order to revitalise the *hanji* production industry, priority was given to increasing awareness of the excellence and beauty of *hanji*, and a *hanji*-themed festival was seen as an ideal platform from which to showcase its attributes and its quality and value as a traditional cultural industry.

In 1996, the city of Jeonju decided to host the first Jeonju Hanji Cultural Festival and has organised it every May since then. Its vision is to enhance the city's attractiveness as a tourist destination through establishing an entertainment and recreational culture using *hanji*, based on the success of Jeonju's *hanji* culture and a celebration of its thousand-year history. The objectives are to increase the number of tourists, to establish *hanji*-themed event programmes in order to enhance local pride, to increase the number of stakeholders from a wide geographic area, to boost the local economy, to enhance the attractiveness of *Han*-style tourism through the success of *hanji* production and culture, and to develop the *hanji* industry by creating more demand and improving the competitiveness of local manufacturers (Jeonju Hanji Cultural Festival 2016).

A wide range of festival experiences have been designed to achieve these objectives. Experiments with *hanji* utilisation can be seen in fashion shows, parades, competitions, craft shows and special exhibitions, with participants mainly coming from the local craft communities, the Western contemporary art world and the education and manufacturing sectors. A seminar for the *hanji* industry targets local entrepreneurs and businesses for the sharing of skills and industry information (Jeonju Hanji Cultural Festival 2016), which is similar to other types of industrial events whose primary aim is the marketing of businesses, industries and products as well as the shaping of future innovations and development.

The festival's programme for general attendees is more diverse. Family-oriented programmes, for example, include a traditional door and window-making competition (traditional doors and windows are made of wood and *hanji;* these can still be found in *hanok* houses), experiencing the traditional daily tea ceremony, the tasting of confectionary and traditional alcohols so that attendees can test *hanji*-made dishware, and folk games using balls, ropes and other items made from *hanji*.

The festival takes place in Jeonju Hanok Village, another distinctive *Han*-style asset and landmark in Jeonju; the best place to experience Korean heritage and traditions. The theme of the Hanji Cultural Festival is indeed harmonised by the venue. The stalls selling *hanji* products, gifts and souvenirs are not alien to the landscape, and the traditional shrine and *hanok*-style architecture used for the event venues are well integrated into the heritage theme.

Despite the uniqueness of this festival's theme, rooted in the industrial heritage and craftsmanship associated with *hanji* production, the Hanji Cultural Festival is more successful at creating recreational activities and less successful at balancing its industrial and cultural elements. In addition, the identity of the festival has not been firmly established due to insufficient marketing efforts, resulting in low awareness of the festival among local communities and potential tourists. The festival is also referred to as a nonspecific-place festival, adopting Relph's (1976) concept of *placelessness* (as cited in Ma and Lew 2012), because a wide range of the products presented and sold at the festival are not developed from the symbolic items of Jeonju; instead, they are part of one-off experiences and a means of the festival income. Furthermore, a survey of the industry's experiences of the Hanji Cultural Festival reported that information collection and cultural experiences were the important factors behind participants' performances in the festival, but that overall satisfaction was entirely dependent on cultural experiences (Kim 2009). This suggests that insufficient information about the history and traditions of *hanji*, its markets and businesses is available at the festival.

The Jeonju International Sori Festival

Sori, as a genre of Korean music and sound, refers to epic chanting, a form of traditional Korean musical drama performed by a singer and a drummer. *Pansori* was an oral tradition that was practised between the 17th and late 19th century in Korea, and is part of the modern history of the Korean arts industry. *Pansori* was made a Korean Intangible Culture Asset in 1964 and proclaimed as a UNESCO Intangible Cultural Heritage of Humanity in 2003 (Um 2012). '*Pan*' in Korean means a place where people gather together and '*sori*' means sound and song, or singing. *Pansori* is performed by one singer, with his/her style, narratives, and gestures also being part of the overall performance (Um 2008).

Jeonju is the birthplace of *pansori* and has long been hosting *pansori* contests and similar folk music events. Since the emergence of *pansori*, the potential global appeal of '*sori*' has been noted and the central government has strategically supported Jeonju in promoting *sori* as part of its *Han*-style strategy. There is recognition that *sori*, as a symbolic brand of Jeonbuk province, has potential as a new cultural product with a rich history and musical content of *pansori*, and that the region has the human and physical resources to support *pansori* businesses and institutions as a cultural industry, as demonstrated by the hosting of a *sori*-themed festival every year since 2001 in the capital city of the province, Jeonju. The festival was established by Jeonbuk province and has been run by the Sori Festival Organising Committee which comprises regional professionals including province and city government officers, the chair of Korean music association, academics, media, the folk music conservation community and so forth.

The size and budget of this festival is relatively large compared to similar festivals in other countries. The festival aims to promote the region as the heartland of *pansori*, along with active exchange and collaboration between international folk music industries. The Jeonju International Sori Festival has been evolving in an attempt to provide a modern interpretation of traditional *sori*, festival design and content development. Consequently, it has expanded the initial scope of *sori* beyond *pansori* by encompassing various genres of Eastern and Western folk music to create a mixture of traditional and contemporary sound arts and music industries.

The programme includes international folk music collaboration, classic *pansori*, musicals, Korean pop music performances, installations and performances using sound and video arts, improvisations, orchestras, choirs and more. It is evident that the characteristics of the festival today are similar to those of a contemporary music festival, with its staged performances and shows. The festival has gained a significant global reputation and was placed in the top 25 international festivals between 2012 and 2015 by *Songlines*, a British World Music magazine (Jeonju International Sori Festival 2016).

To some extent the success of the Jeonju International Sori Festival can be found in its strong regional identity and authentic characteristics, shaped by its contemporary approach to traditional *pansori*. Indeed, the dynamic programmes of the festival showcase how *pansori* can be harmonised with other international music genres. Thanks to this festival and its media coverage, *pansori* in Korea is more widely appreciated for its cultural heritage value than as popular culture. This is similar to the success story of the Tatebayashi noodle Grand Prix in Japan, in which the uniqueness, identity and authenticity of the region's heritage were well encapsulated in the theme and characteristics of the event that also took a modern leisure festival approach (Kim 2015).

Pansori singers are not as numerous as classical or popular music singers as they require special voice timbres that can only be mastered through long, rigorous training. It is evidently difficult for *pansori* to be in the mainstream music industry in modern society. The Jeonju International Sori Festival is therefore an important opportunity for *pansori* to showcase their skills and to attract a wider audience to their music, as well as changing the perception of *pansori* among both Korean and international audiences, so that they become a familiar and enjoyable part of everyday life. It is also a platform for those in the music industry to experience the harmony between different genres. Its success is demonstrated by the overall occupancy rate attained in 2016, which was recorded as 97%, while 86.3% of tickets for the paid performances were sold, an increase of 15% on the previous year. Moreover, the success of the children's shows was outstanding with a 100% occupancy rate (Yoon 2016).

The International Fermented Food Expo

Hansik (Korean food, including its ingredients, dishes, regional cuisines and cooking methods) is one of the major elements of the *Han*-style strategy that aims to build international recognition of Korean tourism products as well as its trade value. Jeonju's unique cuisine and food style has led to it gaining international recognition and being designated a UNESCO Creative City of Gastronomy since 2012. Jeonju is considered the capital of Korean gastronomy and cuisine (Pearson and Pearson 2016). Historically, Jeonju has been renowned for its wide range of traditional foods, but the great majority of marketing has focused on *Bibimbap* as a local signature dish, because of its accessibility and taste for international visitors, as well as its rich nutrition and visual appeal, with its colourful ingredients.

Meanwhile, Korean food is distinctive with its various preserved and fermented cooking methods, with *Kimchi* being the most well-known fermented Korean food. Besides this, Korea also boasts a wide range of traditional fermented foods, including salted fish and seafood, pastes and sauces, fermented vegetables made using pastes and sauces, condiments and juices. While *à la carte* dishes have been promoted and sold as part of tourism product development, less attention has been paid to specialised cooking methods and foods made using fermentation skills for the purposes of industrialisation. Fermented foods exemplify *Han*-style cooking. The health benefits of fermented foods recently reported in scientific journals has increased global awareness of this type of food (OECD 2012), while the versatility of fermentation methods has been experimented with in order to increase the intake of fermented foods by using them in various areas of food production as a new platform of the food production industry, such as bakeries, confectionaries and snacks, tea, grain powders, cheese and drinks.

The annual International Fermented Food Expo (IFFE) has been held in Jeonju for the past 14 years by the Jeonbuk Institute for Food and Bio Industry, and is seen as a successful platform for fermented food promotion and global exchange and trade, receiving as it does 344 exhibitors from 19 countries, and presenting more than 3,000 fermented food products for promotion and sales (IFFE 2016a).

Jeonbuk Province hosts the largest agricultural sector in Korea as well as a specialised fermented food production village (Sunchang Gochujang Village). The Jeonbuk Institute for Food and Bio Industry was founded in acknowledgement of the distinctive food-related resources of the region and established in Jeonju in 2000 with the formal approval of the Ministry of Commerce Industry and Energy, which is also part of the industrial technology infrastructure development plan of the Ministry of Knowledge Economy. The institution aims to promote the region's food industry by strengthening research and development, improving industry networks and supporting small and micro businesses. The IFFE, as part of the effort to promote regional food and food production, has demonstrated the global trade potential of fermented foods. The objectives of the expo are to place Korea in a leading position among the countries with the largest food industries, contribute to the fermented food sector by promoting the excellence of Korean food culture and history and boost the regional economy.

The expo is comprised of four areas: (1) the strategic identifying and supporting of businesses in the food industry; (2) global fermented food brand exhibitions and competitions; (3) conferences for information and skill sharing, and academic-industrial collaboration; and (4) networking with international governments and food trade sectors (IFFE 2016a). The programme includes trade exhibitions, public exhibitions, academic conferences, new food science contests, B2B consultations, B2C activities, international and regional food courts and fermented food-making experiences.

The considerable achievements of the expo can be seen in its economic outcomes. According to the five-year event report (IFFE 2016b), the five-year total economic value of the expo, from 2010 to 2014, was approximately US$36 million in foreign export contracts, while total on-site consumer sales and expenditure was US$13 million. The economic impact of the expo on the host region over these five years is estimated to have been approximately US$13 million in value added, 733 jobs created, and US$25 million in terms of a food production trigger effect. The overall satisfaction of the exhibitors and industry participants was high with 87.5% of respondents reporting positive experiences, particularly when it came to the growth of participating companies and the marketing effect of the expo. More than 83% of exhibitors and participants intended to return to the expo. The event has received a considerable number of visitors, approximately 500,000 participants and 20,000 international and domestic buyers every year (IFFE 2016b).

As the only fermented food-themed expo in the world, the success of IFFE has been recognised by the Korean exhibition industry, while the city and its local government have received multiple awards, such as the International Certified Exhibition award (won for five consecutive years from 2011 to 2015), and the Promising Korean Exhibition award (won from 2012 to 2015) from the Ministry of Trade, Industry and Energy. The expo was also awarded the 2014 Korea's best-selling product award, a consumer power hit award organised by *Chosun Ilbo* (one of the major newspapers in Korea); indeed, the IFFE was the only exhibition to win across all of the award categories.

Although the IFFE is characterised by its strong trade function through the active participation of a variety of industry stakeholders, it is also an important opportunity for the enhancing of local pride in the excellence of the region's food heritage and its versatile use in both Eastern and Western food. Local newspapers report that the IFFE reinforces the image of Jeonju as a gastronomic city. Some local participants have even commented that the IFFE is distinctive and unique among food exhibitions, that they are proud of their local fermented food and glad that the IFEE is held in Jeonju (Lee 2016).

Likewise, the locality and regional identity associated with this unique fermented food culture, as well as its social and cultural values and meanings, are greatly encapsulated in the creative effort of exhibition design and organisation of the International Fermented Food Expo (IFFE) in Jeonju. This is demonstrated by the three core values that the IFFE (2016a) aims to achieve: (1) the fusing of tradition with modern technology in the creative economy; (2) for the core of the sixth largest industry in Korea to solve the agricultural problems of the region; and (3) to develop leading food products for domestic and international food markets.

Conclusion

Festivals and events have become an increasingly significant tool in socio-economic development and transformation. Many of them, however, fail to provide an essential understanding of the themes and festival experiences of visitors within the relevant historical and geographical contexts. The three industrial events presented in this chapter are all rooted in regional industrial heritage (traditional paper production, traditional sound and music and fermented food production) in Jeonju, South Korea. They were all initiated to maintain a sense of authenticity and continuity of the regional industrial and cultural heritage upon which each industrial event is based. At the same time, they aimed to support related industries (*hanji* paper production, *hanji* arts production, *pansori* music, fermented food production such as chili paste), creating a more sustainable environment and improving their competitiveness. To some extent, they all contributed to the building of a new vibrant image and the boosting of regional economic development in Jeonju and the surrounding area, albeit to different extents.

However, it is apparent that not all of the aforementioned industrial events in Jeonju are successful from geographical, cultural and historical perspectives. The Jeonju Hanji Cultural Festival and the International Sori Festival focus on liminal leisure experiences and entertainment that are nevertheless intense and extraordinary, and are separate from everyday life (Morgan 2008). Immediately consumable products that are more generically popular than those associated with local industrial heritage events shaped by local identity and symbolic meaning and significance, were the centre of these two industrial events. This is more serious in the case of the Hanji Cultural Festival, where the industry and the representation of its heritage were somewhat superficial. Thus, the role of the festival was limited to the creation of local cultural experiences and leisure for local communities and festival goers, which is not very different from any contemporary commercial festival that simply relies on marketing and entertainment with little cultural meaning (Ma and Lew 2012). Consequently, the festival seems to fail to differentiate the local identity of Jeonju as a distinctive place with a long history and tradition of the *hanji* production industry.

In comparison, the IFFE, using an exhibition or expo format, not only highlights business networks and industry development, but also enhances cultural tourism experiences for visitors, and community pride and a sense of identity for local communities. The science of fermented food was communicated through the showcasing of dynamic products and various festival programmes, while fermented food as intangible heritage and cultural assets was the core value of the entertainment programmes offered. The IFFE has been evaluated as an authentic industrial event that shows a unique mixture of trade and tourism effects based on food heritage and cultural identity within their historical and geographical contexts. The contemporary and scientific interpretation of fermentation presented at the event has contributed to the changing of audiences' perceptions of fermented food, while variations of fermented food around the world are successfully presented as an alternative food culture in the future.

References

Backman, K.F., Backman, S.J., Uysal, M. and Sunshine, K.M. (1995) 'Event tourism: An examination of motivations and activities', *Festival Management & Event Tourism*, 3(1), 15–24.

Chang, P.K. (2000) 'Local autonomy and directions of regional festival policy in Korea', *The Journal of Culture and Tourism Research*, 2(1), 31–53.

Gursoy, D., Kim, K. and Uysal, M. (2004) 'Perceived impacts of festivals and special events by organizers: An extension and validation', *Tourism Management*, 25, 171–181.

Hashimoto, A. and Telfer, D.J. (2008) 'From sake to sea urchin: Food and drink festivals and regional identity in Japan', in C.M. Hall and L. Sharples (eds.), *Food and Wine Festivals and Events Around the World* (pp. 249–278), Oxford: Elsevier.

International Fermented Food Expo (2016a) *Introduction to IFFE*, www.iffe.or.kr/2016_korean/?doc=wpage/int01.html (accessed 1 March 2017).

International Fermented Food Expo (2016b) *IFFE Result Report 2010–2014*, www.iffe.or.kr/_data/download/5Years_Event_Results.pdf (accessed 1 March 2017).

Jeonju Hanji Cultural Festival (2016) *Introduction to the Festival*, www.jhanji.or.kr/bbs/board.php?bo_table=main01_01 (accessed 1 March 2017).

Jeonju International Sori Festival (2016) *The Festival in Media*, www.sorifestival.com/ (accessed 1 March 2017).

Kim, H.C. (2001) 'Analysis of recognition on theme tourism in Jeon-buk province', *The Journal of Culture and Tourism Research*, 3(1), 151–169.

Kim, J.S. (2009) 'A study on the satisfactions and intentions to re-attend of the businessmen in Jeonju Hanji Cultural Festival', *Proceedings of the 2009 Korean Academic Association of Business Administration*, 4, 1009–1026.

Kim, S. (2015) 'Understanding the historical and geographical contexts of food festival tourism development: The case of the Tatebayashi Noodle Grand Prix in Japan', *Tourism Planning & Development*, 12(4), 433–446.

Kim, S. and Iwashita, C. (2016) 'Cooking identity and food tourism: The case of Japanese udon noodles', *Tourism Recreation Research*, 41(1), 89–100.

Kim, S. and Nam, C. (2015) 'Hallyu revisited: Challenges and opportunities for the South Korean Tourism', *Asia Pacific Journal of Tourism Research*, 21(5), 524–540.

Lee, J., Kyle, G. and Scott, D. (2012) 'The mediating effect of place attachment on the relationship between festival satisfaction and loyalty to the festival hosting destination', *Journal of Travel Research*, 51, 754–767.

Lee, Y. (2016) 'The Rich contents of the 14th International Fermented Food Expo', *Jeonjuilbo*, www.jjilbo.com/news/articleView.html?idxno=148222 (accessed 23 October 2016).

Ma, L. and Lew, A.A. (2012) 'Historical and geographical context in festival tourism development', *Journal of Heritage Tourism*, 7(1), 13–31.

Ministry of Culture, Sports and Tourism Republic of Korea (MCST) (2013) *Korean Tourism Industry 2012 Annual Report*, Seoul: MCST.

Morgan, M. (2008) 'What makes a good festival? Understanding the event experience', *Event Management*, 12(2), 81–93.

OECD (2012) *Food and the Tourism Experience: The OECD-Korea Workshop*, OECD studies on Tourism, Paris: OECD Publishing.

Park, I. (2016) 'Jeonju Hanok village attempting to reaccreditation of Cittaslow', *Hankyoreh*, www.hani.co.kr/arti/society/area/674671.html (accessed 21 January 2016).

Pearson, D. and Pearson, T. (2016) 'Branding food culture: UNESCO creative cities of gastronomy', *Journal of International Food & Agribusiness Marketing*, 28(2), 164–176.

Relph, E.C. (1976) *Place and Placelessness*. London: Pion.

Shim, W.S. (2011) *A Case Study on the Tourism Policy of Foreign Countries and Future Directions*, Seoul: Korea Culture and Tourism Institute (KCTI).

Smith, M. and Forrest, K. (2006) 'Enhancing vitality or compromising integrity? Festivals, tourism and the complexities of performing culture', in D. Picard and M. Robinson (eds.), *Festivals, Tourism and Social Change: Remaking Worlds* (pp. 133–151), Clevedon: Channel View.

Um, H. (2008) 'New pansori in 21st century Korea: Creative dialectics of tradition and modernity', *Asian Theatre Journal*, 25(1), 24–57.

Um, H. (2012) 'Performing pansori musical drama: Stage, story and sound', in H. Um and H. Lee (eds.), *Rediscovering Traditional Korean Performing Arts* (pp. 72–79), Seoul: Korea Arts Management Service.

Yang, M. (2002) 'A study on the evaluation and analysis of the vent of Jeonju cultural festivals', *Journal of Tourism Management Research*, 14(2), 106–126.

Yoon, G. (2016) '15% more paid audiences in 2016 Jeonju International Sori Festival', *Jeonbuk Joongang Newspaper*, www.jjn.co.kr/news/articleView.html?idxno=695874 (accessed 9 October 2016).

13 Exploring family farms and sustainable entrepreneurship in Australian farmers' markets

Vanessa Ratten, Veland Ramadani and Alain Fayolle

Introduction

Farmers' markets offer consumers an alternative shopping experience that reconnects them to the food system. Abello, Palma, Waller and Anderson (2014: 1) describe farmers' markets as 'a local source of fresh, nutritious products and typically include vegetables, fruits, herbs, flowers, plants, baked goods, honey, nuts, meat and poultry products as well as dairy products and eggs'. Farmers' markets enable growers and producers to sell their products to get a better share of profits, with small farms more likely to sell at farmers' markets compared to larger farms. This is due to large farmers growing a greater quantity of produce that enables them to negotiate better profit margins than small farmers. For some small farmers, the farmers' markets are their only source of income and they can be more flexible when they are recreational or part-time business endeavours and do not need a regular income.

Most of the literature on farmers' markets has focused on consumer preferences for locally grown and organic produce (Curtis and Cowee 2011; Dimitri and Greene 2002; Loureiro and Hine 2002). This is due to farmers' markets enabling seasonal products to be sold in a local region, providing opportunity for human contact with the producers and for consumers to connect with the food system, which is a form of sustainable entrepreneurship. Sustainable entrepreneurship involves innovative activity that balances the triple bottom line of having ecological, environmental and social goals, making it a complex process, as there are often trade-offs between economic and social development (Binder and Belz 2014). In this chapter, we aim to add to the understanding of sustainable entrepreneurship by addressing the research question: how do family farms at farmers' markets develop and recognise sustainable opportunities?

The purpose of this chapter is to explore sustainable entrepreneurship strategies of farmers' markets stallholders to determine the effect on performance. This will enable a better understanding about how social capital in a community affects rural entrepreneurship. This chapter begins by reviewing the literature and outlines the study's theoretical perspective. Next, the methodology of the study is stated. In the findings, two main business strategies for family farms are found, which are developing social capital and ethical marketing consumption. Subsequently, limitations, directions for future research and implications for public policy planners are stated. The next section will further discuss the role of sustainable entrepreneurship and farmers' markets.

Literature review

Sustainable entrepreneurship

There are few studies examining the role of sustainable entrepreneurship in the context of farmers' markets (Campbell 2015). As more consumers are driven by ethical consumption, it is expected that an understanding about sustainability will help to increase productivity and provide more opportunities for farmers' markets. Farmers' markets have evolved from being roadside stands to mainstream community events. Part of this evolution has been influenced by increasing social and environmental concern about sustainable food production methods. Farmers' markets enable local farmers to sell directly to consumers and test new strategies such as prices and products. This interaction between farmers and consumers at farmers' markets enables consumers to become better educated about the food system and enjoy the socialisation.

Sustainable entrepreneurship is an emerging field of research that bridges sustainable management and entrepreneurship (Thompson, Kiefer and York 2011). Belz and Binder (2017) suggest that there are two contrasting perspectives about how to define sustainable entrepreneurship. First, there is the definition of sustainable development and the triple bottom line, with entrepreneurship being a minor issue. Second, it is defined as the process of entrepreneurship within the triple bottom line. This latter perspective is adopted in this study and we utilise the definition of sustainable entrepreneurship as 'the recognition, development and exploration of opportunities by individuals to bring into existence future goods and services with economic, social and ecological gains' (Belz and Binder 2017: 2). This definition links sustainable entrepreneurship to social entrepreneurship, but focuses more on the environmental factors of the opportunity recognition process. More emphasis is placed on the simultaneous pursuit of economic viability, social equity and environmental drivers in sustainable entrepreneurship (Thompson et al. 2011).

Social capital

Social capital involves the actual or potential resources a person has based on their interpersonal relationships (Bourdieu 1980). This includes the social networks a person has from their mutual acquaintances. In farmers' markets, there is a network of relationships between family farms and customers that is based on social interactions. Customers who visit farmers' markets more often increase their nutritional knowledge about fruit and vegetables. Personal relationships are influenced by the interactions between sellers and buyers, which creates more trust. These personal relationships enable education about health related benefits of food products sold at local markets (Alonso and O'Neill 2011). Farmers' markets enable personal relationships to develop as social and economic interaction is part of the exchange process and are considered more personal and friendlier settings than supermarkets as they are smaller with greater attention placed on customer service. Lyon, Collie, Kvarnbrink and Colquhoun (2009), in a survey of consumers at Scottish farmers' markets, found that the main reasons for shopping at farmers' markets were the direct interaction with local produce growers and the high quality products available for purchase. McGarry Wolf, Spittler and Ahern (2005) found that Californian consumers were motivated to shop there because they perceived the products to be environmentally friendly and locally grown.

Ethical consumption

Ethical consumption involves the acceptance of responsibility for understanding the social and environmental impact of products (Turner and Hope 2014). Consumers are becoming more interested in the inputs and costs involved in producing a product. Their choice involving ethical consumption can include minimising their consumption of energy and water, recycling and fair trade options. The ethical part of consumption decisions for consumers involves the collective concern and care people have about the environment in which they live (Jagers 2009). This means ethical consumption is a form of solidarity in which consumers, producers and sellers share the same concerns about their environmental footprint. Ethical consumption has focused on how individuals are responsible for what and how they buy products and as consumerism has globalised, more individuals are stressing the role of ecological citizenship, which involves placing ecological concerns in the mind of consumers. Ethical consumption is part of the alternative consumerism that has become popular in response to health concerns about environmental impact (Gabriel and Lang 1995).

Research setting

Our research is based on an analysis of interviews with owners and other family members who have businesses at farmers' markets. All the interviews were conducted in farmers' markets located in Melbourne and its surrounding area. The state of Victoria, of which Melbourne is the capital city, is an area renowned for its fruit and vegetables. Sometimes called the 'fruit bowl' of Australia, there are a number of family farms within a 1–6 hour drive from Melbourne. Melbourne is a good location to study farmers' markets as there is a tradition of these markets.

Methodology

We conducted a study of 12 family-owned farms who sold their produce at farmers' markets. The case studies were selected using a convenience sample and personal connections to identify family farms at farmers' markets. This purposeful sampling technique enabled an in-depth analysis of the key research propositions (Yin 2003).

Snowball sampling was then utilised as each interviewee identified other family-owned farms selling produce at the farmers' markets. This enabled the cases to be confined to family farms and it maintained the similarity of sustainability pressures. Further cases were sought until data saturation was achieved and there were enough data to analyse the responses. The data were collected via one-on-one semi-structured interviews with family businesses at farmers' markets located in the Melbourne and surrounding areas. Semi-structured interviews were chosen as they enabled a breadth of data to be collected (Yin 2003). These data enabled a better understanding of sustainable entrepreneurship in farmers' markets.

A qualitative approach was chosen as it enabled a discussion of sustainable entrepreneurship in the context of family businesses in farmers' markets. This allowed the respondents' perspective to be understood better by delving into the relevant areas of interest (Alvesson 2003). The interview process was structured so avenues of interest could be discussed in more detail, enabling a more in-depth evaluation of farmers' markets and sustainable entrepreneurship. Most interviews lasted around 30 and 40 minutes, depending on the availability of the family business owner at the farmers' market. The interviews were with representatives of family farms and were transcribed prior to the analysis and then categorised by the location of the farmers' market. Analysis of each of the interviews was conducted to see the main themes generated, such as ethical orientation and social networks. The next stage involved identifying the commonalities and differences between the family farm businesses at the farmers' market. This was an important process in allowing grouping of data based on individual perspectives (Yin 2003). The role of ethics, environment and sustainability was analysed to see if there were any patterns emerging.

Findings

As more family farms utilise farmers' markets to supplement their income, we wanted to understand the role of sustainable entrepreneurship. In the cross-case analysis, there were two main strategies used by family farm owners at farmers' markets related to sustainable entrepreneurship: (1) developing social capital and (2) marketing ethical consumption. All the family farms in the study followed one of these strategic approaches as part of their sustainable entrepreneurship development approach. All the farms in the study had been owned by the family for at least three years, with all families being regular attendees at farmers' markets for the past two years. Table 13.1 depicts the type of farm, number of workers and more details about the family business for each interview. For the family farms we studied, five followed a social capital strategy and seven had an ethical consumption marketing approach to their sustainable entrepreneurship activities. Social capital strategists responded to the need for greater interaction with the environment by focusing on sustainability issues raised in local communities. Ethical consumption marketing meant that farm owners took greater care about emphasising the organic and sustainable farming methods in which they engaged.

Table 13.1 The family farms at the farmers' markets

Farm case no	Type of farm	Workers	Current generation	Years at farmers' market	Interviewees
Developing social capital					
3	Fruit and vegetables	2FT/1PT	1st	4	Farm owner
5	Nut	4FT/0PT	1st	2	Farm owner, daughter
7	Dairy	6FT/1PT	2nd	4	Farm owner
8	Fruit and vegetables	2FT/1PT	2nd	2	Farm owner
11	Fruit and vegetables	4FT/4PT	2nd	2	Farm owner, 2 sons
Marketing ethical consumption					
1	Chicken	5FT/3PT	2nd	5	Farm owner
2	Fruit and vegetables	2FT/1PT	2nd	3	Farm owner
4	Fruit and vegetables	2FT/4PT	1st	2	Farm owner, daughter
6	Fruit and vegetables	4FT/8PT	1st	4	Farm owner, son
9	Dairy	2FT/7PT	3rd	4	Farm owner
10	Fruit and vegetables	2FT/1PT	2nd	2	Farm owner
12	Fruit and vegetables	4FT/1PT	3rd	2	Farm owner, son

FT = full-time, PT = part-time

Each of these marketing strategies for the family farms at the farmers' markets will now be discussed.

Developing social capital

Family farms that had developing social capital as their main strategy for sustainable entrepreneurship focused on connected relationships. Building and maintaining relationships is a common business practice for family farms and farmers' markets enable this social interaction. Most of the five cases that followed this strategy were located further away from Melbourne; therefore, they held social capital in high regard, as many country towns are smaller and people often know each other better than in urban towns. The following response illustrates the developing social capital strategy:

> We come to the farmers market every weekend but the location changes around Melbourne. Initially we thought it would help the local region by bringing together farmers from our region but by coming together we can interact and build relationships around our food . . . our vegetables mean that people know who we are but more importantly the town we are from. I like

the social element of the markets. (It) is laid back (relaxed). If I've sold all the produce I shut up (close) early. I like that.

(Farmer no. 3)

Most of the family farms that followed this strategy were focused on the relationships they derived from being part of the community at farmers' markets. By grouping together, the family farm owners felt they were stronger than selling their product alone:

> We sometimes travel with other families to the markets but often we come alone. But being at the markets allows us to interact in a social fashion with the other growers.
>
> (Farmer no. 8)

Family farms with this strategy used their social connections to learn more about sustainability with less emphasis on competition. We heard some family farms say that they learn at the farmers' markets how consumers perceive sustainability farming practices:

> The customers, many haven't been to a farm, some never, so they see sustainability as something different to us. We try to use water wisely and emphasise efficiency as part of our farming practices. But we are part of a community. We learn by following and watching others.
>
> (Farmer no. 11)

As farms were no longer the sole source of income, some interviewees said they felt they could be more interested in sustainability because they had the financial resources to buy more ethical products, which are typically more expensive:

> I have another job, so our farm is for the family but we aren't solely dependent on it. We try to incorporate alternative farming practices that are good for the land but we have the money to do this and selling at farmers' markets helps. If we see other farmers with sustainability practices, we try to innovate in the same way. Recently we did this by planting drought resistant plants that wouldn't be so dependent on the weather.
>
> (Farmer no. 5)

Most of the family farms following the developing social capital strategy moved their focus to sustainability as they had the financial resources to engage in these practices. We note that most of the family farms who stressed social capital also had supplemental incomes in addition to the farmers' market revenue. This enabled them greater flexibility in their sustainable farming practices.

Marketing ethical consumption

Family farm owners at farmers' markets who followed this strategy made a choice to focus on ethical consumption of their products. This was emphasised by their continued presence at farmers' markets and the discussions they had with consumers about ethical consumption. By marketing the ethical consumption of their produce, they expected better profit margins from the farmers' markets. This strategy enabled family farms to incorporate family values together with ethical consumption in their marketing. The following example shows how ethical consumption was marketed:

> The reason people shop at farmers' markets is that they want something different. Most want better products, better service. Part of this is our ethics and related to this is sustainability.
>
> (Farmer no. 9)

Farmers following an ethical consumption marketing strategy believed it was the only way to operate at farmers' markets:

> Consumers at farmers' markets are interested in sustainability. They want to be ethical and involved. I know as I've talked to so many consumers who ask where the fruit comes from, who farmed it, you know all the questions related to the ethics of do we actually grow what we are saying we grow.
>
> (Farmer no. 12)

Focusing on the marketing of ethical consumption at farmers' markets differentiated the family farmers from other businesses that competed on price. There were a number of consequences of this strategy. It enabled specific features of the fruit to be highlighted, such as being organic and not using pesticides. It drew attention to the role of the family in farming and changes to sustainable farming methods. Overall, the interviewees told us that ethical consumption influenced sales at farmers' markets as consumers liked to know about the food chain. For example:

> I know we have grown and sold these ethically. The price is reasonable. The quality is good. We produce small sizes but this is part of our business. We are not larger growers. We care about our products more so because of our reputation. Our brand is focused on quality.
>
> (Farmer no. 2)

The next section will further discuss each of the two marketing strategies for family farms at farmers' markets by linking the data analysis to the literature currently in existence around sustainable entrepreneurship. The summary of each of these strategies and the findings are depicted in Table 13.2.

Table 13.2 Summary of findings

Strategy	Description of strategy	Number of farms	Rationale for family business	Rationale for farmers market
Developing social capital	The family farm focuses on the social networks and connections they have in order to expand their sustainability practices.	5	Farming is part of the tradition and business expertise of the family and developing mutual connections is important.	The farm uses social networks and relationships within the local, regional and international community to connect with consumers.
Ethical consumption marketing	The family farm focuses on the ethical benefits of consuming their products.	7	Farming is considered ethical if it includes sustainable management practices that integrate environmental, social and economic effects. Sustainable entrepreneurship is viewed as a positive aspect of the family business.	The farm is managed using a sustainability perspective by linking community and environmental effects. Farm focuses on sustainability from using it as part of their ethical marketing in farmers' markets.

Discussion

This study focused on how family farm businesses use sustainable entrepreneurship from a social capital and ethical consumption marketing perspective. We found that family farms took different paths in terms of their sustainable entrepreneurship policies. We identified two main strategies used at farmers' markets that link to sustainable entrepreneurship: developing social capital and ethical consumption marketing. These strategies allowed family farms to utilise the specific characteristics of consumers who come to farmers' markets for their economic and social success. Our findings support the role of sustainability in the entrepreneurship process of business. The richness of the qualitative data helps to stress the importance of sustainability in making decisions for family farms. Gómez-Mejia et al. (2007) highlighted that owners of small private businesses want to protect their socio-economic wealth and our findings suggest that family farms have a similar feeling towards social capital development.

Few studies in the family farm literature have considered sustainable entrepreneurship in the context of farmers' markets. The strategies we identified involve significant consequences to family farms but also managers of farmers' markets. We found that family farms utilise their connection to the land and community to promote their sustainability initiatives. Recently, Glover and Reay (2015) proposed that diversification strategies are important for family dairy farmers. Our study showed that social capital and marketing ethical consumption increase the value creation for family farmers at farmers' markets. This is helpful in building marketing communications strategies for farmers' markets as they compete with online shopping sites that also have ethical marketing campaigns. As competition amongst farmers increases in the global market, local family farms can stress their social connections to community, land and place as a way to strengthen their business endeavours. This will be important in promoting sustainable entrepreneurship for family farms who sell their products at farmers' markets.

Conclusions

This chapter has several practical recommendations for farmers' market managers and public policy planners. Farmers' markets should focus on the sustainable and ethical consumption of the products sold as a marketing strategy to increase sales. As more consumers are focusing on organic and locally grown food, this is a helpful marketing strategy, which will increase word-of-mouth communication about the benefits of farmers' markets. Family farm managers should market the sustainable elements of their products by increasing awareness about socially orientated individuals who place high importance on organic and sustainable farming methods. Family farmers could also market their products by having a certified standard that maintains consumers' confidence about sustainable farming. This might mean that higher profits for farmers' market businesses are made from certified sustainable produce.

This study has some limitations that give rise to future research suggestions. First, it analyses perceptions of sustainable entrepreneurship by focusing on social capital and ethical consumption. This means that other secondary motivations influencing sustainable entrepreneurial activity at farmers' markets were not considered and could be addressed in future research. Second, the study examined farmers' markets only in Melbourne, Australia and did not look at other geographic locations. Despite this limitation, the findings are likely to be applicable to farmers' markets in other countries, but more research is needed to see if the cultural conditions affect the propensity of family farmers at farmers' markets to be more interested in sustainable entrepreneurship.

References

Abello, E.J., Palma, M.A., Waller, M.L. and Anderson, D.P. (2014) 'Evaluating the factors influencing the number of visits to farmers' markets', *Journal of Food Products Marketing*, 20(1), 17–35.

Alonso, A.D. and O'Neill, M.A. (2011) 'A comparative study of farmers' markets visitors' needs and wants: The case of Alabama', *International Journal of Consumer Studies*, 35(3), 290–299.

Alvesson, M. (2003) 'Beyond neopositivists, romantics, and localists: A reflexive approach to interviews in organisational research', *Academy of Management Review*, 28(3), 13–33.

Binder, J. and Belz, F.M. (2014) 'Sustainable entrepreneurship: What it is', in P. Kyrö (ed.), *Handbook of Entrepreneurship and Sustainable Development* (pp. 30–71), Cheltenham, UK: Elgar.

Belz, F.M. and Binder, J.K. (2017) 'Sustainable entrepreneurship: A convergent process model', *Business Strategy and the Environment*, 26, 1–17.

Bourdieu, P. (1980) 'Le capital social', *Actes De La Recherche en Sciences Sociales*, 31(1), 2–3.

Campbell, J. (2015) 'Cooperate or compete: The relationship of strategic orientation and firm performance for farmers' market vendors', *Journal of Small Business & Entrepreneurship*, 27(1), 27–42.

Curtis, K.R. and Cowee, M.W. (2011) 'Buying local: Diverging consumer motivations and concerns', *Journal of Agribusiness*, 29(1), 1–22.

Dimitri, C. and Greene, C. (2002) 'Organic food industry taps growing American market', *Agricultural Outlook*, October, 4–7.

Gabriel, Y. and Lang, T. (1995) *The Unmanageable Consumer*, London: Sage.

Glover, J.L. and Reay, T. (2015) 'Sustaining the family business with minimal financial rewards: How do family farms continue?', *Family Business Review*, 28(2), 163–177.

Gómez-Mejia, L.R., Haynes, K., Nuñez-Nickel, M., Jacobson, K.J.L. and Moyano-Fuentes, J. (2007) 'Socioemotional wealth and business risks in family-controlled firms: Evidence from Spanish olive oil mills', *Administrative Science Quarterly*, 52, 106–137.

Jagers, S.C. (2009) 'In search of the ecological citizen', *Environmental Politics*, 18(1), 18–36.

Loureiro, M.L. and Hine, S. (2002) 'Discovering niche markets: A comparison of consumer willingness to pay for local (Colorado Grown), organic, and GMO-free products', *Journal of Agricultural and Applied Economics*, 34(3), 477–487.

Lyon, P., Collie, V., Kvarnbrink, E. and Colquhoun, A. (2009) 'Shopping at the farmers' market: Consumers and their perspectives', *Journal of Food Service*, 20(1), 21–30.

McGarry Wolf, M., Spittler, A. and Ahern, J. (2005) 'A profile of farmers' market consumers and the perceived advantages of produce sold at farmers' markets', *Journal of Food Distribution Research*, 36(1), 192–201.

Thompson, N., Kiefer, K. and York, J.G. (2011) 'Distinctions not dichotomies: Exploring social, sustainable, and environmental entrepreneurship', *Advances in Entrepreneurship, Firm Emergence and Growth*, 13, 205–233.

Turner, B. and Hope, C. (2014) 'Ecological connections: Reimagining the role of farmers' markets', *Rural Society*, 23(2), 175–187.

Yin, R. (2003) *Case Study Research: Design and Methods*, 3rd edition, London: Sage.

14 Beyond branding

The role of booktowns in building a relational marketplace

Melissa Kennedy

Introduction

There have never been as many books as there are in the world today. According to Richard Booth, the founder of the world's first 'book town' in Hay-on-Wye in the UK, 'ninety-five per cent of the world's books were published after 1961' (Booth and Stuart 1999: 270). Since Booth's observations, digital technology and new forms of production, consumption and distribution have augmented book choice and supply via e-books and online sales. Concern for the fate of printed books has not only confronted the local book industry but has also extended to the international network of 'book towns' (Seaton and Alford 2001; Thomas 2014), where predominantly rural villages rely on clusters of bookshops as a rural development strategy. Given that books are the key 'commodity' exchanged in a booktown economy, a vibrant local book industry is vital to the ongoing production of booktowns. In turn, booktowns can also champion the local book industry through creating a new marketplace for book distribution, particularly in meeting growing demands for 'slow' or 'creative' tourism experiences centred around relational encounters with local people, products and place.

This chapter looks beyond the branding benefits of industrial events to explore their strategic role in mobilising action and building a relational marketplace around book distribution. Specifically, it focuses on the case study of the Australian booktown of Clunes, and its annual festival, which is regarded as 'Australia's largest book trading event' (Creative Clunes 2015). The chapter is structured as follows: first, a background to the booktown movement and its intersection with the creative tourism and slow tourism economies is outlined. Second, the study site of Clunes is described. Following this, the methodological approach of Actor-Network theory is introduced. Finally, the festival's strategic role in fostering relational exchanges between the book industry, booktown and consumers is explored.

Booktowns, rural development and tourism

Despite the spread of booktowns throughout Europe from the 1980s, the emergence of booktowns in the southern hemisphere is a relatively recent phenomenon. The first booktown was conceived in the Welsh village of Hay-on-Wye in 1961 by Richard Booth, an entrepreneur concerned with the effects of globalisation and restructuring in rural economies (Booth and Stuart 1999). Booth's clustering of bookshops in Hay-on-Wye's notable buildings such as the old fire station, cinema and castle, led to the market town's transformation as a tourism destination. The unique concept led to a surge in tourists (approximately half a million people per year) and a substantial boost to accommodation and other related enterprises in the town such as bookbinding and crafts (Seaton 1999). Given the distinctiveness of the concept and the success of Hay-on-Wye, booktowns attracted academic and policy interest as a rural development model in the 1990s. This led to the first substantive report into booktowns, which identified commonalities between seven booktowns across Europe such as: scenic appeal, available property and a peripheral location (Seaton 1999). There are currently 22 accredited and prospective booktowns listed throughout Europe, Asia, Australia and New Zealand (International Organisation of Book Towns 2016).

Booktowns have been acknowledged for their contribution to rural development outside of Hay-on-Wye. Studies have highlighted important positive benefits for rural locales such as economic development and cultural heritage preservation. The French booktown of Montolieu has been recognised for its stimulation of the local economy and population through boosting home renovations and maintaining the viability of the local school and retail services (Merfeld-Langston 2014). The small coastal village of Fjaerland in Norway is reported to have attained significant place promotion and visitation as a booktown (Vik and Villa 2010). Economic stimulation is also accompanied by caution concerning rural gentrification through rising house prices and lack of affordability for young booksellers in the case of Montolieu (Merfeld-Langston 2014). This is echoed by concern from the community of Maleny in Queensland, where booktowns were suspiciously viewed by some locals as threatening an increase in rents (Frank 2016). Negotiation with other tourism enterprises that come into conflict with the idyllic image of a booktown is another issue (Vik and Villa 2010). Booktowns therefore face challenges in stimulating economic diversity along with attaining 'buy in' from local businesses and community.

Festivals offer a significant opportunity for the economic diversification of booktowns and place branding, as well as fostering local engagement and pride (Kennedy 2011). Literary festivals have become a relatively recent and successful phenomenon in Australia due to a favourable climate, and utilisation by the book industry as 'unofficial trade fairs' (Ommundsen 2009: 20–21). For consumers, the popular appeal of literary festivals is theorised as part of 'middle brow' or middle-class cultural consumption desire (Driscoll 2014). Furthermore, the desire for participatory, rather than passive experiences is regarded as driving a 'creative turn' in tourism, described as 'an encounter, relationship and negotiation with the symbolic/cultural domain in tourist destinations' (Russo and Richards 2016: 5). The OECD defines creative tourism as:

> tourism directed to an engaged and authentic experience of a place with participative learning in the arts, heritage and special character of a place.
>
> (OECD 2014)

Alongside participatory learning, 'relationality' is emphasised through the exchange of ideas, culture, skills and knowledge (Richards 2014: 88).

The growing shift towards the appreciation of local exchanges offers new prospects in moving beyond the branding benefits of festivals, to understanding how initiatives such as booktown events are valorised as relational experiences. This desire for relationality resonates with the broader 'Slow Tourism' trends. As an offshoot of the Italian-born 'Slow Food' movement, Slow Tourism aims to remediate the disconnected nature of mass tourism, by engaging in:

> a range of spatio-temporal practices, immersive modes of travel and ethical relations that are premised on the desire to connect in particular ways and to disconnect in others.
>
> (Fullagar, Markwell and Wilson 2012: 3)

Booktowns are considered an exemplar of the types of conscious consumption shaping this new tourism field, enacted through the ethical and slow perusing of secondhand books in rural locales (Frank 2016). Tourism desires are therefore increasingly shaped through the interplay between people, product and place. The remainder of this chapter seeks to uncover the strategic role of events in mobilising and fostering such relational exchanges through a case study of the Clunes Booktown Festival.

Clunes: background

Clunes is a small town located in central Victoria, Australia, approximately 140 kilometres from the state capital of Melbourne. The town was established as a pastoral settlement in 1839 and transformed through the discovery of gold in 1851. At the peak of the gold rush, the population of Clunes swelled to around 6,000, falling to an estimated current population of 1,393 in 2011 (Department of Environment, Land, Water and Planning 2016). The gold rush legacy has endowed Clunes with rich heritage streetscapes (Figure 14.1), leading it to be recognised as

Figure 14.1 Clunes streetscape
Source: Photo courtesy of Melissa Kennedy

'one of the most intact 19th-century towns in the Central Goldfields, boasting numerous sandstone, bluestone and brick buildings' (Traveller 2007). Following the depletion of mineable gold in the 1860s, the town transitioned to an agricultural and manufacturing economy, which has contracted in line with global economic restructuring and exacerbated by the protracted 'millennium' drought. The impact of population decline and the drought became a driving impetus in the reimagining of Clunes as a booktown, requiring 'a willingness to dream, to imagine, and to act' (Brady 2012 cited in Johnston 2016: 138).

The introduction of the booktown concept in 2006 signalled a transition to a cultural tourism economy. The construction of a booktown identity for Clunes was thus driven by the imagining of a new economic future, as explained by one of the founders:

> Our whole idea was to build an economy based on culture. Its focus is on a group of the same industries, the same type of shops, cluster tourism, cluster marketing and things like that.
>
> (Creative Clunes Respondent 4)

The booktown model was introduced by four community members who were inspired by the success of Hay-on-Wye and recognised that the town fulfilled many of the established booktown 'Critical Success Factors' such as a declining economy; stock of available buildings; scenic appeal and connections to the publishing industry (Seaton 1999). Although the concept of a booktown was unusual, cultural tourism was not an unconventional strategy for Clunes based on its wide main street and notable and well-preserved built fabric. Over the years the town has been used as a setting for movies such as *Mad Max* (1979) and *Ned Kelly* (2003), as well as national and international television series. Its proximity to the state capital of Melbourne and the regional centres of Geelong, Bendigo and Ballarat is also a key asset in attracting tourists on day trips.

Ten years since the booktown concept was trialled as a festival 'Booktown for a Day' with an estimated 6,000 attendees, it has grown to attract approximately 18,000 patrons, along with high-profile authors, political speakers and creative workshops. Furthermore, Creative Clunes, the organisation driving the initiative, has recorded a number of achievements including: accreditation of Clunes as an international booktown in 2012; cultural exchange projects with international booktowns like Paju Book City in South Korea; and partnerships with arts bodies closer to home such as the Wheeler Centre – a flagship institution associated with Melbourne's status as a UNESCO City of Literature.

While the first booktown festival was ultimately a branding exercise for Clunes as a booktown (Kennedy 2011), in this chapter I engage with actor-network theory to demonstrate the festival's strategic role in bringing together the book industry, community cultural entrepreneurs (Creative Clunes) and tourists as part of a relational network or 'hybrid collectif' (Callon and Law 1995). This approach moves beyond the branding benefits of industrial events to understanding their strategic role in mobilising collective action around bookselling.

Methodology: actor-network theory

Actor-network theory (ANT) is 'an empirical version of poststructuralism' (Law 2009: 145), which rejects pre-determined interpretations of social worlds (Latour 2003). Rather than a fixed theory or framework, ANT is a 'sensibility to the messy practices of materiality and relationally in the world' (Law 2009: 142). ANT's core premise is a shift from static categorisations of social activities to the 'reassembling' of social relations (Latour 2005). This approach involves an open process of the tracing of associations that 'enrol' or bring heterogeneous actors together as a collective (Latour 2005; Murdoch 1997). Furthermore, ANT not only confounds the composition of social worlds but extends into the nonhuman sphere through a framing of 'generalised symmetry' between humans and non-humans in effecting action (Nimmo 2011: 112). ANT's emphasis on processes of collective action and distributed agency is particularly instructive for exploring the process of relation forming between people, places and objects in rural economies. It is increasingly engaged in tourism studies, particularly through the concept of 'tourismscapes', where attention is paid to how people, objects and spaces are ordered together and perform tourism (Van der Duim 2007). ANT is therefore an instructive approach towards understanding how 'material resources' (Van der Duim 2007: 971) and relations are interlinked across space in the production of a booktown.

The multi-faceted and human/nonhuman networks promulgated by ANT are conceptualised as a 'hybrid collectif' or collective (Callon and Law 1997: 8). Callon and Law describe this amalgamation of diverse actors as 'an emergent effect created by the interaction of the heterogeneous parts that make it up' (1995: 485). Attention is thus shifted to analysing how hybrid collectives are comprised rather than pre-determined or positioned as oppositional categorisations such as individual versus collective, or agency versus structure (Callon and Law 1997). The ordering of hybrid collectives involves a process of translation, which entails:

> bringing together entities that are sometimes radically different, and convincing them that they have an interest in connecting and relating.
>
> (Barnes 2005: 71–72)

Given that booktowns are recognised as having the dual purpose of bookselling and rural development (Vik and Villa 2010), it is important to consider how these goals are aligned between actors in the production of a booktown. Translation therefore offers important insights into how the concept of booktowns have been transferred across space to new contexts and have mobilised diverse actors from the book industry, tourists, community and government, as well as the material properties of the 'book' and 'town'.

The following section carries forward actor-network theory's principle of translation into an empirical context, by considering the Clunes Booktown Festival's strategic role in mobilising a hybrid collective of actors around book distribution. This involves tracing the inter-relations between the book traders, booktown and consumers, described as 'specific translations of objects, people and ideas, as they come together from a variety of origins, and sometimes split apart' (Barnes 2005: 72). This tracing of these relations is considered over two stages. First, the mobilisation of the hybrid collective is investigated through the inaugural festival 'Booktown for a Day'. This will be followed by discussion on how the associations fostered around bookselling contribute to a more relational understanding of creative tourism economies beyond consumer perspectives. Data are drawn from a research evaluation of the 2010 Booktown Festival (Kennedy 2010; Kennedy 2011), festival programmes and semi-structured interviews conducted with key informants from September 2015 to July 2016.

Mobilising a movement: Clunes Booktown Festival

The booktown strategy for Clunes was driven by four new residents who united over books as a cultural development strategy for the town (Kennedy 2011). The confluence of these actors in coming together is reflected by one of the key founders who recalled:

> A group of people tended to come together at the one time. Perhaps you know not knowing that the other was interested in establishing a theme if you like for the town along the idea of literature or specifically books.
>
> (Creative Clunes Respondent 3)

At that initial meeting, the discussion evolved from the idea of a monthly book market to becoming a booktown. It was acknowledged that whether the initiative was a book market or booktown, support for the idea by book traders would be vital and required testing. This lead to plans for a trial event 'Booktown for a Day' in May 2007:

> We sort of came to the conclusion that whether it was a monthly book market or concept of a booktown, surely we would have to test it to see whether people would be interested in participating in the book town concept. You had to be prepared for people to come to the book market or move to Clunes and set up shops etc. So that's when we decided 'well look why don't we see – we'll try for one day – see what happens'.
>
> (Creative Clunes Respondent 3)

The organisers received an overwhelming response from book traders with around 50 registrations, exceeding the group's original aspiration for 15 (personal communication). On the day of the event, Clunes transformed into a booktown by turning an array of private and public buildings (including the town hall and courthouse) into temporary shops. Visitor numbers of 6,000 also surpassed expectations. As a result, the organisers recognised that the festival not only offered an opportunity to engage with book traders, but that they had 'stumbled across a niche' with the public by offering an event focused around books (personal communication). After the trial, it was apparent that there was enough demand for the festival to take place annually over a full weekend each May. Pivotally, the positive response to the festival led the organising committee to formalise their booktown strategy through the establishment of a nonprofit 'Creative Clunes'. Their vision statement describes the centrality of the festival in reimagining Clunes as a booktown:

> We aim to create and develop the town as a vibrant rural cultural hub for books writing and ideas. We will do this by developing and managing a high level of cultural and artistic experiences for the local community, the regional community and visitors, and by annually staging a nationally and internationally recognised festival-of-the-book. We aim to make Clunes one of the great Booktowns of the world.
>
> (Creative Clunes 2016a)

By enrolling (or bringing together) a diverse array of actors from industry, community and government to produce the festival, this trial event mobilised a hybrid collective or relational network in reimagining Clunes as a booktown. The enrolment of book traders into the festival was therefore central to the testing of the booktown concept and its ongoing production over the last 10 years. Importantly, the festival acted as a strategic device to familiarise book traders with the initiative with the view of attracting the critical mass of permanent bookshops required for international booktown status. This was a slow process, requiring the 'buy in' of booksellers to the initiative. As one of the permanent book traders explains, setting up an ongoing book shop in the town was not solely for economic reasons, there was a social and strong community element driving participation:

> I think the thing was too that opening a shop here, even on a reduced basis was a way to still use my expertise and do something for the town as much as anything. So we are crying out for people to establish permanent bookshops and they come and go, but I'm here for the moment.
>
> (Clunes Book Trader 1)

From the perspective of this informant, enrolment in the collective suggests that participation in the initiative is reciprocal – a business opportunity as well as contributing to the overall rural development objective. Furthermore, the part-time trading hours of the local bookshops are reflective of the limited flow of tourism revenue outside of weekends. Maintaining the critical mass of bookshops and fulfilling tourist expectations of a booktown offering, especially midweek, are key challenges in the production of a booktown. The festival therefore is of inherent strategic value in maintaining the ongoing viability of the local bookshops and the booktown itself. This is reinforced by the above informant who reflected, 'the festival is vital, absolutely vital for me and just generally for the town. That's a huge draw card' (Clunes Book Trader 1).

Producing a relational marketplace through festivals

The production of a booktown festival involves the assemblage of a broad variety of actors including: authors; book traders; international booktown members; entertainers; local businesses; community members and volunteers; schools and universities; festival patrons; and government and private sponsors. The creation of a booktown also draws extensively upon the material components of books as the commodity to be exchanged and the rich built heritage fabric of Clunes as the physical setting. In considering the strategic role of the event in supporting the book industry and the booktown concept itself, the rest of this chapter focuses specifically on how the festival fosters relations between book traders, visitors and the material resources of a booktown.

Book traders are central to the production of the festival. The event attracts an array of stallholders offering a diverse range of new, second-hand and collectable books with encompassing genres such as arts and literature, children's books, Australiana, automobiles, military history and vintage cook books (Creative Clunes 2016b). The ongoing support of the event by book traders over its 10-year existence is largely indicative of its appeal to industry, with stallholders remaining constant at around 50 participants from around the state and interstate (Creative Clunes 2016b). A study on the festival in 2010 found that the majority of book traders were either very satisfied (29%) or satisfied with their sales experience (57%) (Kennedy 2010: 38–40). Although income from sales was variable, a number of traders recognised the added value of industry and consumer interactions such as networking opportunities with other traders, connections with 'book-orientated customers' and the identification of a 'target market' (38–40). More recently, the appeal of the event for book traders was emphasised by Mark Rubbo, Managing Director of the Melbourne-based independent bookstore 'Readings':

> I think it's the best literary event in Australia. Sales have been great, there's a fun atmosphere and the people who are here are people who are so keen and interested in books.
>
> (Creative Clunes 2016c, see Figure 14.2)

The establishment of a formal partnership with Readings has in turn broadened awareness of the festival through the bookstore's metropolitan network, as relayed by an interview participant:

> People . . . would say things like 'I've always meant to go but it is always so far' . . . and now there are actually people coming up from Melbourne for the festival because [Readings] are involved in it, so definitely it has spread a lot of awareness of Clunes and what's happening here by Readings becoming involved.
>
> (Creative Clunes Respondent 9)

The creation of a unique marketplace centred on books as the material resource is a core attribute of the festival for traders. While the Booktown Festival has an extensive

Figure 14.2 Readings book stall, situated in the middle of the main street of Clunes
Source: Photo courtesy of Melissa Kennedy

programme of high-profile author talks, exhibitions and educational activities (Creative Clunes 2016c), the focus remains strongly on books as the central object to be celebrated and exchanged. This is emphasised in the positioning of the event in programme as a 'festival-of-the-book' (Creative Clunes 2015: 3) and the slogans: 'For the love of books' and 'Australia's largest book trading event in the Southern Hemisphere's Only Booktown' (Creative Clunes 2015). The appreciation of books is clearly reciprocated from a consumer perspective. In the aforementioned survey, 'books' were listed by visitors as the highest factor of enjoyment in the festival (Kennedy 2010: 21). Participants highlighted the variety, volume and price of books on offer, as well as the immerse experience of the event through the 'excitement of book-hunting' and 'finding a treasure', reminiscent of the town's gold rush predecessors (Figure 14.3). Unsurprisingly, Clunes Booktown Festival patrons are found to have a higher orientation towards book buying and collecting compared with other literary festivals in Victoria, which indicate a greater value placed on author engagement (such as the Melbourne Writer's Festival) (Driscoll 2014: 190–191).

The material setting of Clunes is a significant asset in the production of the booktown. The inter-relations between the book and the townscape are reinforced in an interview with a member of Creative Clunes:

> The festival is an essence about the book, it's a celebration of the book in all its forms, variations and meanings . . . so to me anyway Clunes Booktown

Figure 14.3 Book buyers searching for a treasure at the festival
Source: Photo courtesy of Melissa Kennedy

> Festival is multi-faceted because it is about the celebration of the book, not
> just the intrinsic and intangible value of what is inside and . . . this is happen-
> ing in a space . . . where you have the incredibly charming visual aesthetic of
> all of these older buildings.
>
> (Creative Clunes Respondent 8)

The interplay between books and the local aesthetic also elicited strong appreciation from festival visitors. After 'books', the 'atmosphere' of Clunes

(linked to 'historic', 'rural' and 'relaxing') and its built fabric recorded the second and third highest responses in a visitor survey (Kennedy 2010: 21–22). Interactions with the setting and history of Clunes are reflected in visitor comments such as:

> I like the way all the old buildings are open.
>
> (Female 40–49 Melbourne)

> The history of the town goes with the books.
>
> (Male 30–39 Melbourne)

> I enjoy learning about Clunes.
>
> (Female 60–69 Melbourne)

While the festival emphasis is on the exchange of books, being around a 'likeminded community' and engaging with authors also elicited appreciation from attendees (Kennedy 2011: 215). Outside the exchange of books, the trading of ideas and skills offer 'creative tourism' experiences to book lovers (OECD 2014: 44). As a result of these immersive experiences, a unique 'festivalscape' or ambience is also produced (Lee, Lee, Lee and Babin 2008), (Figure 14.4).

Figure 14.4 The festivalscape of inter-relations between visitors and town

Source: Photo courtesy of Melissa Kennedy

Discussion and conclusion

This chapter has identified that industrial events, such as book festivals, provide valuable opportunities for the book industry to engage in a marketplace outside of online platforms. The growth of 'creative tourism' trends centred on relational exchanges between people, product and place (Richards 2011), add to the influence of these events. Drawing upon a case study of the Clunes Booktown Festival, it has shown how the trial festival was instrumental in assembling a hybrid collective of human and nonhuman actors around the twin objectives of book distribution and rural development. While e-sales are becoming inherent to the viability of the book industry worldwide (Merfeld-Langston 2014), and indeed booktowns (Seaton and Alford 2001), the annual bookselling event is influential in breaking down binaries between distribution and consumption. In this setting, the market is 'resocialised' with interdependencies between actors brought to the fore (Gibson-Graham 2006: 95). Book traders have been enrolled into a rural development concept and in turn are offered face-to-face encounters with conscious consumers. Intersecting with principles of the 'Slow' movement, this process of ethical encounter contributes to the visibility of market transactions where interconnections and wellbeing are foregrounded over distant and disembodied exchange (Gibson-Graham, Cameron and Healy 2013: 105).

This research moves beyond the branding attributes of industrial events to offer a deeper understanding of the relations generated between community cultural entrepreneurs, book traders and consumers in the production of a book festival. While literary events are recognised for their role in facilitating participatory exchange between authors and consumers (Ommundsen 2009), this chapter has explicitly emphasised another opportunity for exchange, between that of distributors (booksellers) and consumers, in an era where the viability of the second-hand book industry is increasingly perceived as threatened.

References

Barnes, T. (2005) 'Culture: Economy', in P. Cloke and R. Johnston (eds.), *Spaces of Geographical Thought* (pp. 61–81), London: Sage.
Booth, R. and Stuart, L. (1999) *My Kingdom of Books*, Wales: Y Lolfa.
Brady, T. (2012) 'Clunes Address' *World Booktown Symposium*, Paju Booksori, September.
Callon, M. and Law, J. (1995) 'Agency and the hybrid collectif', *The South Atlantic Quarterly*, 94(2), 481–507.
Callon, M. and Law, J. (1997) 'After the individual in society: Lessons on collectivity from science, technology and society', *Canadian Journal of Sociology*, 22(2), 165–182.
Creative Clunes (2015) *Clunes Booktown Festival Program 2015*, www.clunesbooktown.com.au/wp-content/uploads/2015/03/Clunes-Booktown-2015-Program1.pdf (accessed 30 November 2016).
Creative Clunes (2016a) *Creative Clunes*, www.clunesbooktown.com.au/creative-clunes/ (accessed 30 November 2016).
Creative Clunes (2016b) *Clunes Booktown Festival Program 2016*, www.clunesbooktown.com.au/clunes-book-town-festival/2016-festival-schedules/ (accessed 30 November 2016).

Creative Clunes (2016c) *Clunes Booktown Festival*, www.clunesbooktown.com.au/clunes-book-town-festival/ (accessed 20 November 2016).

Department of Environment, Land, Water and Planning (2016) *Towns in Time – Clunes*, www.data.vic.gov.au/data/dataset/towns-in-time-clunes (accessed 30 November 2016).

Driscoll, B. (2014) *The New Literary Middlebrow: Tastemakers and Reading in the Twenty-First Century*, Basingstoke: Palgrave McMillan.

Frank, J. (2016) 'Book culture, landscape and social capital: The case of Maleny', *Queensland Review*, 23(1), 35–48.

Fullagar, S., Markwell, K. and Wilson, E. (2012) *Slow Tourism: Experiences and Mobilities*, Bristol: Channel View.

Gibson-Graham, J.K. (2006) *A Postcapitalist Politics*, Minneapolis, MN: University of Minnesota Press.

Gibson-Graham, J.K., Cameron, J. and Healy, S. (2013) *Take Back the Economy*, Minneapolis, MN: University of Minnesota Press.

International Organisation of Book Towns (2016) *Member Book Towns and Individuals*, www.booktown.net/members.html (accessed 5 November 2016).

Johnston, J. (2016) *Public Relations and the Public Interest*, Abingdon: Routledge.

Kennedy, M. (2010) *Research Audit: Clunes Back to Booktown 2010*, La Trobe University Bendigo: Community Planning and Development Program.

Kennedy, M. (2011) 'Binding a sustainable future: Booktowns, themed place-branding and rural renewal: A case study of Clunes Back to Booktown', in J. Martin and T. Budge (eds.), *The Sustainability of Australia's Country Towns: Renewal, Renaissance, Resilience* (pp. 207–226), Ballarat: VURRN Press.

Latour, B. (2003) 'Is re-modernization occurring-and if so, how to prove it? A commentary on Ulrich Beck', *Theory, Culture & Society*, 20(2), 35–48.

Latour, B. (2005) *Reassembling the Social: An Introduction to Actor-Network-Theory*, Oxford: Oxford University Press.

Law, J. (2009) 'Actor network theory and material semiotics', in B.S. Turner (ed.), *The New Blackwell Companion to Social Theory* (pp. 141–158), London: Blackwell.

Lee, Y.-K., Lee, C.-K., Lee, S.-K. and Babin, B.J. (2008) 'Festivalscapes and patrons' emotions, satisfaction, and loyalty', *Journal of Business Research*, 61(1), 56–64.

Merfeld-Langston, A. (2014) 'Judging a book town by its cover: Marketing French villages du Livre', in P. Whalen and P. Young (eds.), *Place and Locality in Modern France* (pp. 125–136), London: Bloomsbury.

Murdoch, J. (1997) 'Inhuman/nonhuman/human: Actor-network theory and the prospects for a nondualistic and symmetrical perspective on nature and society', *Environment and Planning D: Society and Space*, 15(6), 731–756.

Nimmo, R. (2011) 'Actor-network theory and methodology: Social research in a more-than-human world', *Methodological Innovations Online*, 6(3), 108–119.

OECD (2014) *Tourism and the Creative Economy*, Paris: OECD Publishing.

Ommundsen, W. (2009) 'Literary festivals and cultural consumption', *Australian Literary Studies*, 24(1), 19–34.

Richards, G. (2011) 'Creativity and tourism: The state of the art', *Annals of Tourism Research*, 38(4), 1225–1253.

Richards, G. (2014) 'Creating relational tourism through exchange: The Maltese experience', *Journal of Hospitality and Tourism*, 12(1), 87–94.

Russo, A.P. and Richards, G. (2016) 'Introduction', in A.P. Russo and G. Richards (eds.), *Reinventing the Local in Tourism: Producing, Consuming and Negotiating Place* (pp. 1–14), Bristol: Channel View.

Seaton, A. and Alford, P. (2001) 'Technology by the book: BookTownNet and SME cultural tourism networks', *Information Technology & Tourism*, 4(2), 107–121.

Seaton, A. (1999) 'Book towns as tourism developments in peripheral areas', *The International Journal of Tourism Research*, 1(5), 389–399.

Thomas, H. (2014) 'Hay-on-Wye: A town of books or festivals?', *BBC News*, 29 May 2014, www.bbc.com/news/uk-wales-mid-wales-27624226 (accessed 1 November 2016).

Traveller (2007) 'Clunes', *The Age*, 11 December 2007, www.theage.com.au/news/Victoria/Clunes/2005/02/17/1108500206319.html (accessed 15 November 2016).

Van der Duim, R. (2007) 'Tourismscapes: An actor-network perspective', *Annals of Tourism Research*, 34(4), 961–976.

Vik, J. and Villa, M. (2010) 'Books, branding and boundary objects: On the use of image in rural development', *Sociologia Ruralis*, 50(2), 156–170.

15 Selling sustainability and the green economy

A case study of Ecofest, New Zealand

Jennifer Laing, Judith Mair and Warwick Frost

Introduction

Encouraging sustainable behaviour is increasingly a priority for society. One mechanism for achieving this goal is to organise events with a sustainability focus, which aim to foster behaviour change amongst attendees. These sustainability festivals, otherwise known as eco-festivals or *ecofests*, generally provide information for attendees on how to engage in sustainable behaviour, often involving workshops or lectures, but also showcasing local sustainable businesses and their products (Mair and Laing 2013). They are surprisingly understudied, given the growing interest in green events more generally (Laing and Frost 2010).

This chapter focuses on a qualitative case study of the Ecofest in Nelson, New Zealand, an event which was staged annually between 2001 and 2014. Future plans for staging the event are unfortunately currently 'on hold' (Tasman City Council 2017), with Brian McGurk, Councillor and Chair of the Planning and Regulatory Committee of the Nelson City Council, arguing that it essentially 'preaches to the converted' and 'only 37 per cent were first-time visitors to Ecofest. We're keen to take a much more holistic approach to sustainability that engages with all sectors of the community' (quoted in Nelson Live 2015). Yet, the event provides an important historical example of a successful ecofest, given that it won the Green Ribbon Award in 2004, given to 'recognise the outstanding contributions made by individuals, organisations, businesses and communities to protecting and enhancing New Zealand's environment' (Ministry for the Environment 2017).

The aim of this chapter is to consider the benefits of attending ecofests from a business and a societal perspective. In addition, we seek to chart the reasons why this event fell out of favour in this region of New Zealand. Data were gathered at the 2010 Nelson Ecofest through interviews conducted at the event with attendees. Exploring the reasons why people attended the event and what they sought from attendance helps us to understand the potential outcomes of these events for attendees and the ramifications of cancelling the event.

Sustainability festivals and the green economy

The 21st century has seen a growth in the *greening* of events, where there is 'increasing interest by organisers of events in highlighting their green credentials and an increasingly sophisticated market that is more knowledgeable about sustainability practices than ever before' (Laing and Frost 2010: 261). Such widespread interest in terms of events parallels similar greater engagement with green issues in tourism and leisure (Bergin-Seers and Mair 2009). Whilst there has been growing research into how events utilise certain green aspects in their staging (see, for example, Draper, Dawson and Casey 2011; Mair and Laing 2012; and Jones 2014), little attention has been given to industrial events that specifically focus on promoting and selling green products. Such *sustainability events* (Mair and Laing 2013) are integral to the expansion of the green economy, operating both as alternative sales distribution networks and as educational opportunities to engage with new customers.

Industrial events specialising in sustainability are now common throughout the Western world, reflecting widespread consumer interest in the green economy. Many are promoted as *alternative*, offering different lifestyles and relationships in opposition to the conventional mass market. As with many industrial events (see Chapter 1), they allow direct connections between producers and consumers, often bypassing established wholesalers and retail outlets. From our observation, these events generally cover five main product areas, which may either form a specialised focus of an event or be mixed under a more general sustainability banner. The products and systems marketed at these events are usually aimed at the household unit, again emphasising alternative production, rather than the conventional mass economy. The five main areas are:

1   Organic food production for homes and small-holdings
2   Alternative building methods, such as mud-brick and rammed earth
3   Renewable energy production and storage
4   Institutional arrangements, such as barter systems and car share schemes
5   Domestic products and appliances such as environmentally friendly cleaning products, compostable toilets and water-saving showers.

These sustainability events are mainly aimed at consumers. Attendees are not homogeneous, rather in most cases they are likely to encompass a range of *shades of green* (Bergin-Seers and Mair 2009). Given the limited research so far, there is a need to better understand potential attendees

> including their motivations, the influence of their interest in green issues on their decision-making processes with respect to attending green events and their expectations as to the green 'content' of events, as well as levels of satisfaction with current offerings.
>
> (Laing and Frost 2010: 265)

In one of the few empirical studies of sustainability events, Mair and Laing (2013) examined their role in promoting behaviour change, potentially affecting pro-environmental behaviour amongst those attending. They applied the Transtheoretical Model or TTM (Prochaska 1979; Prochaska and DiClemente 1983) to a case study of the annual Sustainable Living Festival held in Melbourne,

Australia. The model, also referred to as the 'Stages of Change' model, postulates that an individual moves along and sometimes backwards and forwards through a sequence of five stages as they adopt voluntary changes in their life. These stages are labelled: (1) pre-contemplation; (2) contemplation; (3) preparation; (4) action and (5) maintenance (Andreasen and Kotler 2008; DiClemente 2007). This model also refers to the dimensions that act to change attitudes and affect behaviour (Prochaska, DiClemente and Norcross 1992; Chib, Chiew, Kumar, Lim and Ale 2009). Attitudinal dimensions include *consciousness raising* (becoming aware that a problem exists), *dramatic relief* (an emotional stimulus or inspiration for change), *environmental re-evaluation* (understanding that change will affect society in a positive way) and *self-evaluation* (understanding that change will affect one's self-identity in a positive way), while behavioural dimensions include *helping relationships* (using social support to assist with change), *reinforcement management* (finding rewards for making a change), *counter-conditioning* (substituting new behaviours and thought processes) and *stimulus control* (changing one's environment to encourage new behaviour rather than old habits).

The Mair and Laing (2013) study found that people in the early and late contemplation stages, who were already motivated to engage in pro-environmental behaviour, and appreciated the costs or barriers in doing so, were most likely to be open to persuasive attempts at the event to encourage change in attendees. Those in the action and maintenance stages were already performing the desired behaviour and thus only required the support and encouragement that the event offered to continue with this behaviour, particularly through 'helping relationships', 'counter-conditioning' and 'stimulus control'. The event also validated 'their lifestyle choices, which contributes to 'reinforcement management" (Mair and Laing 2013: 1123).

Given that this study was quantitative, there is a gap in the literature relating to our understanding of the phenomenon of sustainability events. A qualitative research approach would, therefore, be useful in order to drill down more deeply into the perspectives and motivations of attendees. This chapter addresses that gap, through a qualitative case study of the 2010 Nelson Ecofest in New Zealand.

Methods

The study was divided in two stages. This chapter focuses on the first stage, which was qualitative, given that little was known about the subject or phenomenon and exploratory research needed to be undertaken (Jordan and Gibson 2004). It was undertaken within a paradigm of *pragmatism*, which is 'not committed to any one system of philosophy and reality', but is focused on solving a problem and the 'practical implications' of a study (Creswell 2013: 28). This allows the researcher the flexibility to choose the methods that they need to address the research question at hand. In this case, there was a second quantitative stage of the study involving a survey administered at another site, which is outside the scope of this chapter, but is discussed in Mair and Laing (2013). Each site was considered a separate case study.

200   *Jennifer Laing et al.*

Qualitative data for the first case study were principally collected through short structured interviews conducted with 42 attendees of the Ecofest at Nelson in 2010. Two of the researchers undertook this task. Participants were randomly approached by a researcher and asked about their expectations and satisfaction levels with the event; their current levels of sustainable behaviour (using a measure of sustainable practices and facilities implemented by Bergin-Seers and Mair 2009); their perceptions of what they had learned as a result of attending the event; whether they intended to make any behavioural changes following the event; and their attitudes towards sustainability and climate change. All data were coded according to themes derived both from the literature and from the emergent data (Miles and Huberman 1994).

The two researchers attending the event also conducted observations in situ, focusing on the messages that the event was sending to attendees and the range of organisations and businesses involved in the event. This included examining and analysing signage (Figure 15.1) and booths (Figure 15.2) and the taking of photographs to document what was observed. Attendees at the event were also observed, in order to understand typical behaviour (Figure 15.3) and how they reacted to and interacted with the activities on offer and the products and businesses being showcased. Photographs also assisted here to prompt the researchers during the data analysis phase, along with field notes that recorded their impressions and reactions while gathering data. This chapter however will focus on the interview data.

Figure 15.1 Signage for alternative home builders, Nelson Ecofest
Source: Photo courtesy of Jennifer Laing

Figure 15.2 Interaction between exhibitor and attendee, Nelson Ecofest

Source: Photo courtesy of Jennifer Laing

Figure 15.3 Exhibitor's booth, Nelson Ecofest

Source: Photo courtesy of Jennifer Laing

Case study context

The Nelson/Tasman region of New Zealand, at the top of the North Island, is an appealing place to live in and visit 'due to three national parks and plenty of natural (e.g. coastlines with beautiful beaches) and cultural (e.g. wine and seafood industries and a diverse and popular arts and crafts culture) attractions' (Blumberg 2005: 48). Tourism is one of the top four most important industries in the region, along with horticulture, fishing and forestry (Blumberg, 2005). The Ecofest, while always a collaborative effort between the Nelson City Council and the Tasman District Council, was initially held just in Nelson, the largest town in the region with a population around 46,000 (Nelson City Council 2016). Subsequent Ecofests were split between two sites – Motueka and Nelson – and held on two different days, due to the original venue, the Trafalgar Centre in Nelson, being permanently closed due to earthquake safety concerns (Neal 2013).

In its heyday, the Ecofest attracted around 6,000 visitors a year (Ministry for the Environment 2017), with a peak of 8,000 in 2009 (Bradley-Smith 2015) and included over 120 exhibitors showcasing environmentally friendly products and services, along with seminars and workshops on sustainability. The aim was to support 'community engagement in a range of topics such as self-sufficiency at home, waste management, water conservation, solar and alternative energies, sustainable transport and local conservation issues' (Ministry for the Environment 2017). In 2012, the Tasman District Council noted in its newsletter that the Ecofest formed 'part of its commitment to environmental education and improving the health and wellbeing of the residents of Tasman' (Newsline 2012: 4). There was a clear objective to deliver environmental messages and to educate the public on how to live more sustainably. Interestingly, the economic case for staging the event was not made by the organisers in promoting the event, even though it was well supported by local businesses.

Attendances dropped to 2,000 in 2014, although this was partly attributed to a new format and a change in venue (Bradley-Smith 2015). The decision by the Nelson City Council to cease staging the event was not unanimous. One of the councillors who supported its demise noted: 'Ecofest was suffering from event fatigue. What we need to do is breathe life, funkiness and sexiness into our 2060 [sustainability] strategy' (quoted in Bradley-Smith 2015). Another councillor voted to retain the event, but wanted the focus to be changed from a business event: 'I'd like to see less of a trade show and more of a festival. It would be an opportunity to reward our leaders [in sustainability]' (quoted in Bradley-Smith 2015). There was also a perceived need to attract a new demographic: 'This isn't a negative at all, it's a really positive step . . . you have to engage the younger generations' (quoted in Bradley-Smith 2015). This move was supported by the Council's Environmental Programmes Officer, who 'said staff believed ongoing education initiatives, rather than the one-stop-shop approach, would better meet the council's environmental goals' (quoted in Bradley-Smith 2015).

This study will consider a snapshot in time – the Ecofest staged in 2010 – and explore the role of the event both in potentially changing behaviour and in building and maintaining a market for environmentally beneficial products and services.

After presenting our findings based on data collection at the 2010 event, we will then move on to consider the ramifications of cancelling the event and the potential outlook for these kinds of events long-term.

Findings

Motivation for attending the event

The business side of Ecofest was understood by the attendees as an important part of the event, with P12 noting that the event facilitated 'green purchasing opportunities, networking, knowledge, e.g. the business sustainability talk'. P39 expanded on this aspect: 'I am interested about new technologies/improvements and to talk to people. I think it's important to go with the flow . . . We have to use more ecological products and preserve it [the planet]'. Only one participant expressly stated that they didn't attend Ecofest for the industry show: 'There is a lot of consumption based around it – you can see an industry [built] around consumption. I skip a lot of these things' (P38). Interestingly, the general attraction of the commercial elements appeared to have been discounted by Council representatives when deciding whether to continue with the event (Bradley-Smith 2015).

Innovation was a key push factor for attending the event, generally linked to the commercial exhibits. P15 sought 'everything new that helps me to live a life more sustainable', while P32 mentioned 'I want to see new models on the market and the new inventions out there. Are there any new ideas I haven't thought about?' For P23, the Ecofest provided a vehicle for 'new innovative and different ideas. There are always new products on the market – this is the place to go to see them'. Much of this interest in the latest thinking was linked to the home. For example, P28 wanted 'to see more up-to-date stuff, as we built our home 10 years ago and we want to see how things are evolving', while P11 sought out 'new ideas, I'm a DIY person'. Some appreciated the randomness of what they would find there and did not necessarily anticipate looking at particular products or meeting businesses. As P37 commented: 'I am nosy – this event is interesting as you never know what you are going to find. It is my curiosity'. P36 agreed: 'I was looking for a solar water pump and found various products I didn't expect to find.' For P42, 'I will have a look around and see what is out there'. A variety of products and businesses on display was also important to respondents. P2 complained that 'the food area could have been better – [there were] not enough variety of organics'. Seeking out innovations may assist with stimulus control, through increased access to 'products and services to help make pro-environmental behaviour changes easier and more routine' (Mair and Laing 2013: 1117).

Some attendees *sought advice* that was broad and related to their values, which might be a form of environmental re-evaluation, with the event 'publicising and demonstrating that pro-environmental behaviour can have a positive impact on society' (Mair and Laing 2013: 1117). They didn't necessarily know or were not able to articulate precisely what forms this advice might take. Thus, P21 mentioned wanting to find out about 'Alternative power options. Sustainable building options. General ways of accommodating earth for human occupation. Emphasis on sustainability, not exploitation'. Most however, were seeking quite specific or *targeted advice*, particularly those who were building or renovating their houses and needed to find out about the latest developments on green technology and sustainable building, as well as the businesses who were active in this market. Those who mentioned this were possibly in the pre-contemplation and contemplation stages of behaviour changes (Andreasen and Kotler 2008; DiClemente 2007; Mair and Laing 2013), where they had yet to adopt these innovations in their living space or environment, or were more advanced (in the action or maintenance stages) and were merely looking to upgrade what they had. These innovations might be conceptualised as a form of consciousness raising or alternatively act as counter-conditioning or stimulus control (Mair and Laing 2013) with respect to behavioural change. For example, P4 sought out 'things you can retrofit', while P41 referred to their desire 'to get ideas for renovations – keep up to date. We are renovating an old house and selling our new one'. For P8, it was about 'ideas, inspiration and information. How to combine our old house with new technology'. A few people had moved into the area from overseas such as P38, who advised: 'When we buy a house (have just moved from the UK), I will make sure that it is as energy efficient as possible. We are buying an old house to do up'. The Ecofest provided a convenient place for a newcomer to find out what was available in the region. This was echoed by P25: 'It shows me what the region is offering'. Attendees wanted to buy local where possible.

There was also high interest in attending *seminars or demonstrations*, which acted as a pull factor for attendees. Topics mentioned included growing food and gardening, where a practical demonstration helped to reinforce the learning. P9 said that they 'just came for a look and to listen to the talks', while P20 referred to 'Lectures (like to go to those), the demonstration tent, gardening mainly – growing food and learning about green issues'. For P6, it was about 'vegetarian info and demonstrations'. This provision of information, as well as elements of training and skill development complemented rather than competed with the exhibits section of the event. As above, those who mentioned the value of the seminars were possibly in the pre-contemplation and contemplation stages of behaviour changes (Andreasen and Kotler 2008; DiClemente 2007; Mair and Laing 2013), where they attended demonstrations about activities or practices which they were thinking about adopting in the future.

Encouragement was mentioned as a motivation and also an outcome of attendance. Many attendees used the event as a source of positive feedback for their lifestyle choices, which suggests that Ecofest provides 'dramatic relief' as an inspiration for change (Mair and Laing 2013). For example, P18 said that they attended 'for encouragement and new ideas'. P27 also mentioned this: 'Yes, finding a lot of innovative products at the grass roots level. In the States, there are a lot of big commercial things. Here, there is a focus on local things you can do simply. This is very encouraging'. They expanded on why they sought out this validation of their existing behaviour, while at the same time learning from others: 'A lot of stuff I am familiar with but it is nice seeing it so readily available. I have moved from the US and like the fact that there is a different consciousness – I am attracted by this. It is a healthier lifestyle here' (P27). For P28, 'it is good to see people doing the architecture that we had to fight for 10 years ago'. In some cases, this attendance was linked with *reinforcing knowledge*, which directly references reinforcement management as a conduit for behaviour change (Mair and Laing 2013). P21 mentioned that 'I haven't learned a lot but it reinforced what I know. I learnt that you can get a laptop case which recharges using solar energy. It is very encouraging to see what there is. These events are more about encouragement . . . I am hoping it reaches people in a position to seriously change their options, such as people building a house'. This suggested that they fell within the action or maintenance stages of pro-environmental behaviour change (Andreasen and Kotler 2008; DiClemente 2007; Mair and Laing 2013).

Other motivations mentioned were connected to *relationships* with others, which suggests that Ecofest may support the processes of behaviour change through 'helping relationships' (Mair and Laing 2013). P19 wanted 'to meet like-minded people', while P38 drew out the social benefits of attendance: 'It is a social event where I can meet interesting people'. Information might be sought out in order to help others or a particular cause, and thus has an altruistic element to it. P40 observed: 'I want to find out what is new and what we can do to help'. It could be argued that these kinds of people wanted to affect the behaviour change of others that they met in everyday life, and hunted for ideas on how to do this through attending the Ecofest. This supports Henderson's (2011: 253) observation that altruism is one of 'three psychographic predictors of "green" consumer behaviour'.

Expectations and satisfaction

The data revealed a divergence of opinions about whether there were enough businesses taking part in the Ecofest. Although P37 noted 'There is a much bigger range of suppliers than there used to be', P11 was more critical, observing that: 'organisers should be trying to attract more business people [rather than leisure people]'. P11 went on to explain however that they had a twinge of conscience in encouraging consumer demand, even if it is for environmentally sustainable products: 'It's an oxymoron having businesses scale up unnecessary consumption of eco-products, but hopefully it will raise awareness'. This suggests there is a tension in promoting business involvement in an ecofest, in that it may paradoxically increase consumption. There was also debate about the businesses' level of expertise in dealing with the public and providing adequate information. While P24 observed: 'The people know their product well – good product knowledge', P13 was not so sanguine: 'Some of the stallholders need to be educated about educating the public'. This may be an element that is difficult for the organisers to influence, unless they wanted to run training sessions beforehand. Of more concern, one participant complained about what they saw as fraud: 'You see some businesses pretending to be eco-friendly – we found them last time. For example timber companies and those claiming to be organic!' (P29). This is something that is within the organisers' control. Businesses taking part could be vetted beforehand in terms of their pro-environmental claims. This goes to the heart of the credibility of the event as a source of information and encouragement.

For some participants, the demonstrations and seminars were not broad enough to address their general interest in sustainability. For example, P17 noted that they 'would also like to see a public forum on social issues. We need to have more general discussion'. Others like P20 were happy with what was presented: 'The quality of the lectures has been amazing. The people are nationally known'. Learning about forgotten skills or lifestyles of the past was attractive. P26 saw the demonstrations in nostalgic terms: 'I liked seeing things like showing people how to make jam. I grew up with that'. It was felt to be important that attendees could be active in their learning, rather than passively sitting back at lectures or seminars. P27 suggested: 'They might combine it with more hands-on courses that make people more self-reliant i.e. courses to make iron or weave wool or grow food. They could expand that more'.

Attendees liked the fact that attending Ecofest would *improve understanding* amongst those who might not have been so advanced in pro-environmental behaviour: 'Public awareness is important – Live simply so that others can simply live' (P19); a reference to 'consciousness raising' (Mair and Laing 2013). The interviewees felt that these attendees would become more environmentally aware as a result of attending the event. According to P38: 'The hope is that these events move people a bit further along. I am at the high end of the scale. You get people starting out, but you need people at all ends of the scale'. The reference to *scale*, which was unprompted by the researcher interviewing P38, was interesting, in that the interviewee clearly visualised differences between pro-environmental behaviour in these terms and referred to themselves as being at the top of the scale (action/maintenance stages).

This did not mean that most people had nothing to learn, even if they were at the higher end of the scale in terms of pro-environmental behaviour. In particular, it appeared that the lectures and demonstrations on offer were extremely useful in developing attendees' practical skills. P38 mentioned 'I learned how to make cheese and ginger beer', while P2 'liked the fashion show, and learnt about fabrics and couch finishings'. The majority of our interviewees felt that they had learned something new at the event, which suggests that it went beyond mere reinforcement of knowledge. The most common responses were that they had learned about worm farms and composting options, about cleaning and laundry products (particularly laundry balls), about gardening, and about new or innovative sustainable products. Specific things mentioned included 'smart lighting' (P12), 'to be more vigilant about waste and heating use' (P4), 'all the laundry stuff – you don't need to use powder. You can do a lot of cleaning with natural products' (P22) and 'nutrient dense gardening' (P10). Even those who had a higher level of knowledge said that they learned something: 'I am operating at a higher starting point [than most people] but have learnt a bit, such as how to make cheese, wall insulation to go over the existing one and how to grow mushrooms' (P38). For some, it was a revelation that environmental initiatives did not need to be expensive: 'Being sustainable doesn't have to cost much' (P7). They also did not need to be huge to make a difference: 'There are easy things to implement, like the year without waste' (P8).

The only sustainable option that seemed to be difficult for attendees was to use public transport. In many cases, this was the result of a paucity of local public transport, rather than any lack of desire to use it. Instead, they tended to seek out other low-impact transport options. This finding was supported by the 2013 Nelson Census, which found that 'Compared with the national average, Nelson has a higher percentage of people travelling to work by walking, jogging or cycling. In Nelson, 9.6 percent walked or jogged, compared with 6.8 percent for New Zealand, and 8.7 percent biked to work, compared with 2.9 percent for New Zealand' (Nelson City Council 2016).

Influence of the event on future behaviour

Participants were also asked whether they intended to adopt any sustainable practices or products as a result of their visit. Only three participants stated that they would not adopt anything new, while three further participants felt that they were doing everything they could already. For example, P33 noted: 'There is nothing here that I haven't already got', while P26 commented 'I do these things anyway, so it won't change very much what I do'. The rest indicated that they may, or would, adopt something new in the future, based on their visit, which suggests counter-conditioning may have occurred as a result of attending the Ecofest (Mair and Laing 2013). Examples mentioned of what might be adopted by the participants included 'the alternative to polyurethane, natural house, eco timber finishes, upholstery fabric' (P2); 'The composting toilet – I will implement that in our new house we are building' (P23) and a 'worm fertiliser, water tank and self-flushing system' (P41). P36 was 'hoping to improve the insulation in my house as a result and get some cleaning products'. For P27: 'Now we are settling in, I am thinking about solar panels, LED lighting and garden boxes. I am pretty conscious already, but perhaps may do more recycling'. P28 was more complacent but still referred to changes they hoped to implement: 'There is nothing else for us to do apart from cutting back on cleaning products. Once we retire, we will get some chooks!'

In order to further assess attendee views on sustainability (and thus to understand the views/ethos of those attending), interviewees were asked whether they felt that sustainability was an important issue to them personally. They were also asked to explain why this was the case. Almost all stated that it was an important issue. For example, P17 noted 'It's about caring for the planet – I don't like consumerism. It's about not wasting resources. The GFC was good for society – it helps us re-focus on what's important'. Several referred to their role in stewardship of the environment. P18 stated 'I have a long term vision of being a good steward of creation', while P19 said: 'I feel for the coming generations, and want to improve the quality of our own life. It's about living closer to the Earth. There is some onus on us. And it's nice not to waste. We have no TV, no mobiles, no dishwasher'. For some, this was a long-standing way of life and was passed on through their family lifestyle and habits: 'I have practised these things since I was a child. My father practices this (he was before his time). You have got to live in the world and sustain good soil habits' (P28).

While it is natural that people may respond this way because they feel that this is the answer that they should give in their explanations, the so-called 'social desirability' of answers, most respondents were able to articulate specifically why it was indeed an important issue for them. The most common responses were that we have limited/finite resources and we need to start using them more sparingly, that we need to act to save the environment/the planet, that we must reduce waste, that we must act now for the sake of future generations, and that we should make an effort to 'tread lightly' and have minimal impact. Climate change assisted with that, according to P38: 'It is a stimulus to change our cultural norms. Gives us a lesson in needing to change'.

There were however a number of climate change sceptics, which the researchers found surprising, given the stated levels of pro-environmental behaviour. This suggested an area which future sustainability festivals could address. For example, P35 noted 'I am a sceptic about the anthropomorphic influence. It is a natural phenomenon. This doesn't mean that we shouldn't prepare for it and do things about pollution. Some countries are really polluting the environment'. P41 made a similar comment:

> We are not totally responsible for global warming. It is important that we look after the environment but humans are arrogant if we believe that we can beat Mother Nature. Whether we cause it is debatable. Politicians see it as a cash cow – an excuse to tax people.
>
> (P41)

Several indicated that they had moved to New Zealand from places abroad (mainly the United Kingdom and the USA), because they felt it offered an environment conducive to a sustainable lifestyle. In terms of a commitment to change, this is probably at the top level of the scale. As an example, P37 advised: 'It is part of the reason we moved here from the UK. There are more and more pollutants in the UK. NZ is taking care of the land and there is less pollution . . . The big thing is that the sky is blue here, compared to the UK – there is always a tinge to it. You don't realise when you live there how dirty it is'. There was also a doomsday mentality present amongst some participants, based on what they told us. P27 asserted vigorously: 'It is a shame, but nobody is listening out there. When the world goes to hell, it is time to live in a remote place (like New Zealand) with good food supplies'.

Conclusion

The Ecofest in 2010 appeared to attract individuals who were already significantly committed to sustainable behaviour, such as monitoring their energy use, limiting their water use, buying recycled products and doing their own recycling. For example, P3 stated that they were 'already aware of most of it'. Fewer respondents had invested in significant sustainable purchases (not surprisingly given the cost of many of these items). However, most noted that they purchased low energy globes, checked the energy efficiency of appliances when purchasing, had a compost bin and had installed water-saving devices such as low flow shower heads or dual flush toilets. Thus, it appeared that the vast majority of attendees were those who may be considered (using the TTM categories) as being in the action or maintenance stages, or at the very least the pre-contemplation and contemplation stages. They were actively engaged in sustainability and considered it an important personal issue.

Critics, such as the councillors mentioned earlier (Bradley-Smith 2015) may suggest that this event is simply 'preaching to the converted'; however, it is important to note that according to the TTM, even those in the action and maintenance stages of change require certain processes to support and encourage them, and prevent recidivism. Therefore, whilst this small event may not be particularly successful at attracting new converts to sustainability, nonetheless, it played an important role in promoting sustainable behaviour by offering several of the processes required for change, including 'helping relationships', 'reinforcement management' and 'stimulus control'. It also appears that many of the people interviewed still felt they had something to learn or wanted to adopt something new as a result of attending the Ecofest. In addition, our findings suggest that not all attendees were in the action/maintenance stages, with some potentially lower down the scale in the pre-contemplation and contemplation stages of behaviour change (Andreasen and Kotler 2008; DiClemente 2007; Mair and Laing 2013).

The decision to discontinue Ecofest was based in part on the fact that it was mostly appealing to those who were already engaged in this type of behaviour, the so-called 'preaching to the converted' argument. However the decision was broader than that:

> Councillor McGurk said Ecofest had been a valuable platform to engage with the community on sustainable issues in the past. However, declining visitor numbers, increasing costs and difficulties measuring the environmental gains of the event meant it was time to look at new ways to effectively deliver environmental messages.
>
> (Nelson Live 2015)

The fact that the event had benefits for local businesses seeking to raise awareness of their products, as well as the learning opportunities offered by Ecofest, even for people who were at the higher end of the scale in terms of environmental behaviour, and the benefits of having this behaviour validated by their peers, appears to have been overlooked. In addition, the reasons for the decline in attendance, including the potential link to changes in the venue, did not seem to form part of the background to the decision to stop staging the Ecofest. Previous research suggests that festivals and events fail, or are discontinued, for a range of reasons, some of which are pragmatic, including a lack of community support, negative publicity or poor management or governance (Frost and Laing 2015), whilst others are more related to either overdependence on a single source of funding (like a sponsor or grant scheme), or where there are simply too many other events providing competition (Carlsen, Andersson, Ali-Knight, Jaeger and Taylor 2010). In this case, the Ecofest was solely reliant on local government support, therefore, when that support was withdrawn, the event could no longer proceed. However, our findings also suggest that there may have been an element of poor management decision-making in the sense that consumers felt that the range and quality of businesses taking part in the event were not of a suitable standard, and therefore this might have also played a part in declining attendance.

Eco-businesses in the region will need to find other ways to get their messages out to potential consumers, or make a persuasive case to the Councils as to why these events should be supported in the future. Future research could extend this study further by concentrating on businesses formerly or currently involved with ecofests, to examine their rationale for involvement and whether these events are meeting their needs. It might also be useful to explore the organiser's perspective on the decision to cancel the Ecofest and their views on the role of these types of events; going beyond what was reported in the media.

The question remains open as to whether ecofests are the best way to achieve behaviour change in relation to pro-environmental behaviour. Certainly they seem to fill a niche, if only to make sure that people maintain their existing behaviour and are given direction and encouragement as to how this might be done. We currently have no data on whether this move away from ecofests has become a trend in other destinations, either because these events are declining in popularity or are being replaced by other ways of delivering environmental messages. This again would be a useful area for future research.

References

Andreasen, A.R. and Kotler, P. (2008) *Strategic Marketing for Nonprofit Organizations*, Upper Saddle River, NJ: Prentice Hall.

Bergin-Seers, S. and Mair, J. (2009) 'Emerging green tourists: Their behaviours and attitudes', *Tourism and Hospitality Research*, 9(2), 109–119.

Blumberg, K. (2005) 'Tourism destination marketing: A tool for destination management? A case study from Nelson/Tasman Region, New Zealand', *Asia Pacific Journal of Tourism Research*, 10(1), 45–57.

Bradley-Smith, A. (2015) 'Council cancels Ecofest "to breathe life, funkiness and sexiness" into sustainability', *Nelson Mail*, 15 May, www.stuff.co.nz/nelson-mail/news/68548994/council-cancels-ecofest-to-breathe-life-funkiness-and-sexiness-into-sustainability (accessed 27 January 2017).

Carlsen, J., Andersson, T., Ali-Knight, J., Jaeger, K. and Taylor, R. (2010) 'Festival management, innovation and failure', *International Journal of Event and Festival Management*, 1(2), 120–131.

Chib, A., Chiew, H.J., Kumar, C., Lim, G.C. and Ale, K. (2009) '[Minus] plastic: Influencing pro-environmental attitudes among Singaporean youth', *Environmental Education Research*, 15(6), 679–696.

Creswell, J. (2013) *Qualitative Inquiry & Research Design: Choosing among Five Approaches*, 3rd edition, Thousand Oaks, CA and London: Sage.

DiClemente, C.C. (2007) 'The transtheoretical model of intentional behaviour change', *Drugs and Alcohol Today*, 7(1), 29–33.

Draper, J., Dawson, M. and Casey, E. (2011) 'An exploratory study of the importance of sustainable practices in the meeting and convention site selection process', *Journal of Convention & Event Tourism*, 12(3), 153–178.

Frost, W. and Laing, J. (2015) 'Avoiding burnout: The succession planning, governance and resourcing of rural tourism festivals', *Journal of Sustainable Tourism*, 23(8/9), 1298–1317.

Henderson, S. (2011) 'The development of competitive advantage through sustainable event management', *Worldwide Hospitality and Tourism Themes*, 3(3), 245–257.

Jones, M. (2014) *Sustainable Event Management: A Practical Guide*, London: Routledge.

Jordan, F. and Gibson, H. (2004) 'Let your data do the talking: Researching the solo travel experiences of British and American women', in J. Phillimore and L. Goodsen (eds.), *Qualitative Research in Tourism: Ontologies, Epistemologies and Methodologies* (pp. 215–235), London: Routledge.

Laing, J. and Frost, W. (2010) '"How green was my festival": Exploring challenges and opportunities associated with staging green events', *International Journal of Hospitality Management*, 29(2), 261–267.

Mair, J. and Laing, J.H. (2012) 'The greening of music festivals: Motivations, barriers and outcomes: Applying the Mair and Jago model', *Journal of Sustainable Tourism*, 20(5), 683–700.

Mair, J. and Laing, J.H. (2013) 'Encouraging pro-environmental behaviour: The role of sustainability-focused events', *Journal of Sustainable Tourism*, 21(8), 1113–1128.

Miles, M.B. and Huberman, A.M. (1994) *Qualitative Data Analysis: An Expanded Sourcebook*, Beverly Hills, CA: Sage.

Ministry for the Environment (2017) *Green Ribbon Awards*, www.mfe.govt.nz/more/awards/green-ribbon-awards (accessed 27 January 2017).

Neal, T. (2013) 'Quake fears cause closure of Trafalgar Centre', *Nelson Mail*, 13 December, www.stuff.co.nz/nelson-mail/news/9514769/Quake-fears-cause-closure-of-Trafalgar-Centre (accessed 24 April 2017).

Nelson City Council (2016) 'Population and demographics', *Nelson City Council*, www.nelson.govt.nz/council/plans-strategies-policies/strategies-plans-policies-reports-and-studies-a-z/population-and-demographics (accessed 24 April 2017).

Nelson Live (2015) 'The end of Ecofest', *Nelson Live*, 14 May, www.nelsonlive.co.nz/2015/05/end-ecofest/ (accessed 27 January 2017).

Newsline (2012) 'Ecofest 2012', *Newsline*, 280, 27 July, 3. Motueka: Tasman District Council.

Prochaska, J.O. (1979) *Systems of Psychotherapy: A Transtheoretical Analysis*, Homewood ILL: Dorsey.

Prochaska, J.O. and DiClemente, C.C. (1983) 'Stages and processes of self-change of smoking: Toward an integrative model of change', *Journal of Consulting and Clinical Psychology*, 51(3), 390–395.

Prochaska, J.O., DiClemente, C.C. and Norcross, J.C. (1992) 'In search of how people change: Applications to addictive behaviors', *American Psychologist*, 47(9), 1102–1114.

Tasman City Council (2017) *Ecofest*, www.tasman.govt.nz/environment/environmental-education/sustainable-business/ecofest/ (accessed 27 January 2017).

16 Exhibitions, trade shows and industrial events in a digital age
Setting a research agenda

Warwick Frost and Jennifer Laing

The Melbourne International Flower and Garden Show

Established in 1995, the Melbourne International Flower and Garden Show is held annually each autumn. It was one of a number of events that were developed in the 1990s by the state and city governments as part of a new events strategy. This strategy was prompted by Melbourne's failure in bidding for the 1996 Olympics Games. Faced with the realisation that the city might never be successful in gaining mega-events, policy-makers turned towards the development of a portfolio of hall-mark events. This led to the creation of a 'calendar' of sporting and cultural hall-mark events, spread across the year and linked to existing destination attributes and images (Frost and Laing 2011). The International Flower and Garden Show is not the only industrial event to form part of Melbourne's annual calendar of events. The Melbourne Fashion Festival, the Melbourne Food and Wine Festival and the Australian International Airshow are other examples. This suggests that trade shows, exhibitions and other industrial events may play a role in developing des-tination brands. In this case, the businesses showcased – horticultural, fashion retail and gastronomic – underpin some of the key experiences that Melbourne is known for and which attract visitors to the city (Frost and Laing 2016).

We attended the Show in 2017 as part of fieldwork for this book. Walking past the various exhibits, we were struck by how much emphasis there was on selling to attendees on the day. Apart from plants for sale, there were tools, garden orna-ments, greenhouses, watering and composting systems and service providers (such as florists specialising in weddings). Each booth had a *spruiker* (an Australian word of unknown origins for a one who is demonstrating products whilst deliver-ing a persuasive sales pitch). In addition, the booths had two or three sales atten-dants who would come out from behind their counters to engage with attendees. In some cases, they were intent on delivering the *hard-sell* to anybody who had merely paused to look at a display. Others were more casual, perhaps realising that potential customers might be frightened off by such aggressive tactics. In an era where online sales are growing, it is more important than ever that these events reacquaint customers with the benefits of face-to-face contact, where a knowledge-able person is available to answer questions and can demonstrate the features and benefits of products and services in a real life setting.

The wide range of products on sale was surprising and there were some curious patterns. Spring is the key season for planting garden beds in temperate Australia and so it was strange to even be considering buying plants in autumn. This was especially so given that we had just experienced a long dry summer and most gardens would not be ready for any sort of plantings for a while. Contemplating this, we found it unusual that this industrial event is not held in spring, as occurs with the Chelsea Flower Show in London and Canberra's Floriade. The use of a calendar of events in this case leads to strange anomalies, such that the date for a garden event is possibly determined by the number of competing events and finding a time when Melbourne is relatively quiet, rather than opting for the most opportune time for planting and gardening, and thus for businesses to make a sale. We commented to each other that there were only a few exhibitors selling vegetable seedlings, clearly because the main growing season was now over (Figures 16.1 and 16.2).

With tools and systems for watering and composting, the key selling point was always that they were labour-saving. Indeed, it seemed that the selling proposition for these was directed at gardeners who were struggling to keep control of their garden and were keen to grasp a product that promised solutions. One further pattern of note was that technical terms like organic and permaculture were bandied around as general sales descriptors, with any educational content for these alternatives either unavailable or downplayed. Given the often important educational role played by these types of events, this was a lost opportunity.

Figure 16.1 Seeds and plants for sale, Melbourne International Flower and Garden Show
Source: Photo courtesy of Jennifer Laing

Figure 16.2 Demonstrating a worm farm, Melbourne International Flower and Garden
　　　　　Show

Source: Photo courtesy of Jennifer Laing

　　With the plants and products on display, the emphasis was often on innovation
and newness. This is not surprisingly a feature of many industry-themed shows,
where novelty and trends are at the forefront and may even have been part of the
planning process for the event. Bathelt, Golfetto and Rinallo (2014) term this
process *concertation*, where those involved, often on an industry-wide basis, collectively decide what the trends to be featured will be. At the Melbourne International Flower and Garden Show, this was particularly apparent with displays by
garden designers. A highly popular part of the show, major garden designers construct prototype gardens. Incorporating the latest trends, these are generally given
the main prominence in media coverage, particularly on the television news. In
2017, we felt there was a sameness to them, each featuring stonework, water

features and a similar range of plants. This made them possibly less interesting and thought-provoking than they might otherwise have been.

The show was indeed a mediatised event. Though we were attending on a quieter weekday, we were delighted to see two television garden presenters in Don Burke and Costa Georgiadis. The latter was filming a sequence for *Gardening Australia*, the weekly show he hosts on the ABC television station in Australia. We also noted that two large booths featured companies selling plants, landscaping and garden travel packages that were branded with the names of well-known television presenters. This also appears to be a feature of modern industrial events, where attendees expect to see some celebrity faces or experts to lend some cachet and credibility to the proceedings.

As with a range of industrial events, various prizes were being competed for. These fell into two categories: professionals and students from technical colleges. Inside the main exhibition building, the competitions were focused on floristry (Figure 16.3). For the static displays, the prizes had already been awarded, allowing onlookers to make their own judgements on the merit or otherwise of the decision-makers. In addition, a student competition was taking place, in which in the manner similar to modern cooking television shows, the contestants had a set short time and limited ingredients. Outside, the prototypes of professional garden designers were positioned next to a group of displays from competing students in that field. For young, aspiring designers, this opportunity to have their work presented and critiqued alongside more established leaders in the field would not have been available if it weren't for the Show.

Figure 16.3 Floristry display by technical college students, Melbourne International Flower and Garden Show

Source: Photo courtesy of Jennifer Laing

The Melbourne International Flower and Garden Show was staged in the magnificent setting of the Royal Exhibition Buildings in Melbourne. Purpose-built for exhibitions in 1880 and the venue for Australia's first parliament in 1901, it was restored for the Centenary of Federation in 2001 and achieved World Heritage listing in 2004 (Frost 2012). Whilst it provided a stunning backdrop for exhibitors, the Royal Exhibition Building did however limit the amount of space that was available for businesses to create displays. For example, unlike Canberra's Floriade, which is held outdoors beside Lake Burley Griffin, there was insufficient room to create massive beds of flowers, which draw tourists to Canberra because of the spectacular vistas that these produce (Coughlan and Mules 2001). The Melbourne event was essentially a consumer show, built around attendees' interest in the exhibitors' products and services, rather than the garden displays. Another contrast with Floriade was that the Melbourne International Flower and Garden Show does not create a new theme for each year's event, instead relying on the brand recognition that the name of the event evokes. Each staging of Floriade involves new partnerships between Events ACT and various external bodies, and this helps to determine the annual theme. In 2015, the theme was reflections, linked with the Centenary of World War One, and the Floriade organisers worked with the Australian War Memorial 'to help enhance the theme but also help to promote those individual attractions as well throughout that process' (personal communication with a representative of Visit Canberra, 2015). This type of strategy might however divert attention away from the overt link with place that the Melbourne International Flower and Garden Show seeks to highlight to attendees. The event organisers therefore do not have to share the limelight with other tourist attractions or organisations in Melbourne.

Despite the selection of this event as a prestigious hallmark event in Melbourne's event calendar, it has not been studied in an academic sense. This is a common state of affairs for many high-profile industrial events, which have often been passed over by researchers in favour of work on other types of events. Even industrial events that fall within the mega-event category, such as world's fairs and expos, are largely under-researched. One of the aims of this book is to draw together current research in this area and inspire or stimulate future studies to address this dearth of research.

Setting a research agenda

We conclude this book with an examination of themes that we believe warrant further examination. These themes have been touched upon in the various chapters as areas that need further discussion and research. Accordingly, we conclude by presenting an agenda of eleven key issues for future research.

Missing and uneven sectors

The research across the typology of industrial events is highly uneven. On the one hand, there has been quite a deal of research into trade shows, whereas, on the other hand, certain sectors are characterised by a paucity of research. Particularly prominent in being under-researched are industry-themed consumer shows (with the exception of food and wine events) and product launches. Indeed, the latter has been almost completely ignored by researchers, despite their importance as a promotional tool and the amount of money that is often spent on their staging (Frost and Laing 2011).

Within these sectors, there are also noticeable strengths and weaknesses. The literature on world's fairs is dominated by historical approaches, particularly of a number of iconic events. In contrast, the World's Fairs of the last 50 to 60 years have received little attention, probably due to geographical shifts in where these events are held. In recent years, there has been some increase in research interest in this sector and it will be interesting to see if this trend continues. Research into trade shows has also increased markedly in the 21st century. Most of these new studies, however, are quantitative and there is scope for empirical studies taking a qualitative approach to understanding their importance from both a demand and supply side. Even then, there are notable deficiencies in the literature. As Skov notes, 'I have been puzzled by the gap between the importance ascribed to fairs by fashion world members and their almost complete invisibility in academic analysis' (2006: 764). In regards to industry-themed consumer events, the sector has been dominated by studies into food and wine events, perhaps because of their tourist appeal and ubiquity within destinations. Accordingly, there is great potential for research into consumer-focused events that is based on other products and industries.

Measuring economic impact

Conventionally, the economic impact of events has been measured primarily in terms of the tourism expenditure generated. The logic behind such an approach is that it is only tourists who bring money into the economy, essentially seeing visitor spending stimulated by the event as akin to an export. In contrast, local expenditure – including construction, marketing and ticket sales to locals – are just reallocations within the economy and do not generate extra income. Here the rationale is that locals would have spent that money on something else within the economy if the event had not taken place. Although this reasoning is fairly simple, there is a tendency for the over-estimation of economic impacts, resulting in scepticism as to the reliability of these studies. The usual cause of this inflation is that these studies are commissioned by decision-makers who want to justify any public funding they have received on the grounds that they are generating a significant economic benefit (Crompton 2006; Frost and Laing 2011).

Industrial events, however, operate in a different paradigm and this raises questions as to how we might evaluate their economic impact. For most of the events covered in this book, the main objective has been to generate sales, with tourism either a secondary, or even minor, objective. Consequently, conventional methods of evaluation might not be a good fit for these events. An example of this was discussed in Chapter 3. In 2013, the High Point Furniture Market commissioned a university to measure the event's economic impact. The result was calculated at $US5.39 billion. In terms of the conventional tourism-focused approach, such a figure seems way too high, essentially about half that claimed for the 2012 London Olympic Games. On the other hand, if we view this in terms of the sales and orders generated through this trade show, this seems more reasonable. Selling furniture was, after all, the chief objective of this trade show. Going a step further, innovation is a major objective of many of these events. Should the impact of the event on encouraging innovation be quantified? If so, how might that be done? As we write, a book on new approaches to valuing events has just been published (Lundberg, Armbrecht, Andersson and Getz 2017). This is likely to stimulate a great deal of discussion about the efficacy of various approaches and it provides scope for research into the economic impact of events that are not primarily tourism-focused.

The value chain

The commercial paradigm of industrial events challenges event researchers to take new approaches to understand the processes and impacts of these events. This may require the use of concepts and models from Economics, Cultural Studies, Sociology, Management and other disciplines. An example of this can be seen with the sociological study of fashion trade shows by Skov (2006). She argues that these events can be seen as interfaces along the *value chain* of production and marketing. This allows fashion trade shows to be seen as facing two directions, where 'downstream indicates proximity to consumer markets whereas upstream takes us in the opposite direction in the supply chain towards raw materials' (Skov 2006: 765). In the downward movement of production on this value chain, trade shows are stages in which further value is added as products move from manufacture to retailing. Given that most events research focuses on tourism and social impacts, this is a very different way of looking at the phenomena. As research into industrial events is extended, such studies and concepts will shape future work.

Innovation

Whilst industrial events are seen as drivers of innovation, there is little research into how this process occurs. Economic historians Frost and Dingle (1995) suggest that international exhibitions drove international technological diffusion in the 19th century. To demonstrate this, they provide the example of the 1888 Centennial Exhibition in Melbourne featuring a large electricity generating plant to light up the building's exterior, which then contributed to the spread of electrical power early in the next century (Figure 16.4). While it is a good instance, it is frustrating that it is not explored in more detail. Who displayed it? What did attendees think? Did it gain much newspaper coverage? Most importantly, did it influence any of those entrepreneurs who introduced electricity to Melbourne over the next few decades? It would be ideal if we had a causal chain linking an attendee with a later innovation. However, we do not. Similarly, Roche (2000: 46) provides a detailed table of technology featured at various world's fairs from 1851 to 2000. Again, there is little detail of how that technology spread as a result of being displayed at these events. Airshows, as in the Australian International Airshow, are another

Figure 16.4 The Melbourne Exhibition Building illuminated to demonstrate innovation in
electrical lighting

Source: Photo courtesy of State Library of Victoria

example of events that highlight new technology or innovation, yet this process is
yet to be unpacked in the literature.

The challenge for researchers in entrepreneurship and innovation is to trace
these linkages. We need a better understanding, particularly to assist the organisers
of future events. How are the displays conceptualised by innovators? Do they see
an event as a solitary opportunity, or is it part of a broader strategy utilising a
number of occasions and media channels? The almost complete lack of research
into product launches adds further to our frustration. We need to understand how
they fit in the processes of dissemination of innovation.

Entertainment or business?

Many of the events covered in this book can be characterised in two ways. First,
they are critical elements within an economic system, allowing buyers and sellers
to better understand each other and encouraging the spread of innovative and
economically effective products and services. In contrast, a second perspective is
that they are primarily a form of entertainment, catering for desires for fun,

novelty, shopping as leisure and possibly even escapism. Of course, many events will combine both, but the question as to which foci is the more dominant shapes our understanding and attitudes towards them. In essence, it decrees whether we see these events as integral to business or simply as another leisure option.

Accordingly, there is scope for rethinking studies of attendee motivation in this context. Is there a significant divide between those attendees with a business focus and those seeking entertainment? Does that vary according to the type of industrial event? Is it that both are important in motivating attendance? Such questions are particularly important for organisers as they plan the staging of these events.

Festivalscape and boothscape

The design and staging of events may be conceptualised in terms of a *festivalscape*, which comprises the physical environment and ambience in which the event takes place (Mason and Paggiaro 2012). The efficacy of this festivalscape is often a key factor in the satisfaction of attendees and the effectiveness of the event. Accordingly, event organisers and venue operators are vitally interested in the design and layout of facilities. Taking this further, some researchers have argued for a *boothscape*, in which the individual exhibitor's display area is seen as a major success factor (Gilliam 2015; Woo and Jun 2017). This is an excellent example of an issue which has concerned industry players for a long time, but is only now starting to be examined in the research literature (Figures 16.5 and 16.6).

Figure 16.5 The boothscape, an individual exhibitor's booth at the Melbourne Leisure Fest
Source: Photo courtesy of Warwick Frost

Figure 16.6 The festivalscape, various exhibitors' booths in the indoor area at the Melbourne
          Leisure Fest
Source: Photo courtesy of Warwick Frost

Such considerations bring into play the concept of the *Experience Economy* (Pine
and Gilmore 1999). Very popular within sections of industry, this theory advocates
that there are commercial benefits for selling *experiences* to consumers that are
produced and staged like a play. The consumers are the audience who are entranced
by the performance and actors. Surprising elements and special effects are included,
'staging the unexpected' (Pine and Gilmore 1999: 96), to create the impression that
this is a bespoke production. However, the experiences are carefully scripted to
control quality. Like a play, the actors concentrate on reading their lines while
maintaining an illusion of naturalism. Whilst this concept has become widespread,
it has also attracted a great deal of criticism. Such staged experiences have been
described as unsatisfactory and inauthentic, suggesting Disneyland and Las Vegas,
whereas many consumers want more engaging experiences that they seek out or
construct themselves (Frost et al. 2016). All this suggests that there is great scope
for research into organisers of industrial events who follow the principles of the
experience economy and how this affects the attendees' experiences.

Social worlds

It may be valuable to examine attendees or even exhibitors at some of these events
as members of *Social Worlds*. This concept was developed by Unruh (1979) to
describe groups of people who come together to share common interests that they

are passionate about. These groupings tend to be loose and even informal. They may form clubs and in more recent times they have used peer-to-peer social media to create virtual communities with a wide geographical reach. Some of these industrial events offer the opportunity for such like-minded people to come together and interact with fellow fans. An associated concept is that of *serious leisure* (Stebbins 1992), where amateur enthusiasts treat their passion like a career, engaging in continuous improvement through training and research, motivated by a goal of reaching an elite level. Regular and committed attendees, accordingly, might fall into this category. In some cases, exhibitors might also see themselves as fans, even though they are primarily using the event as a business opportunity.

The most obvious manifestations of these concepts are at popular culture themed events. As Jenkins (2012) argues, an event like Comic-Con may be seen as a *homecoming*, where fans keep returning year after year to meet face-to-face with those who share their interests. Such events also function as an introduction to these social worlds for newcomers. Whilst popular culture themed events may grab our attention, it is important to understand that social worlds extend to other industry-themed consumer events. These include food, wine and beer festivals. In recent years, there has been the rise of the *Foodie*, who is self-consciously fascinated by food and associated products (Getz, Robinson, Andersson and Vujicic 2014). Similar groups – possibly overlapping – exist for coffee, wine and beer. Social worlds and serious leisure may also extend to attendees at events that focus on gadgetry, an area that could repay further research. Chapter 6 on Motorclassica is an example of an industrial event involving fans, the study of which could have been framed using this literature.

Tourists and destinations

Events are often strongly linked with tourism, yet throughout most of this book, business objectives have been highlighted and the role of tourism downplayed. Nonetheless, in some circumstances, tourism may be an important secondary factor. As mega-events, the rationale for public funding of World's Fairs is often that they will bring in tourists. Trade shows generate business tourism. Industry-themed consumer shows draw in visitors to a destination. All of these events require further research to establish their relationship with tourism and destination development, as the case of the Melbourne International Flower and Garden Show at the beginning of this chapter illustrates.

At present, research into industrial events, tourism and destinations is fragmented. Craik (1992) found that the tourism benefits of World's Fairs were overstated and it is unfortunate that little further work in this area has occurred. A recent study by Ferrari and Guala (2017) examined linkages with destination image in the context of the Milan Expo. The impact on the destination image of trade shows has been studied by Jin, Weber and Bauer (2012). For industry-themed consumer events, there has been a deal of research into how food and wine festivals affect destination branding (see for example, Lee and Arcodia 2011) and tourist motivations (Yuan, Cai, Morrison and Linton 2005). However, there has been practically no research into tourism and other industry-themed consumer events, including – most surprisingly – popular culture events.

The Asian century

With the ongoing development and diversification of Asian economies, it is important to understand how industrial events are being transferred and potentially evolving with this regional shift. The most obvious manifestation of this is World's Fairs. From the middle of the 19th century through to the late 20th century, these were typically staged in major Western cities, particularly in the USA and Europe. However, two parallel shifts changed this. The first was a rapid fall in their popularity, mainly in the USA, but also apparent throughout the Western world. The second was that starting with Osaka in 1970, Asian countries became interested in hosting World's Fairs.

Some research has started to take place regarding this new generation of Asian World's Fairs (Lee, Kang and Lee 2013; Lee, Mjelde and Kwon 2017). There is also recent research on Asian trade shows (Jin et al. 2012) and industry-themed consumer shows (Song, Bae and Lee 2017). However, this amounts to a quite small amount in the mainstream tourism and events literature. Furthermore, this research is focused on East Asia, indicating a paucity of studies for Southeast Asia, South Asia and the Middle East. Underpinning this problem is the likelihood is that research is being undertaken by academics in this region, but it is not being published in major journals and presses.

There have been some long-running and highly successful Asian industrial events that are barely mentioned in the events literature. One example is the Hong Kong Industrial Products Exhibition, which was first staged in 1938 by The Chinese Manufacturers' Association. It was an annual event until 1974, apart from a five-year hiatus associated with the Japanese occupation of Hong Kong during World War Two and the associated chaos in its aftermath. Attendance was huge at times – in 1968–69, visitation almost reached two million. Understanding why the event was first staged, why it ran for so long, and why it eventually closed, are all questions for future studies. Another is the China Import or Export Fair (Canton Fair), which has been understudied to date despite its political, economic and sociological significance (Jin and Weber 2008; Peng, Cheng and Qin 2013; Zhang, Qu and Ma 2010). The challenge in the future is to extend research on industrial events into these regions, make it accessible for a global audience and to examine possible differences in patterns and experiences.

Social impacts

As noted in our introduction, there are social dimensions to industrial events. The problem is, however, that these are mainly considered in the grey literature of media reports, rather than the academic research literature. The examples we gave in Chapter 1 – of the controversy over the potential censorship of the Busan Film Festival and the undesirability of gun shows – have not been subject to academic scrutiny. While there have been some research studies, such as a food and wine event that seeks to change the image of the night-time economy (Hollows, Jones, Taylor and Dowthwaite 2014), there is much more scope for research into such social impacts. This includes both those that are planned (for example through the activities of social marketing sponsors) and those that have unintended outcomes.

The Digital Age

As we move further into the Digital Age, this raises a range of questions for the future of industrial events. Is there still a need for the physical inspection of samples, tasting and trialling products, talking with exhibitors and networking? A number of chapters mentioned the role of face-to-face seminars and workshops at industrial events, but is this still an effective method of communication and engagement? Is there an increasing use of technology in exhibit stands, or is the boothscape still fairly low tech? And is there any move towards virtual trade shows?

The use of social media is an area that needs further study. There is evidence that the organisers of food and wine festivals are increasingly using social media (Frost et al. 2016; Strickland, Williams, Laing and Frost 2016). How effective this is needs to be evaluated, as do the markets that it reaches and those which it does not. Attendee-generated social media – often peer-to-peer – is apparent at some of these events, most notably popular culture events like Comic-Con (Jenkins 2012). Differences in control and effectiveness between business-to-business, business-to-consumer and peer-to-peer social media are other critical areas for further research. The rise of industry bloggers as taste-makers, as in the fashion industry (see Chapter 5), also needs to be better understood.

Conclusion

Despite their long history, ubiquity and importance to businesses and destinations, industrial events, with a few exceptions, remain understudied in the events literature. The reasons for this might include their sometimes prosaic character and the nascent stage of development of events research more generally, as well as a common focus on conventions and conferences as examples of business events. The term *Industrial Events* has been coined – drawing on the existing concept of industrial tourism – to encapsulate the range of events that seek to promote businesses, industries and products.

As the chapters in this book attest, industrial events cover a range from fashion shows to farmers' markets, from World's Fairs to the product launch of the latest computer. We see this book as a first step towards a deeper understanding of these events. Up to now, most of the focus in Events Studies has either been on events that have a primary objective of attracting tourists to a destination, or ones that have major social impacts. In this book, we have advanced the idea that there are a group of events that fall outside these perspectives, yet are still significant in their impacts and importance. This book is a call to take a new view of these events, understanding that they primarily have a commercial imperative.

References

Bathelt, H., Golfetto, F. and Rinallo, D. (2014) *Trade Shows in the Globalizing Knowledge Economy*, Oxford: Oxford University Press

Coughlan, D. and Mules, T. (2001) 'Sponsorship awareness and recognition at Canberra's Floriade Festival', *Event Management*, 7(1), 1–9.

Craik, J. (1992) 'Expo 88: Fashions of sight and politics of site', in T. Bennett, P. Buckridge, D. Carter and C. Mercer (eds.), *Celebrating the Nation: A Critical Study of Australia's Bicentenary* (pp. 142–159), Sydney: Allen & Unwin.

Crompton, J. (2006) 'Economic impact studies: Instruments for political shenanigans?', *Journal of Travel Research*, 45(1), 67–82.

Ferrari, S. and Guala, C. (2017) 'Mega-events and their legacy: Image and tourism in Genoa, Turin and Milan', *Leisure Studies*, 36(1), 119–137.

Frost, L. and Dingle, T. (1995) 'Infrastructure, technology and change: A historical perspective', in P. Troy (ed.), *Technological Change and the City* (pp. 14–31), Sydney: Federation.

Frost, W. (2012) 'Commemorative events and heritage in former capitals: A case study of Melbourne', *Current Issues in Tourism*, 15(1/2), 51–60.

Frost, W. and Laing, J. (2011) *Strategic Management of Festivals and Events*, Melbourne: Cengage.

Frost, W. and Laing, J. (2016) 'The food revolution in Melbourne, 1980–2015', in M. Sahakian, C. Saloma and S. Erkman (eds.), *Food Consumption in the City: Practices and Patterns in Urban Asia and the Pacific* (pp. 124–140), London: Routledge.

Frost, W., Laing, J., Best, G., Williams, K., Strickland, P. and Lade, C. (2016) *Gastronomy, Tourism and the Media*, Bristol: Channel View.

Getz, D., Robinson, R., Andersson, T. and Vujicic, S. (2014) *Foodies and Food Tourism*, Oxford: Goodfellow.

Gilliam, D. (2015) 'Trade show boothscapes', *Journal of Marketing Management*, 31(17/18), 1878–1898.

Hollows, J., Jones, S., Taylor, B. and Dowthwaite, K. (2014) 'Making sense of urban food festivals: Cultural regeneration, disorder and hospitable cities', *Journal of Policy Research in Tourism, Leisure & Events*, 6(1), 1–14.

Jenkins, H. (2012) 'Superpowered fans: The many worlds of San Diego's Comic-Con', *Boom: A Journal of California*, 2(2), 22–36.

Jin, X. and Weber, K. (2008) 'The China import and export (Canton) Fair: Past, present, and future', *Journal of Convention & Event Tourism*, 9(3), 221–234.

Jin, X., Weber, K. and Bauer, T. (2012) 'Impacts of clusters on exhibition destination attractiveness: Evidence from mainland China', *Tourism Management*, 33(6), 1429–1439.

Lee, C.-K., Kang, S. and Lee, Y. (2013) 'Segmentation of mega-event motivation: The case of Expo 2010 Shanghai China', *Asia Pacific Journal of Tourism Research*, 18, 637–660.

Lee, C.-K., Mjelde, J. and Kwon, Y. (2017) 'Estimating the economic impact of a mega-event on host and neighbouring regions', *Leisure Studies*, 36(1), 138–152.

Lee, I. and Arcodia, C. (2011) 'The role of regional food festivals in destination branding', *International Journal of Tourism Research*, 13(4), 355–367.

Lundberg, E., Armbrecht, J., Andersson, T. and Getz, D. (Eds.). (2017) *The Value of Events*, London and New York: Routledge.

Mason, M. and Paggiaro, A. (2012) 'Investigating the role of festivalscape in culinary tourism: The case of food and wine events', *Tourism Management*, 33, 1329–1336.

Peng, Q., Cheng, L.X. and Qin, H.H. (2013) 'The impacts of large-scale exhibitions on hotel room rates: A case study of Canton Fair', *Tourism Economics*, 19(2), 245–256.

Pine, B. and Gilmore, J. (1999) *The Experience Economy: Work Is Theatre & Every Business a Stage*, Harvard, MA: Harvard Business School Press.

Roche, M. (2000) *Mega-Events & Modernity: Olympics and Expos in the Growth of Global Culture*, London and New York: Routledge.

Skov, L. (2006) 'The role of trade fairs in the global fashion business', *Current Sociology*, 54(5), 764–783.

Song, H.J., Bae, S.Y. and Lee, C.-K. (2017) 'Identifying antecedents and outcomes of festival satisfaction: The case of a cosmetics and beauty expo', *International Journal of Contemporary Hospitality Management*, 29(3), 947–965.

Stebbins, R. (1992) *Amateurs, Professionals and Serious Leisure*, Montreal: McGill-Queen's University Press.

Strickland, P., Williams, K., Laing, J. and Frost, W. (2016) 'The use of social media in the wine event industry: A case study of the High Country Harvest Festival in Australia', in G. Szolnoki, L. Thach and D. Kolb (eds.), *Successful Social Media & Ecommerce Strategies in the Wine Industry* (pp. 74–92), New York: Palgrave Macmillan.

Unruh, D. (1979) 'Characteristics and types of participation in social worlds', *Symbolic Interaction*, 2(2), 115–130.

Woo, G.J. and Jun, J.-K. (2017) 'How to create a profitable boothscape', *International Journal of Contemporary Hospitality Management*, 29(3), 966–985.

Yuan, J., Cai, L., Morrison, A. and Linton, S. (2005) 'An analysis of wine festival attendees' motivations: A synergy of wine, travel and special events?', *Journal of Vacation Marketing*, 11(1), 41–58.

Zhang, L., Qu, H. and Ma, J. (2010) 'Examining the relationship of exhibition attendees' satisfaction and expenditure: The case of two major exhibitions in China', *Journal of Convention & Event Tourism*, 11(2), 100–118.

Index